Computing Taste

Computing Taste

ALGORITHMS AND THE MAKERS
OF MUSIC RECOMMENDATION

Nick Seaver

The University of Chicago Press   CHICAGO AND LONDON

The University of Chicago Press, Chicago 60637
The University of Chicago Press, Ltd., London
© 2022 by The University of Chicago
All rights reserved. No part of this book may be used or reproduced in any
manner whatsoever without written permission, except in the case of brief
quotations in critical articles and reviews. For more information, contact
the University of Chicago Press, 1427 E. 60th St., Chicago, IL 60637.
Published 2022
Printed in the United States of America

31 30 29 28 27 26 25 24 23 22   1 2 3 4 5

ISBN-13: 978-0-226-70226-1 (cloth)
ISBN-13: 978-0-226-82297-6 (paper)
ISBN-13: 978-0-226-82296-9 (e-book)
DOI: https://doi.org/10.7208/chicago/9780226822969.001.0001

Library of Congress Cataloging-in-Publication Data

Names: Seaver, Nick, 1985– author.
Title: Computing taste : algorithms and the makers of
music recommendation / Nick Seaver.
Description: Chicago : University of Chicago Press, 2022. |
Includes bibliographical references and index.
Identifiers: LCCN 2022017125 | ISBN 9780226702261 (cloth) |
ISBN 9780226822976 (paperback) | ISBN 9780226822969 (e-book)
Subjects: LCSH: Music—Philosophy and aesthetics. |
Recommender systems (Information filtering). | Music—Social aspects.
Classification: LCC ML3877.S43 2022 | DDC 781.1/7—dc23/eng/20220408
LC record available at https://lccn.loc.gov/2022017125

For Gus and Poppy

Contents

Prologue

In the office, there is always music.

It plays from speakers tucked among exposed wooden rafters, filling two floors of an old brick building with a shared soundtrack. The music flows over clusters of tables scattered with screens, papers, and empty bottles. It reaches everywhere across the open-plan office, muted only by the large headphones some engineers wear or the doors that close off a few small meeting rooms and private offices.

Upstairs, the volume is usually turned down; the people here are older, the shirts have more buttons, these "nontechnical" employees make sales calls or greet visitors. Downstairs sit the engineers, wearing company T-shirts, typing rapidly, and staring into pairs of monitors. The music is loudest at one end of this floor, playing over a ring of couches from a speaker balanced on top of a kitchen cabinet.

Here, people take breaks from their desks, and visitors camp out under a screen that displays the office playlist. Anyone logged on to the corporate network can add to it, from the CEO to the interns to me, a visiting anthropologist. The result is an omnivorous mess: bright and airy pop gives way to dark and dense black metal before the playlist is overtaken by a run of songs with "pizza" in the title. (The office manager has ordered pizza for lunch.) Pounding club music segues into the sounds of a barbershop quartet, followed by the main theme from the video game *Sonic the Hedgehog*.

The open-plan office is a notorious symbol of technology start-up culture. Around the world, scrappy teams of coders seek and spend funding from offices assembled in repurposed industrial buildings. In the molted shells of capitalisms past, these adolescent companies try to demonstrate their flexibility and agility in part through their furniture. Teams and tables are readily reconfigured, people constantly change seats, and if the companies grow, they spread easily through these buildings' open spaces, replicating their cells of tables out to the exterior brick walls.

Embodied in the open plan is a theory about how companies should work and grow. The desks and the walls, the headphones and the screens—all of it traces the contours of contemporary software production, which is as much about managing people as it is about writing code. The open plan symbolizes freedom from hierarchy and rigidity, a willingness to rapidly change. With almost everyone sitting in the same big room, spontaneous encounters are said to lead to unexpected insights and innovation. But the shape of the office is perhaps more symbolic than economic: studies have indicated that, in practice, open plans harm productivity by distracting workers from their work.[1]

: :

So, when I first walk into the company I will call Whisper, I see a stereotypical start-up office.[2] The building's infrastructure is bared: ventilation ducts hang above the desks, and cables snake along the walls. Later this summer, a mysterious ooze will seep between the boards of the unfinished wooden ceiling. There is no receptionist or front desk, only a sea of tables and people typing at them. As at many software start-ups in the United States, most of these people are white men.

Whisper is a music recommendation company. The people at the tables are building a set of large databases that contain information about music and its listeners. Reporters sometimes call this data collection and analysis apparatus a "musical brain." With its brain, Whisper calculates the relative popularity of artists, measured in play counts or online chatter; it analyzes musical sound, estimating tempo and key; it profiles listeners, estimating their favorite genres. The system is always growing, analyzing more music, acquiring new data sources, and deriving new measures.

Whisper's customers are music streaming services—companies like Spotify or Deezer—which use all this data, combined with some of their own, to answer an apparently simple question: What's next? This is the question that music recommender systems are built to answer, and it appears everywhere in the industry—in slide decks, on company-branded sweatshirts, in advertisements. While music recommendation takes many shapes, its prototypical form is a never-ending sequence of tracks, following a path of algorithmic suggestions. In the world of music streaming, these endless playlists are called "radio."

Whisper's office playlist began as a way for the company to listen to its own radio, through an internal program named Caviar. In the software industry, using your own product is often called "dogfooding"—as in "eating your own dog food"—and it is regarded as a way to ensure quality and to experience a user's point of view. The story goes that Whisper's CEO once declared, "Our recommendations aren't dog food, they're caviar!," and the name stuck. Across the office, Caviar's purple interface can be seen on many workers' secondary screens. When the tracks queued by humans run out, a "robot" account uses the company's radio algorithm to keep the music flowing. But during a typical workday, this rarely happens, and the robot is often in disrepair, so most of Caviar's caviar consists of music chosen by Whisper's workers.

Caviar is everywhere; it is escaped only by putting on headphones or moving into a private meeting room, where it can still be heard playing faintly in the background. As I interview people in these rooms, everyone has something to say about it. The CEO tells me that he could recount the company's entire history through the evolution of its shared listening situation, through the accumulation of speakers and code contributed by volunteers. When a small satellite office opens up across the country, Caviar gets upgraded to work there, too, linking the two offices together. A junior engineer, walking me through Caviar's source code, which has grown into a makeshift tower of ad hoc rules and jury-rigged functions, explains the system's significance to me in an inadvertently anthropological register: "It's like Caviar is a symbol of the whole company culture, if that makes sense." It does, I reply.[3]

Over the year before my arrival, Whisper has grown dramatically. The tables are packed, and people are worried that the company culture is being lost. So, even though Caviar is plainly a distraction—a source of jarring sonic transitions and tempting diversions from work—it is widely cherished as an essential part of Whisper's culture and collective identity. This makes it much like the office itself, a symbol of openness and creativity whose practical value is beside the point.

But despite this apparently anarchic egalitarianism, there are rules and structure. In the patchwork mess of Caviar's source code, one can find traces of the office's evolving playlisting norms, sedimented into software. Songs by the pop-rock band Coldplay are automatically rejected; if a user tries to skip a song queued by someone else, they are discouraged by a pop-up confirmation window. When someone has queued many tracks in a row, their selections are pushed down the list to make room for others—unless they are one of the company's founders. At some point, a feature was introduced that let anyone click a button to play the sound of an air horn over the currently playing song, like a Jamaican dancehall DJ. After an overly enthusiastic reception of the new feature, the number of air-horn clicks allowed per day was limited. Open plans are never quite so open as they seem.

Every summer, when a new group of interns arrives, Caviar is thrown into disarray for a few weeks as the newcomers learn the system's tacit rules. I come to Whisper in one of these groups, as an outsider with few concrete obligations, so I spend a lot of time with Caviar. After several weeks and desk changes, I've become comfortable enough with its norms and my status in the office to queue Gary Numan's 1979 "Observer," a song whose lyrics describe the alienation of observation. Liam, an engineer and one of Caviar's more active users, queues another song from the same album in reply—Numan's "Engineers," which takes the point of view of an engineer isolated from human concerns.

We're playing, tracing relations among songs and showing off our musical knowledge, expressing ourselves vaguely and ironically. Most of the people who hear this exchange won't even notice that it has happened.

: :

One morning, a squelching comes across the speakers. Over a halting beat, a woman's singing voice is doubled, and the copy shifts up into a child's register. The pitch of the duplicated voice wheels around over a rubbery-sounding synthesizer motif until the song abruptly stops, displaced by a brief and detuned cover version of Céline Dion's 1996 power ballad "It's All Coming Back to Me Now." The medley stays its erratic course for nine minutes, with more clangorous beats, tuneless yet singsong vocals, and elastic synthetic timbres. (A cover of another 1996 power ballad, Toni Braxton's "Un-Break My Heart," is crushed through digital distortion; it is followed by closely recorded breathing and kissing sounds, synthetic harpsichord, and music-box chimes.) The music is saccharine, chaotic, and relentless. It is, I note to myself, something like a condensation of the experience of listening to Caviar.

"I am old enough that people have invented music that I don't understand and hate," Ed, a senior engineer in his thirties, posts to the office chat. The medley comes from the new, divisive "post-ringtone" label PC Music, which specializes in this mixture of glossy pop aesthetics and avant-garde difficulty. Ed says he gets a "serious emperor-has-no-clothes vibe" from it, but he's not sure. His colleague Richard, who as it happens is a trained experimental music composer, is a fan and has started to regularly queue the label's music on Caviar. "And that dude only likes jams," Ed posts to the chat, as we debate PC Music's merits. The summer continues with more snapped-balloon rhythms and unsettlingly doe-eyed vocals.

Eventually, PC Music becomes just one of the many peculiar and fleeting styles that pass through the office queue. Whisper's employees are generally enthusiastic omnivores, eagerly pursuing the idiosyncratic, the niche, and the obscure. They take pleasure in identifying new microgenres like seapunk or vaporwave, and queuing music on Caviar is one way to perform their enthusiasm. (They also simply enjoy annoying one another, sometimes.) To see whether people are queuing music they like or just using Caviar to inflict music on others, one of Whisper's product managers, Tom, has run a skeptic's data analysis. He compares the music people queue on Caviar with their personal listening histories, logged on Whisper's servers; he is surprised to find that they match. Tom also maintains a user profile for all the music played on Caviar, which is sometimes used to represent Whisper's collective musical taste, as though the office were a single, extremely omnivorous listener.

By the end of the summer, I notice Ed queuing a PC Music song on Caviar (between TLC's "No Scrubs" and the yacht rock anthem "Sailing," by Christopher Cross). His tastes have changed, he explains, although it's hard to say why.

: :

I came to Whisper looking to understand how people like Ed and his colleagues thought about taste. If recommender systems were becoming increasingly influential, and if they embodied their makers' theories about how taste works, then it followed that these theories were themselves becoming influential. I assumed that theories of taste would map neatly on to techniques and data sources: if you thought that people liked music because of how it sounded, then you'd make a system that analyzed audio data; if you thought they liked music to fit in with their friends, then you might try to acquire social network data; if you thought that taste varied by context, then you might try to figure out what people were doing while they listened. Many short-lived companies have built and promoted products around theories like these, pushing their own particular techniques.

But what I found at Whisper, and across the industry, was not so straightforward. Not long before his encounter with PC Music, I interviewed Ed and asked him a question I asked all my interviewees: Why do you think people like the music that they like? He gave a very common response, chuckling and sitting back in his chair, as though I'd asked an impossible question. "There are so many answers," he said.

When I asked the same question of Dan, an experimental musician and data scientist who consulted for Whisper, he gave the same answer in many more words:

> Why do people like the music that they like? I mean—I think this sort of platonic ideal in mine and a lot of people's minds is that there's some sort of—you know, I don't know. I mean, this is such a tricky thing—I wanted to talk about some innate sensibility that matches the sensibility of the musicians essentially. You know, there's sort of—It's some sort of almost mystical thing that they're tapping into that expresses something unexpressible, and that strikes a chord with you, but—I mean, of course there's this social dimension too, and there's this, you know—There's a million examples of—It's not so pure in a way or, you know—I mean—I guess the other extreme is, like, because it's cool, you know? There's all this—I feel like the reality is some sort of mix of "Because I really enjoy these sounds and the way I feel when I experience these sounds" and "I also get some sort of pleasure about thinking about who this band is and what they represent and where that places me in this whole scene," and, you know, how that sort of—It's part of creating my image of myself.

It wasn't that there was no accounting for taste. If anything, there were too many ways of accounting for taste—reasons that piled up in Dan's halting response, summing and multiplying into something that was just out of reach. So many answers, as Ed had suggested.

Whisper's infrastructure did not provide one answer to the question of why people like what they like, but instead it embodied the attitude expressed by Dan and Ed. Who could say precisely why anyone liked what they did? Taste might be the result of anything, and the musical brain had to have an open mind, ready to find answers wherever they might lie. However taste worked—no matter whether it worked differently for different people or across different moments in a person's life—a good recommender system would be open enough to recognize it and cultivate it. People's horizons would expand, their affinities would intensify, and their attention would range ever more widely across the world of music. Like Caviar, like the office, algorithmic recommendation was intended to provide an open plan, to allow whatever was going to happen to happen *more*.

But as anthropologists and other cultural critics have long argued, designs on openness bring their own subtle enclosures; supports are also constraints; efforts to be universal always have their own particularities; and systems purporting to empower others often accrue power to themselves. As the makers of music recommendation work, they make choices and bring in ideas that structure the open plan. These choices affect what people hear; they alter the circulation of music; they change what it means to have taste in a world filled with computers.

Introduction

Screw Algorithms!

In August 2013, the audio technology company Beats Electronics announced that it was launching a new music streaming service: Beats Music. In the United States, Beats had become a household name with its popular headphones brand Beats by Dr. Dre, and its logo—a red curlicue letter *b*—seemed to be everywhere: in music videos, in paparazzi photos of celebrities, on the heads of people walking down the street, and on billboards across Los Angeles, where I was living at the time. Critics had panned the headphones' quality, claiming that they were made from cheap components with the bass cranked up, and many suggested that Beats' popularity was really a marketing success. The company had capitalized on the celebrity social networks and cultural cachet of its cofounders, the producer Jimmy Iovine and the rapper and producer Andre Young, better known as Dr. Dre.

Iovine and Dre were music industry veterans who had helped create some of the most popular albums of the 1980s and 1990s, and since then, they had ascended to a level of industry status and net worth that meant journalists typically described them as "moguls" or "impresarios." Iovine pushed back against critiques of his headphones by drawing on his reputation as a producer. He was known as "the man with the magic ears" (Fricke 2012), and he "dismissed those who criticize the sound quality of Beats. Competitors use fancy equipment to determine how headphones should sound, he said, whereas he and Mr. Young simply *know* how they should sound" (Martin 2011). On one side, technology, and on the other, an ineffable, embodied form of expert knowledge. The box that the headphones came in featured a quotation attributed to Dr. Dre, also appealing to his personal experience: "People aren't hearing all the music. With

Beats, people are going to hear what the artists hear, and listen to the music the way they should: the way I do."

As Beats established its new music streaming service, it followed the template set by its headphones business. Beats Music would be headed by a pair of music industry veterans with cultural bona fides: Ian Rogers, who began his career in the 1990s as webmaster for the rap group Beastie Boys before heading a series of digital music ventures, and Trent Reznor, front man of the industrial rock group Nine Inch Nails.

At the time, Beats Music appeared to be a late entrant into an already-saturated market. Over the previous five years, on-demand music streaming services had finally come to seem like viable businesses in the United States, overcoming legal and technical challenges that had been killing companies since the late 1990s. By 2013, though, companies like Spotify and Rdio had arranged licensing agreements with most of the major record labels, and the spread of smartphones and high-bandwidth internet meant that their users could stream music from their catalogs nearly continuously. But these were long and expensive projects; to enter into the competition at this point required deep pockets or industry connections to negotiate the necessary licenses. As one digital music industry expert described the situation to me, there were "too many rats, not enough cheese."

As streaming catalogs grew, offering mostly the same music, these companies struggled to differentiate themselves from one another. One Rdio engineer explained to me that what ultimately set streaming services apart was the "discovery layer" they provided on top of their catalog: the interface and tools that listeners could use to find what they wanted to listen to in collections of tens of millions of songs (see Morris and Powers 2015). This was where algorithmic recommendation, like the services provided by Whisper, came in. The major music streaming services devised personalized "home" screens and algorithmic radio stations that would cater to listeners' particular interests, guiding them through the catalog and introducing them to new music.

To differentiate itself from the rest of the market, Beats drew again on its music industry connections. Where other streaming companies had their origins in "tech" (the founders of Spotify and Rdio, for instance, were already rich from founding advertising and telecom companies), Beats boasted a deeper cultural sensitivity: "We know music—we obsess over it, and devote our lives to it. We understand music is an experience, not a utility. We realize the heart and inspiration it takes to craft music and cherish the connection between the artist and the listener. Musical taste is complex, evolving, and unique. We believe that hearing the right music at the right time enriches your life. It's why we're here: To deliver musical bliss, and move culture" (Houghton 2013). In interviews, Rogers argued that Beats would be "a service, not a server" (The Verge 2014), rejecting what he presented as the overly technological focus of his competitors.[1]

To that end, Beats announced that it would replace the algorithmic discovery layer typical of its competitors with the work of a team of "curators"—music critics, DJs, and celebrities—who would assemble playlists, helping users discover new music by drawing on their own, ineffable cultural expertise. "Screw Algorithms!" read the title of one trade press article covering the announcement, "The New Music Service from Beats Uses Celebrity Curators to Show You New Music" (Titlow 2013). Algorithmic recommendation could never really work, Beats suggested, because algorithms could never understand musical taste the way that human experts could. To recognize and cultivate taste required expert human attention, not algorithmic recommendation.

: :

"Bullshit!," tweeted Oscar, the head of recommendation at a movie streaming company. "Look who they're hiring!"[2]

When Beats Music launched, I had been conducting ethnographic fieldwork for a few years with people like Oscar—scientists and engineers who had built their careers developing the algorithmic machinery that Beats claimed could never really work. I had attended their conferences, where academic and industry researchers presented new methods and grappled with new sources of data; I had interviewed workers, from CEOs to summer interns; I would soon spend a few months embedded at Whisper, watching the people behind the "algorithms" at work.

These people were, unsurprisingly, skeptical of Beats' argument. If Beats wanted to have lots of music and lots of users, there was no way to bring them together without algorithmic help. It was absurd to suggest that recommender systems might be replaced by a team of celebrities; there were simply too many songs and too many people. Were Reznor and Rogers going to make playlists for each user by hand? Even if Beats' curators assembled thousands of playlists, the company would still need some way to match those playlists with relevant users, and it couldn't do that without algorithms.

Sure enough, when I followed Oscar's suggestion and looked at Beats' job listings page, I found it full of advertisements seeking engineers and data scientists, people tasked with building the very algorithmic infrastructures that the company's press releases criticized.

When Beats Music launched, behind schedule, in January 2014, it featured a home screen titled "Just for You." On it were a set of playlists assembled by Beats' curators—who included anonymous workers as well as the talk-show host Ellen DeGeneres and, strangely, the retail chain Target. But the playlists were recommended algorithmically, drawing on the work of data scientists like Jeremy, a Beats engineer I interviewed at a rock-climbing gym in San Francisco's Mission District. Reflecting on his employer's ambivalence about his work, he joked: "Technology is just marketing, anyway."

To accompany the launch, Beats released an advertisement in the form of a manifesto, read by Reznor, which showed a series of roughly animated red-on-black images morphing into each other: silhouettes kissing, turntables spinning, a sailboat tossed on stormy water that turns into a sea of 1s and 0s. The manifesto began by reiterating the company's earlier critiques of algorithms: "Music is much more than just digital files: it breathes and bleeds and feels. [To understand it], you'll need more inside your skull than a circuit board. Because code can't hear the Bowie in a band's influences. It doesn't know why the Stones segue perfectly into Aretha Franklin. And if you're one perfect track away from getting some satisfaction, you'd want more than software to deliver it. You'd want brains and souls. You'd want people driven by a passion for music." The manifesto maintained the importance of human qualities like brains, souls, and passion, but it ended on a more conciliatory note: "We've created an elegant, fun solution that integrates the best technology with friendly, trustworthy humanity—that understands music is emotion and joy, culture . . . and life." Beats Music would not be algorithm-free—as my interlocutors had pointed out, it couldn't be—but it would be a synthesis of human expertise and what it called the "best" technology. It would be, Reznor claimed, "the next step in the evolution that's taken us from 45s to CDs to streaming." As the advertisement drew to a close, a pulsing red heart appeared, pumping blood that spread into the shape of a circuit board (fig. 1). That image reappeared in Beats' online ad campaign: a circuit board coursing with blood, and written across the center: "Technology with Humanity."

That Man-versus-Machine Garbage

The contradictions and ambivalence of Beats Music encapsuled the state of popular discourse about algorithms during my fieldwork among the makers of music recommendation through the first half of the 2010s. Not much earlier, algorithms had been a fairly arcane technical concern,

FIGURE 1. Online advertisement for Beats Music

"a funny word that most people don't hear every day, if at all" (*Ad Age* 2007), as one advertising trade magazine put it. But they quickly became something companies might boast about, eager to demonstrate their technical prowess. And just as quickly, they became objects of substantial popular and academic critique.

It was common to see, as in the Beats marketing materials, algorithms and humans defined in opposition to each other. Humans were one thing, algorithms were another. Among the panels proposed for the industry conference South by Southwest in 2012, for instance, were "Music Discovery: Man vs. Machine," "Editor vs. Algorithm in the Music Discovery Space," and "Music/Radio Content: Tastemakers vs. Automation." News coverage in the popular and trade press routinely described algorithmic techniques as heralding the end of human expertise.

Through all this, it was never entirely clear what an algorithm was, what made a service "algorithmic," and whether it mattered or was just, as Jeremy had joked, "marketing." Nevertheless, the figure of the algorithm attracted much attention and aroused very strong feelings, not only in the world of music streaming but across so many domains that their variety came to serve as yet another symbol of algorithms' importance. Algorithms could be found calculating away and displacing human expertise in medicine and law, in companies' procedures for hiring and firing, and in situations ranging from the life-threatening targeting of drone strikes to the apparently insignificant selection of which song to play next.

When I interviewed Brian Whitman, cofounder of a music recommendation company called The Echo Nest, he recalled the discursive situation bluntly: "Every interview I ever got, or every panel I was on, they would just start with that man-versus-machine garbage—as if these were the only two options you had, basically. And that pissed us off." For the humans cast on the "algorithm" side of the human-algorithm dichotomy, this framing was a constant source of frustration. Not only did that "man-versus-machine garbage" categorically malign their work, but it was also inadequate to describe the many ways that people and software might come together in systems labeled "human" or "algorithmic." As Whitman (2012) wrote on his blog: "Yes, we use computer programs to help manage the mountains of music data, but so does everyone, and the way we get and use that data is just as human as anything else out there." Algorithms were never simply unaccompanied machines; they were always tended to by human minders. Whitman tweeted: "Real fleshy caring humans power all the popular music discovery platforms, including ours. No successful service uses only 'robots.'"

Whitman's argument, broadly shared among people I met in the field, echoed a truism in the social study of technology: most technical systems are best understood as sociotechnical systems—as hybrid agglomerations of elements that are both human and machine (Hughes 1987; Pfaffenberger 1992). While popular and academic critics might pit humans against algorithms, these "algorithms" were full of people making decisions, changing things around, and responding to a never-ending stream of small and large crises. In the rapid development cycles of contemporary software engineering, human actions are woven into the functioning of algorithms continually.[3]

In academia, concerns about algorithms arose across many disciplines in the humanities and social sciences—from sociology to journalism, legal theory to the history of science—constituting a body of work that would come to be known as "critical algorithm studies."[4] Being outsiders to computer science, many of these critics were anxious about their own technical expertise: what exactly was an algorithm anyway? Answering this question was an important step in establishing terms of critique, and early on, many critics turned to textbook definitions as they tried to make sense of algorithms. For instance, a commonly used undergraduate textbook defines "algorithm" like this: "An algorithm is any well-defined computational procedure that takes some value, or set of values, as input and produces some value, or set of values, as output. An algorithm is thus a sequence of computational steps that transform the input into the output" (Cormen et al. 2009, 5). Following such definitions, people often suggest that algorithms are essentially simplistic procedures. The prototypical algorithm in an introductory computer science course is a sorting algorithm—a procedure for putting lists in order, like arranging a deck of cards. This simplicity and this straightforwardness are often why algorithms are imagined to have problems grasping the complexities of social life. Recognizing someone's taste in music seems much more complex than unshuffling playing cards.

But this technically correct sense of "algorithm" does not capture the sociotechnical web of uncertainty and human judgment that characterizes algorithms in practice. We might call these actually existing technical apparatuses "algorithmic systems" to distinguish them from classroom idealisms, but out in the world, even among technical actors, people usually just call them algorithms. Significantly, these algorithmic systems reverse many of the features that define algorithms in textbooks: where a sorting algorithm is simple, well defined, and stable, an actual recommender system is complex, porous, and constantly changing. If algorithms seem to be defined by the absence of a human hand, algorithmic systems are full of people who make choices and change things up.

This reversal is significant: if our objects of interest are algorithmic systems, then limiting ourselves to studying technical details cuts out all of the people, whose motivations and ideas about the world actually change how the algorithm works. More strongly, we might say that, in algorithmic systems, these "cultural" details *are* technical details: the way an engineering team thinks about their work is as significant to the functioning of the system as the structure of a sorting algorithm. If we tried to look past all the people to find the algorithm, we'd miss a crucial part of how and why these systems come to work as they do.

Although algorithms have revived the popular specter of autonomous technology, to conclude that algorithms are sociotechnical is not much of a conclusion at all. It is, however, a useful starting point. We cannot approach algorithms as though their defining quality is the absence of human influence, and critiques that take the opposition of humanity and technology for granted risk reinforcing this cultural common sense rather than analyzing it. As feminist scholars of technology like Lucy Suchman and Donna Haraway have argued, the aim of critical researchers should not be to draw a clearer line between humans and machinery, but to examine "which kinds of humanness and machineness are produced" by our sociotechnical arrangements (Nakamura and Haraway 2003; see Suchman 2007).

Given that all music streaming services relied on a mixture of human and algorithmic processing, the public application of a label could be capricious: whether a system was described as "human" or "algorithmic" depended on who was talking and the point they wanted to make. In the popular press, to be "human" was to be culturally sensitive; to be "algo-rithmic" was to work at large scale.[5] Mike, chief scientist at a streaming radio company I'll call Willow, explained to me that his company gen-erated playlists algorithmically, but it used data about music that had been produced by human experts. As a result, popular critics would sometimes deride the company's playlists as "algorithmic"—lacking hu-man sensitivity—while its competitors would point to its use of human experts as a constraint: Willow could not recommend a song until it had been analyzed by a person. As the popular reputation of algorithms shifted, Willow's marketing materials emphasized different parts of its process.

In 2015, when Spotify released a new recommendation feature called Discover Weekly, anti-algorithm sentiment was high, and in interviews, company representatives rejected the standard dichotomy: "For describ-ing the way we do things at Spotify, 'human vs. algorithm' doesn't even make sense anymore" (Dredge 2015). The product manager Matthew Ogle maintained that Discover Weekly, because it analyzed playlists made by Spotify's users, was "humans all the way down. . . . Our algorithms stand on the shoulders of (human) giants" (Dredge 2015). To understand algorithms as the absence of a human hand didn't make sense, because, as Ogle said, humans were everywhere: they wrote the code, they gener-ated the data, they made the decisions about how a system should work. While this was corporate spin, it was also true. As one engineer put it to me, "Algorithms are human, too."

This book is about those humans—people who occupy a paradoxi-cal position within algorithmic systems and in discourse about them. Although they are often figured as unfeeling agents of rationality, they describe themselves as motivated by a deep care for music. Like many of their critics, the makers of music recommendation recognize that there is something strange about their aspirations—a tension between the closed, formal rationality of technology and the open, contingent subjectivity of taste. Whitman (2012) described it as "the postmodern insanity of a *computer understanding how you feel about music*." The title of this book, *Computing Taste*, is meant to index that tension—between the common-place idea that there is no accounting for taste and the elaborate forms of computational accounting we call recommender systems. That tension is an inescapable part of the cultural milieu in which the subjects of this book work. It is a problem that they try to resolve by drawing on their own experiences from worlds of calculation and feeling, by programming computers and exercising their cultural intuitions about taste and music.

The makers of music recommendation do not, as some critics suggest, simply chop and screw the elusive human stuff of taste into the rigid machinery of computation. Rather, they develop ways of thinking about musical preference, and about software, that try to reconcile them with each other. These ways of thinking are generally informed by a commitment to the open plan I described in the prologue—to techniques aimed at facilitating exploration and discovery, and to thinking about taste as something with potential, to be cultivated and grown.

The thinking of the makers of music recommendation matters because, as they note, there is no such thing as an unaccompanied algorithm. As algorithms change and grow, they do not follow some inexorable algorithmic logic that determines what they will be like. Rather, at every moment, people are making decisions and evaluating their consequences. And, at least within the scope of my fieldwork, these people were not the often-caricatured "data fundamentalists" (cf. Crawford 2013) who set aside their own personal judgment in favor of a naive belief in the objectivity of data and the desirability of automation. The makers of music recommendation are ambivalent actors who seek a path between the supposed opposition of algorithms and humans, computing and taste.

Taste and Technology

Anxieties about the relationship between humans and machines, along with their distinctive capacities, are long-standing themes in the culture from which algorithmic recommendation emerges. In the Western context, the division between rigid, unfeeling machinery and subtle, expressive humanity is a strong cultural value and readily available as an explanatory resource (Haraway 1991; Ingold 2001). In the context of technology, the idea of sociotechnical systems helps complicate this picture: as I've just described, technologies like algorithms look quite different when we drop the assumption that they are the opposite of human action.

Popular understandings of taste are neatly complementary with technology: if technology is the domain of necessary decisions, then taste is a human domain of arbitrary and subjective judgment. We can have taste in music but not in the mechanics of jet engines. Here, too, social scientists like to reverse things, emphasizing the flexibility of engineering and the determinedness of taste. Technologies are shaped by much more than the dogged pursuit of efficiency, and our tastes are actually shaped by forces beyond our own control.

Most social scientists would attribute this position on taste to Pierre Bourdieu, the sociologist whose book *Distinction* (1984) provides the field's common sense about what taste is and how it works. In brief: tastes are not caused by their objects but are consequences of the social order. Fancy people like fancy things, common people like common things, and preferences are a function of status, which serve to reinforce social hierarchy. This "homology thesis" is not the only argument Bourdieu makes about taste (and arguably, it predates him, being found in Thorstein Veblen's 1899 *Theory of the Leisure Class*), but for many social scientists, the homology between taste and status *is* Bourdieu's theory of taste. If we wanted to use this theory to build a recommender system, we might end up with an unsettling design: assess users' social positions and give them the cultural artifacts that correspond to their class fraction.

Critics of this theory suggest that it takes taste to be "an arbitrary election which has to be explained . . . by hidden social causes" (Hennion 2007, 98), leaving an explanatory hole: how is taste acquired in the first place? Research in the pragmatics of taste responds to this perceived lack in the Bourdieusian theory by attending to how people, especially enthusiasts, try to cultivate their own taste in practice, through studies of opera fans (Benzecry 2011), wine tasters (Shapin 2012), or recorded music listeners (Hennion 2001; DeNora 2000).

Music offers a useful domain in which to examine these concerns in part because it embodies the paradoxical relationship between culture and technology from which many concerns about algorithms emerge. As the anthropologist Georgina Born (2005, 8) has argued, music "destabilizes some of our most cherished dualisms concerning the separation not only of subject from object, but present from past, individual from collectivity, the authentic from the artificial, and production from reception." It also destabilizes the separation of culture and technology, being a paradigmatic example of "culture" by any definition and a symbol of human emotional expression while also being ineradicably technical. Music has existed through a variety of technological mediating assemblages, as Born describes them: collective playing of instruments, written notation, the circulation of audio recordings, and so on. Music is already a hybrid of the technical and the cultural, and this has long been a matter of some unease, especially in the Western tradition, with its trademark anxieties about mixture and impurity (Loughridge 2021).

Work in the pragmatics of taste commonly describes how taste is entangled with particular techniques. As the sociologist Antoine Hennion (2004, 6) writes: "Taste closely depends on its situations and material devices: time and space frame, tools, circumstances, rules, ways of doing things. It involves a meticulous temporal organization, collective arrangements, objects and instruments of all kinds, and a wide range of techniques to manage all that." In this theory, taste emerges from instrumented encounters; it does not miraculously manifest in individuals as a consequence of their social position. For the vulgar Bourdieusian, as critiqued by Hennion, the object of preference doesn't matter at all, and the experience of taste in the moment is incidental to the force of social structure, which compels certain tastes in certain people.

To be fair to Bourdieu, this is not what he said. As the sociologist Omar Lizardo (2014, 337) has argued, much of *Distinction* is in fact concerned with how taste is acquired—it is simply buried deep in the latter part of the "sprawling" book's "odd structure." Given Bourdieu's central role in developing practice theory, it would be surprising for him to suddenly come down on the side of structural determinism, arguing that people are simply recipients of large-scale social forces. Instead, Bourdieu's theory of taste hinges on his understanding of the habitus—the set of embodied dispositions that people acquire as they are socialized and that they exercise when making judgments of taste (among other things). For Bourdieu, the concept of habitus provides an alternative to visions of people as either free-willed autonomous subjects or unthinking vehicles of structural dynamics (see Sterne 2003, 376). People acquire the sensibilities that constitute their habitus in worlds full of the myriad entities Hennion describes: a person's taste in music is going to be shaped by how the people around them act, the forms they encounter music in, and a host of other situational factors. Because people in similar social positions grow up under similar conditions, they end up with a similar habitus, and the mystery of how tastes come to mirror social structure is at least partly resolved (Lizardo 2014, 346).

In Bourdieu's use of habitus and Hennion's insistence on the instrumented nature of taste, we find a potential rapprochement between taste and technology. Habitus is, at least in part, a technical concept: the anthropologist Marcel Mauss (1934) used it to encompass his theory of techniques of the body—culturally variable practices like walking, sitting, or swimming. The historian Jonathan Sterne (2003, 370) argues that "technologies are essentially subsets of habitus—they are organized forms of movement." If we understand taste and technology as different kinds of organized technique, they come to appear more similar than we might have thought.

Taste is not only something people have, but it is also something they do. It is a set of techniques for interacting with the world, and the world it interacts with is full of technologies: People have favorite recordings, record labels, radio stations; they encounter the objects of their preference through infrastructures of circulation; they learn to like within particular media ecologies. What it means to have taste thus changes over time: tuning the radio in 1940, buying a vinyl record in 1970, downloading MP3s in 2000, or listening to an on-demand streaming service in 2020 all transform the experience and development of musical preference. As a result, we might anticipate that what it means to have musical taste will change in a world full of algorithmic recommender systems. These systems would not only model taste from the outside, getting it right or wrong; they will actually change how it works as they become part of the circulatory infrastructure of music.

The point of laying out this theory of taste is not to set an academic benchmark against which we might evaluate the vernacular theories of the people I describe in this book. Ideas about taste do not need to be correct (or even explicit) to be built into algorithmic systems, and once there, they can constitute "performative infrastructures" (Thrift 2005, 224) that bring the world into alignment with the theories they embody. By exposing people to music along certain lines and not others, a recommender system working at a large enough scale may make itself come true, regardless of whether its makers have read their Bourdieu. Thinking of taste as an essentially instrumented technique, mediated and organized through countless devices, can help us avoid the essentialist view that technology should just leave taste alone—that computers must always come to taste from the outside, as technical interlopers to be resisted in the name of human subjectivity.

Consequently, this book is about taste in a rather expansive sense, as a mediated, malleable, emergent, collective phenomenon. If taste is entangled with technical concerns, then the way people understand technology can come to bear on how they understand taste. Even when the actors in this book are not explicitly talking about taste—when they worry about information overload or trace the geometries of machine learning—they are participating in the theorization and production of taste in this broader sense. Theories of taste and technology intermingle, sedimented into algorithmic systems or speculated about in conversation.

The Problem of Access

It is customary among critics of algorithmic systems to note that algorithms are very hard to study. Once we have decided that we are interested in, say, the vernacular theories of taste embedded into recommender systems, we are stuck. Algorithms are conventionally described as "black boxes"—obscure, hard-to-access, secret technologies that produce their effects on the world from behind a veil. Although secrecy is generally absent from computer scientists' understanding of algorithms, it has arguably become their defining feature in contemporary algorithmic critique.

As Malte Ziewitz (2016) has argued, secrecy is a key feature of the "algorithmic drama" that animates much of critical algorithm studies: first, algorithms are introduced as powerful and ubiquitous; second, they are described as hidden and mysterious, which makes them all the more powerful and in need of examination.[6] Thus, the central problem for the researcher becomes gaining access, and their goal becomes revelation: by bringing the functioning of an algorithmic system out from behind the veil, we can subject it to critique and lessen its power.[7] In practice, however, the figure of the black box does ethnographers more harm than good: it misrepresents what "access" looks like in practice, and it constrains our methods and the questions we might ask of algorithmic systems. To see what I mean, consider what happened when I first tried to get inside a black box at the personalized radio company Willow.

I was sitting in Willow's lobby, waiting for a meeting with the head of research and engineering, which I had managed to arrange through some persistent emailing. The room was filled with music (one of Willow's radio stations, chosen by the receptionist, I would learn) and by a broad, white desk with a glowing red sign embedded in it. On Air, it read, as though I were outside an actively broadcasting radio studio, which, in a metaphorical sense, I was.

Like many tech companies, Willow's reception desk had a small tablet computer on it for visitors to sign themselves in. The receptionist directed me to the tablet, which displayed a legal agreement and asked for my signature. Thoughtlessly, I clicked through and signed with my finger, as though I were trying to install some software on my computer or paying for a coffee at a café. I sat down in the row of obligatory modernist chairs lined up against the wall to wait for my host.

After a moment, I realized what I'd done and got up to ask the receptionist if I could have a copy of the agreement I'd just signed. I had a vague sense that this must be the law—that an agreement I couldn't keep a copy of was not a real agreement at all. The receptionist's sense of the law was vague too, and she frowned. "I'm not sure," she said. "I've never had anyone ask before." She said she would send a message to the company lawyers.

My host arrived and took me out of the office for lunch. If we had only met downstairs, I would never have encountered the agreement in the first place. After lunch, I returned to the lobby to follow up with the receptionist, who told me, reluctantly, that the lawyers had said I could have a copy of the agreement I'd signed, "but only if you really, really need it." I supposed that I did, and she printed it out for me, asking that I not share it publicly. It occurred to me that this was why she had printed it instead of emailing it to me: a physical document is just a bit harder to post to social media or to forward to a reporter.

On the subway home, I snapped a photo of the document on my lap, scouring it for the juicy details that Willow's lawyers might want to keep quiet. But it was completely unremarkable, a boilerplate liability waiver and nondisclosure agreement: if I got hurt on the premises, it was my own fault, and if I learned any "non-public, confidential, proprietary, and/or trade secret information," I promised not to tell. Just how I was supposed to recognize these various kinds of protected information was never specified.

In Willow's brilliant white lobby, I stood at the edge of the black box: a locked door, a receptionist with an iPad, and two nonlawyers' efforts to understand the law. As the legal scholar Frank Pasquale suggests in his landmark book *The Black Box Society* (2015), the blackness of these black boxes is largely constituted by legal regimes. The rise of unaccountable algorithmic systems can be tied to the history of corporate legal secrecy: since the late 1960s, corporations in the United States have enjoyed a growing set of legal protections that allow them to keep much of their internal operations hidden, firming up the boundary between the firm and the public. The document I had so casually signed was a result of this history.

What my encounter in the Willow lobby made clear was what anthropologists of secrecy commonly argue: secrecy is not a wall holding information back but a "relationship between insiders and outsiders" (Jones 2014, 62)—a pervasive social accomplishment, embedded, as the sociologist Georg Simmel (1906, 454) put it, in "the finest meshes of social forms." Whenever I spoke with someone who worked for a company, we jointly negotiated this boundary, determining what would count as "inside" or "outside" and what rules would govern our exchange. To borrow a phrase from the anthropologist Marina Welker (2014), we were "enacting the corporation," trying to coordinate among various senses of the permissible and the desirable, hoping that we wouldn't have to bring in the lawyers whose enactments are uniquely able to sharpen the border for everyone else.

Once I finally achieved what ethnographers would call "access," entering the offices of Whisper for a protracted stay as an intern, I was still not inside the black box. Although the office had its infrastructure bared— all exposed wiring and ducts—the algorithm always seemed to be somewhere else, an emergent property of the organization that I could only partly see, spread across a messy collection of desks. Conversations in the office were multimodal: laughter might erupt from one corner, in response to something from the company chat server; suddenly, a scattering of people would get up and move to a meeting room to discuss something only they knew about. I might hear the laughter or see some of the chats, but there was always the sense that the discussions I participated in and heard around the office were surfacing from contexts I wasn't privy to. The black box never opened up, and its border just kept thickening: more doors, more people, an infinite regress of boxes.

Conventional ways of thinking about access mislead researchers into thinking that, once they have cracked through the black box's wall, knowledge will be waiting there for the taking. But access is not an event; it is the ongoing navigation of relationships. Access has a texture, and this texture—patterns of disclosure and refusal—can be instructive in itself. When I interviewed junior employees, they were often worried about what they were allowed to say to me, even when I had signed the same nondisclosure agreements they had. In contrast, CEOs and founders usually spoke quite freely, sure in their ability to define the parameters of the permissible and to draw the corporation's limits into strict, punishing existence at will. The social structure of the firm shimmered into view through these interactions.

And while navigating access can be frustrating for ethnographers, it would be a mistake to assume that they are the only people excluded. As the anthropologist Casper Bruun Jensen (2010, 74) has argued, the experience of most people working within broadly distributed, technologically mediated organizations is "characterized by limited presence, partial information and uncertain connections." If ethnographers make it into the office, they will find themselves situated within a shared topography of knowing and not knowing with the insiders, who do not know everything.

In figuring out how to approach algorithmic systems, the would-be ethnographer is up against three stacked imaginaries: algorithms as technically closed black boxes, corporations as sealed-off parts of society, and field sites as naturally bounded locations. The ideologies of access and knowledge that circulate around these powerful border imaginaries can fool us into thinking that just because something is secret, it must be what we want to know. In the algorithmic drama, ethnographers are cast as raiders of the office park who try to gain access to obscure sites in order to shuttle precious secrets out of them.

But this is a flawed understanding of what knowledge is in general and what we might want to know about algorithmic systems in particular. As critics of algorithmic "transparency" initiatives have argued (e.g., Ananny and Crawford 2016), we cannot meaningfully talk about knowledge in the abstract, as though facts were just sitting around in the office, waiting to be uncovered: to talk about knowledge, we need to talk about knowers. And as feminist epistemologists have demonstrated, these discourses of discovery—in which researchers heroically recover facts from a recalcitrant world—give a poor account of the interactive and dynamic processes through which knowledge is made (Harding 1986), evincing what the anthropologist Henrietta Moore (2010, 31) describes as a "masculine preoccupation with penetration, domination, and objectification."

In pursuing dominance over withheld objects, we risk forgetting our interest in understanding cultural practices. This is not a book about the precise configuration of one recommender system at one moment in time—an arrangement that would likely have changed by the time I returned home from the field and has certainly changed by the time I write this book. Rather, it is about more durable ways of thinking that continue to inform how these systems evolve. Ethnographers and other critics have more to do than simply reporting on technical details that engineers already know; by attending to how the people working in these systems think about their work, we can understand how recommender systems take shape.

The Shape of the Field

So, what should an ethnographer do?[8]

It is useful to remember that algorithmic systems are not the first obscure objects that ethnographers have tried to study and that the conditions of partial knowledge and pervasive semisecrecy I've been describing exist in all sorts of field sites. Looking to ethnographies concerned with conspicuously hard-to-access groups, I found helpful models in work on magicians (Jones 2011), Freemasons (Mahmud 2014), and nuclear scientists (Gusterson 1996) that both theorized secrecy itself and suggested tactics for ethnographers dealing with it.[9]

In his efforts to study nuclear scientists in the United States, Hugh Gusterson (1997, 116) faced an intensely secretive organization, spurring an eclectic approach that he termed "polymorphous engagement": "Polymorphous engagement means interacting with informants across a number of dispersed sites, not just in local communities, and sometimes in virtual form; and it means collecting data eclectically from a disparate array of sources in many different ways." Against dominant ethnographic fantasies of access and full participation, this attitude embraced a long anthropological tradition of "pragmatic amateurism" in the field (Gusterson 1997, 116), gleaning information wherever it may be found. For Gusterson, this was at the homes of workers or in local cafeterias; for me, it was often in off-the-record chats with engineers, the reading of press releases against social media updates, and a host of other informal settings where the apparently airtight boundaries of corporations became porous. "Ethnography," as Ulf Hannerz (2003, 213) writes, "is an art of the possible."

People who work at software companies, like most people, are not absolutely secretive; rather, they exercise discretion (Mahmud 2012). They share certain kinds of knowledge with certain kinds of people in certain situations, and they do so in ways that are not entirely determined by legal obligations. Among tech workers in Silicon Valley, for instance, the "frieNDA" (punning on the abbreviation for "nondisclosure agreement") is a common informal arrangement whereby people working at different companies share information with each other that may be technically proprietary. As I continued to speak with people over many years, demonstrating that I knew a lot about their work, they became more willing to share information with me that was questionably secret. In writing about this information, I have sometimes had to exercise my own discretion, compositing people and altering details so as to obscure my sources and protect the confidence of those who confided in me.

But much of what interests scholars of critical algorithm studies—ways of thinking, styles of explanation, responses to critique, and shared common sense—is not secret at all. It is quite available to the researcher who manages to build relationships with people working on these systems. While outside researchers are unlikely to be able to trace out the bulk of a single company's algorithmic system, they can roam across the broader corporate field, piecing together elements from disparate sites. The resulting knowledge is not an exposé of a particular company's configuration at one historical moment but a more generalizable appraisal of cultural understandings that obtain across multiple sites within an industry. These understandings are more durable and more common than specific technical configurations, and thus they are arguably more useful to outside critics than knowledge about what is happening inside one rapidly changing software system at one moment in time.[10] Working at this level of abstraction cannot answer every question we might want to ask of algorithmic recommendation, but it is well suited to my central concern here: How do the people who design and build recommender systems think about music, listeners, and taste?

So, this book is not about one algorithmic system in particular but

about the world of music recommendation in general: a loose conglomerate of academic and commercial institutions in which systems for recommending music are researched, invented, and deployed. Like many
contemporary ethnographies, this one is multisited, tracing a network
of connected locations rather than staying put in a single place (Marcus
1995; Burrell 2009). Between 2011 and 2015, I visited academic labs and
corporate offices in San Diego, Los Angeles, San Francisco, Boston, and
New York, for terms ranging from single lab meetings to a three-month
internship. I attended hackathons, meet-ups, and social gatherings in and
out of work. I attended nine international academic and industry conferences with people I had met in the field, on topics including recommender systems research, music informatics, and applied mathematics.
I took popular online courses in recommender system design and one
at a major public university. I stayed in touch with many of the people
I met in the field through social media, mailing lists, and blogs, just as
they used these platforms to stay in touch with one another. I collected a
personal archive of news coverage, company white papers, and academic
research on music recommendation. And over the course of this research,
I conducted about ninety semistructured interviews with CEOs, aspiring
founders, product managers, software engineers, data analysts, data curators, office managers, consultants, interns, hackers, scientists, graduate
student researchers, and professors.

As I moved through this network, being referred on by interviewees or
encountering strangers at conferences, I began to recognize the contours
of an "invisible college" (Crane 1972) of researchers who had begun their
careers in academia and then moved out into industry, often following
their advisers or bringing their students and coauthors with them. An invisible college is a coherent group of researchers, the boundaries of which
do not correspond to any particular institution but rather collect together
a dispersed set of people. Not everyone in the labs that graduate students
came from worked on music recommendation, and not everyone at the
conferences they attended was part of this group. But within the invisible
college, people knew one another, coauthored with one another, hired
one another, and skipped conference social events to go have drinks with
one another.

If there is an *ethnos* in this ethnography, it is this invisible college—the
people I call "the makers of music recommendation." The fact that this
group extended beyond the walls of corporations offered an opportunity
to see—if not the trade secrets of particular companies—the common
sense they shared with those who remained in academic positions. Members of this group fill the research teams at all the major music stream-

ing services today; almost everyone depicted as a graduate student in this book now works in industry as a professional researcher or software engineer.

Like the industry and academic disciplines of which they are a part, these sites were fairly demographically homogeneous, dominated by white men in their twenties and thirties. I sought to diversify the set of people I interviewed as much as possible, although they still reflect the relative homogeneity of the field. In many cases, the scarcity of members of minoritized groups meant that noting their race or gender in the text would make them uniquely identifiable, so in such cases, I have not done so. My own social position, as another white man in his twenties and thirties who could have easily ended up performing the jobs described here instead of writing about them, doubtless shaped what access I managed to achieve. My hope is that other ethnographers, bringing other perspectives and other questions, will be able to complement the work I've done here, filling out a richer and broader picture of the industry than any one researcher could do alone.

The Plan of the Book

Through the following chapters, I describe how the makers of music recommendation think about various aspects of their work: the digital environment, the purpose of recommendation, the variability of listeners, the nature of sound, the meaning of musical genre, and their own technological agency. To gain purchase on their thinking, I bring them into dialogue with parts of the ethnographic record that may at first seem remote from office work: anthropological theorizing about trapping, myth, cosmology, and many other topics appears throughout these pages as a tool for thinking differently about what has become a culturally dominant form of technical practice. I often seize on particular metaphors—like capturing users or tending to musical landscapes—to help make visible ways of thinking that pervade the industry.

Chapter 1, "Too Much Music," offers a brief history of the origins of modern recommender systems in the mid-1990s, alongside the emergence of the World Wide Web. There, we find what remains the most common argument for algorithmic recommendation: people are overwhelmed by the choices that information technology makes available, and recommender systems promise to help, by mediating between limited individuals and apparently limitless archives. Through analyzing these stories of overload as myths—not historical claims, but accounts of the nature of the world—I draw attention to the cosmology of algorithmic recommendation. The makers of recommender systems imagine themselves and their users to live in a world where everything is informatic, and to exist is to be overwhelmed.

Chapter 2, "Captivating Algorithms," turns to an apparently contradictory understanding of what recommender systems are for: it is common for developers to describe their goal as "hooking" people, enticing and retaining users for a platform. I argue that this shift emerged as part of a broader transformation in the business models and technical infrastructure of digital media services. Drawing on work in the anthropology of animal trapping, I describe how theories about listener behavior are embedded in the technical design of recommender systems. By examining what it means for a recommender system to "work"—and how metrics of success have changed—we can better understand how ideas about listeners and ideas about algorithms are entangled.

Where the first two chapters present visions of listeners as overloaded people in need of help or as prey to be captured, chapter 3, "What Are Listeners Like?," pursues another vision of the listening subject: the "lean-back" listener, whose preferences are defined by her context. For the makers of recommender systems, "context" is a capacious label that applies to all sorts of data, ranging from location to weather to the configuration of a software interface. The techniques in chapter 1 rely primarily on users' ratings of items to be recommended; the techniques in chapter 2 turn to measures of engagement like listening time. In chapter 3, we find omnivorous systems that acquire all sorts of data, figuring listeners as fragmentary and potentially incoherent subjects.

Chapter 4, "Hearing and Counting," turns to a concern that is surprisingly absent from most music recommenders: how music sounds. This chapter examines how musical sound is brought in to recommender systems, as a kind of signal within the informatic cosmology described in chapter 1. This understanding of music is premised on the idea that music and mathematics—and hearing and counting more generally—are fundamentally linked. Where humanistic critics often worry about the reductive effects of quantification, I describe how the connection between numbers and sound also enables a set of interpretive listening practices that are central to algorithmic work.

Chapter 5, "Space Is the Place," moves from the content of individual songs to what developers call the "music space," a shared abstract vision of music distributed by similarity. Algorithmic recommendation is commonly imagined as occurring within spaces like these, where similar users are "neighbors" and plausible recommendations are nearby. Such spaces are widespread in machine learning more generally, where they are treated simultaneously as intuitive models of difference and uncanny computational objects. Understanding musical variation as essentially spatial changes the meaning of familiar terms like genre and preference, rendering them as clusters or regions to be computationally mapped and explored.

Chapter 6, "Parks and Recommendation," builds on that discussion of space by examining a set of spatial metaphors commonly used by the makers of music recommendation: pastoral metaphors that figure technical workers as gardeners or park rangers who tend to the music space and the listeners who travel within it. Many critics have argued that such metaphors naturalize the work of machine learning, mystifying how it actually works. I offer a different interpretation, suggesting that developers find pastoral metaphors useful because they describe an ambivalent form of control: while the people who manage the music space are aware that they determine a good deal of its structure, they also understand their work as tending to lively data sources beyond their influence. Analyzing these metaphors helps us interpret how the makers of music recommendation think about their power and responsibility in relation to the objects of their labor and to music more generally.

In the epilogue, I step back, recounting an interview with one of the central figures in the field, conducted a few years after he left the industry and after I wrapped up my fieldwork. We discuss the souring of his optimistic vision, the limits of the open plan, and the limits of ethnographic research as algorithmic systems sink deeper into corporate structures, growing ever more complex and centralized.

Despite their reputation and their apparent success, the makers of music recommendation were often uncertain about their work and its consequences. They tried to make sense of the world of music and their role in it using the tools they had ready to hand: the various technologies involved in algorithmic recommendation and a particular understanding of the nature of computing and of taste. Throughout this book, my goal has been to trace out the connections between techniques and worldviews within this group, elaborating on the thinking I encountered in the field. This sympathetic approach has its limits: staying close to the people who work in these systems means that I cannot speak authoritatively about their impacts on others who make music or listen to it. But by better understanding how the makers of music recommendation think, we will be in a better position to understand how recommender systems have come to work as they do and why.

CHAPTER 1

Too Much Music

Ganging Up on Information Overload

Ringo was, by most accounts, the first music recommender system.

When it launched, in July 1994, users interacted with Ringo via email. If you sent it a message reading "join," the system would respond with a list of 125 artists to rate on a seven-point scale (from "1: Pass the earplugs" to "7: BOOM! One of my FAVORITE few! Can't live without it"). Those ratings were the start of your profile on the service, representing your musical preferences. By comparing profiles using standard statistical methods, Ringo identified "neighborhoods" of similar users, whose ratings might be used to make recommendations to one another.

After creating your profile, you would receive a welcome message that began like this: "Hi there, Music Lover! Welcome to Ringo, your personal music recommendation service. There is a world of music out there, some of it meant for you, some of it not. What should you check out, what should you avoid? Ringo is here to help answer that question, to recommend artists that you personally will like, to help you wade through the ocean of CDs that's out there" (Shardanand 1994, 83). Ringo was a product of the Software Agents Group at MIT's Media Lab, which was led by the computer scientist Pattie Maes. The group called their new technique "social information filtering," and they described it as a tool for "automating word of mouth." Emailing Ringo, they suggested, was like asking a friend for recommendations, except that, "instead of having to ask a couple friends about a few items, a social information filtering system can ask thousands of other people, and consider thousands of different items, all happening autonomously and automatically" (Shardanand and Maes 1995, 211).[1]

The reason to automate word of mouth, according to the Ringo team, was that people had begun to face an overwhelming accumulation of choices in all areas of contemporary life, including music. All the publications stemming from the Ringo project began by invoking the figure of information overload. For instance, Upendra Shardanand (1994, 13), a master's student in the group, began his thesis like this: "Recent years have seen the explosive growth of the sheer volume of everyday things. The number of products, books, music, movies, news, advertisements, and the flow of information in general, is staggering. This truly is an 'information age.' The volume of things is considerably more than any person can digest. A person could not possibly filter through every item in order to select the ones that he or she truly wants and needs." He went on, listing some more examples of media's staggering availability: the mail-order BMG Compact Disc Club offered 14,000 CDs, the average Blockbuster Video had 6,000 VHS tapes available to rent, and the Library of Congress held 15,700,905 books. "As the world becomes more digital and interactive," Shardanand (1994, 14) continued, "with the promise of the 'information superhighway,' more and more options will become available." Without help, people would be unable to parse all these choices, using "what little time we have to select items worthy of our time and effort" (14). To deal with a problem of this scale, "we need technology" (Shardanand and Maes 1995, 210).[2]

Shardanand and Maes argued that social filtering was better than conventional content-based searching in several respects: First, because it relied on ratings, Ringo's recommendations captured collective notions of quality, preferring music that was highly rated, not only similar. Second, because Ringo knew nothing about sound, Shardanand and Maes suggested that its recommendations were more "serendipitous"; it recommended music that did not necessarily all sound alike.[3] Third, and most importantly, Ringo was domain independent. Because it required only ratings data, this technique could, in theory, recommend anything that you could get people to rate.[4]

Around the same time, a few other research groups were doing just that. In 1992, researchers at the Xerox Palo Alto Research Center (PARC) released a system called Tapestry, which used a technique they called "collaborative filtering" to sort through email. In 1994, researchers at the University of Minnesota, working with another team from MIT, released GroupLens, a collaborative filtering system designed to sort through postings in online newsgroups. Not long after that, the GroupLens team released MovieLens, which recommended movies; at the University of California, Berkeley, the Jester system would recommend jokes.

These systems shared the same basic premises and techniques. Individuals were overwhelmed, and conventional forms of filtering—sorting emails by key terms or music by genre labels—were not up to the task. In the article presenting Tapestry, a figure showed a businessman "being inundated by a huge stream of incoming documents" (Goldberg et al. 1992, 61), flailing in shirt and tie under a cascade of paper. Conventional filtering methods barely attenuated the flow, but a figure labeled "collaborative filtering" showed him finally at ease, leaning back in his chair as a faceless colleague presented him with a neat stack of papers (fig. 2).[5]

What made collaborative filtering "collaborative" was the same thing that made social information filtering "social": the idea that the solution

FIGURE 2. Tapestry's overloaded subject (Goldberg et al. 1992, 62)

to overload lay in linking isolated users together, or, as the title of a review essay later published by the GroupLens team put it, "Ganging Up on Information Overload" (Borchers et al. 1998). "A basic tenet of the Tapestry work," the PARC team wrote, "is that more effective filtering can be done by involving humans in the filtering process" (Goldberg et al. 1992, 61).

Tapestry, which inaugurated the term "collaborative filtering," required users to create their own filters. A worker, for example, might want to filter company-wide messages to only see those that had been annotated as "interesting" by their manager. The problem with such an approach, the Ringo and GroupLens teams would argue, was that it only worked in small settings, where people already knew each other well enough to know which other users shared their interests. "Tapestry," Shardanand (1994, 20) wrote, "only provides an on-line architecture for facilitating 'word-of-mouth,'" not *automating* it.

Implicit in this critique was the idea that users were overloaded not only by items but also by one another. Finding your "neighbors" could be an overwhelming challenge in its own right. The benefit of automated collaborative filtering was that it effectively gathered individuals together into a "large virtual community where users could share recommendations without actually knowing each other" (Borchers et al. 1998, 107).

While Tapestry's basic techniques of shared annotations and manual filter creation would be short-lived, the name "collaborative filtering" stuck. Although the MIT group at first tried to distance itself from the term (Shardanand 1994, 20), Ringo soon came to be considered an "automatic collaborative filter." Within a few years, the term "collaborative filtering" would refer exclusively to these automated variants. Today, recommender systems that generate suggestions from patterns in user data are still called collaborative filters, even though the intentional collaboration that gave them the name has long vanished. These systems envision users as a collective that might collaborate without knowing it, entered into relations they do not realize they have with "neighbors" they do not know.

What made collaborative filtering work, according to its creators, was the fact that "people's tastes are not randomly distributed: there are general trends and patterns" (Shardanand and Maes 1995, 211). Users resembled one another; they clustered into neighborhoods, even when they thought their own preferences were unique. Your taste was not your own—it was something partially shared with countless others. This was, as written in the original GroupLens paper, "a deceptively simple idea: people who agreed in their subjective evaluation of past articles are likely to agree again in the future" (Resnick et al. 1994, 176). Shardanand captured this associative logic in an epigraph to his thesis, borrowed from The Beatles: "I am he as you are he as you are me and we are all together."

Emerging at the same time as the World Wide Web, these early collaborative filters established a durable paradigm for how recommender systems worked and what they were for. Algorithmic recommendation was not only useful, according to its creators; it was becoming *necessary* to mitigate the overwhelming effects of an otherwise utopian age of information access.

The Celestial Jukebox, Brought Down to Earth

When Ringo was released in 1994, sales of CDs were just surpassing audiocassettes in the United States, and music industry pundits were anticipating an abundant digital future. They called it the "celestial jukebox."

In a book that helped popularize the term, the legal scholar Paul Goldstein (1994, 199) described the celestial jukebox as "a technology-packed satellite orbiting thousands of miles above the Earth, awaiting a subscriber's order—like a nickel in the old jukebox, and the punch of a button."[6] From the heavens, the celestial jukebox would allow anyone, anywhere, at any time to listen to anything from its "vast storehouse" of music, "via a home or office receiver that combines the power of a television set, radio, CD player, VCR, telephone, fax, and personal computer" (199). This media chimera heralded a musical utopia in which listening would be seamless, effortless, and bountiful.

The celestial jukebox was not a satellite any more than it was a fax machine. But like actual satellites, it was a potent guiding vision—a destination for technological road maps and economic investment plans, a vanishing point that set the current music industry in perspective.[7] As the media critic Eric Harvey (2014) has argued, "the celestial jukebox merged a beloved cultural form with the immeasurable scope of the heavens, giving notoriously tech-illiterate CEOs and politicians a useful idea around which to build a new industry." Corporate invocations of the celestial jukebox bathed the slick futurity of the satellite in the nostalgic glow of the nickelodeon, imagining a situation in which the practical challenges of real-life music distribution—from the technical architecture of data circulation to the legal apparatus of copyright—had already been escaped. The celestial jukebox marked the azimuth of corporate fancy, a bright spot in the night sky against which existing media infrastructures might be reckoned and toward which they could be oriented.[8]

For a while, it seemed that the main problem with the celestial jukebox was how to get there. As early as 2001, the music streaming service Rhapsody advertised itself online as "THE Celestial Jukebox," offering its subscribers unlimited listening to its catalog for a monthly fee. But Rhapsody and its peers stumbled, struggling with bandwidth constraints and licensing troubles. By the time of my fieldwork, Harvey (2014) could write that "the celestial jukebox is mostly remembered today for how dramatically it failed."

After a decade of halting starts, however, a new generation of music streaming services launched in the United States around 2010, facilitated by smartphones, high-speed internet, and new licensing deals with record labels. These companies claimed the mantle of the celestial jukebox, if not its name, offering more reliable access to significantly more music than their predecessors. Spotify, based in Stockholm, advertised, "All the music, all the time." Rdio, with headquarters in San Francisco, promised "unlimited music everywhere." Deezer, founded in Paris, claimed that users could "listen to all the music you love, anytime, anywhere." A few years later, Beats Music would launch with what it described as "a vast catalog of more than 20 million fully licensed songs." While I was conducting fieldwork, these companies were in a period of tumultuous and dramatic growth: by 2014, 67 percent of music listeners in the United States listened online.[9] It seemed, as one music technology journalist put it, that music listeners had finally reached the "promised land" (Bylin 2014).

But if this was the celestial jukebox, landed on Earth, then its arrival was less lustrous than anticipated. Twenty years after the release of Ringo, as I set out into the field, the makers of music recommendation were bemoaning the same old problems in a new technological context.

In one of my earliest interviews, I sat with Peter, a senior engineer at Whisper, in one of the company's brick-walled meeting rooms. He explained to me how music recommendation was designed to solve a problem caused by the changing economics of the music industry: "Fifteen, twenty, thirty years ago music had to go through this expensive pipeline, right?" Because of all the costs associated with finding, recording, and distributing music, "there were these gatekeepers—you had A&R people, you had the labels, the producers, you had the DJs."[10] Thanks to the work of those cultural intermediaries, he explained, "there was some notion at the end that the stuff that came out was worth listening to." "But now," he continued, "the internet has sort of leveled out the playing field. You don't need trucks. You don't need a label. You don't need anything. If you have a laptop, you can publish music." This was a familiar story, told in the obligatory second-person of internet utopianism (Grossman 2006), but it ended with a problem for a different "you": the listener. "Now," Peter told me, "the slush pile" that used to be filtered out by the machinations of the music industry "is sitting in your inbox."

: :

Too much music. This was the problem that recommender systems were meant to solve—the omnipresent justification for their existence, from the ocean of CDs in the mid-1990s to the massive on-demand streaming catalogs of the mid-2010s. That claim was repeated everywhere: in interviews, research papers, press releases, and conference presentations. One could hardly begin to explain what recommender systems were without first invoking the figure of overload. It was a problem, and it was new, and it was only one part of an all-embracing glut that was growing in every domain, making things even worse.

Sometimes, people would name this problem with terms from psychology like "choice overload" or "the paradox of choice" (Schwartz 2004), which described the surprising results of giving people too many options: "although the provision of extensive choices may sometimes still be seen as initially desirable, it may also prove unexpectedly demotivating in the end" (Iyengar and Lepper 2000, 996). More often, they used the more generic "information overload." But it was a reality that was deeply felt—a commonsense problem that needed little explanation.[11]

As one engineer put it: "30 million songs! With 30 million songs, how do you even begin?" He joked: "You begin of course, by saying, 'Hey, all the music in the world! Cool! I can listen to that Dave Matthews Band album I had on CD but never unpacked after my last move!' And then, forty minutes later, it's over, and there are 29,999,988 songs left."

It was surprisingly easy to forget that on-demand music streaming was relatively new—a utopian fantasy only a few years earlier—or that complaints of musical overload long predated these services. If this was a musical utopia, then it was like the realized utopia that the cultural critic Theodor Adorno had bemoaned in the 1960s: "The fulfillment of utopia consists in general only in a repetition of the ever-same," a dispiriting stasis, like gaining access to most of the world's music and listening only to a familiar Dave Matthews Band album, again and again (quoted in Bloch 1988, 2).[12]

Overload was such a fixture of local common sense that it took me a long time to realize that it might not be a problem at all. Why should access to a large catalog be understood as a burden rather than a resource?

If not knowing what to listen to next was a problem, then who was it a problem for?

We have no shortage of explanations that place the blame at the foot of capitalism itself: in the ceaseless production of desire that capital demands. The musicologist Eric Drott (2018c, 333), for instance, convincingly argues that the promotional materials for music streaming services "transfigure plenitude into a form of lack." These services provide users access to the catalog, and then suggest that the size of the catalog is a problem that they can solve for those same users, keeping the wheels of capital moving. The cultural critic Jonathan Cohn (2018, 50) follows a similar line of reasoning, arguing that recommender systems operate in "bad faith," framing choice as a "burden" to be relieved rather than as the location of users' agency, which recommendations diminish.

These explanations are not wrong; they reach for large-scale dynamics of desire and production. But they do not capture the local reasoning of people working on these systems, who *feel* the reality of overload in their everyday lives and come to understand their work as a form of care for users who are similarly beset by the paradox of choice. If we want to understand the logic of people working in these systems, we cannot reduce their efforts at understanding the world to "bad faith" or the epiphenomena of capitalist machinery. This does not mean that the makers of music recommendation can't be wrong—about themselves, their users, or the cultural dynamics they try to understand. They may indeed be caught up in large-scale processes in which their ultimate function is the ongoing production of consumer desire. But the political economy of the music industry does not directly determine how people working in these settings make decisions or think about their work.

My goal here is to understand how recommender systems make sense to their makers—how they work, who they're for, why they exist. To do this, we need to understand overload. Overload haunts the utopian fantasies of the information age, lurking beneath dreams of exponential growth and threatening to turn computing's successes into failures. It feels real, it feels new, and it feels tightly bound up with contemporary technologies of media circulation. And yet as we've already seen, its newness is old. What seemed like a natural response to on-demand streaming in the 2010s also seemed like a natural response to the ocean of CDs in the 1990s.

What are we to make of the simultaneous novelty and timelessness of overload? And what is there to say about the possibility that overload, self-evident as it seems, may not be a "real" problem at all but an invention?

In what follows, I make a case for thinking about overload as a myth—not a falsehood or mistake, but a particular kind of story about the nature of the world. In anthropological usage, myths are cosmological stories that function beyond the realm of proof. Although we often find claims of overload accompanied by quantitative "evidence," like the number of songs in a streaming catalog, these numbers are not where overload finds its reality. Overload's existence is experienced as a necessary fact of an informational universe. Interpreting overload in this way will help us to better understand the worldviews of the people who build these systems. Taking this myth and historicizing it will help to draw the apparent inevitability of overload into question, locating it not in the timeless nature of the universe but within particular social and technological arrangements. This chapter sketches a history of recommender systems and overload that will bring us to the ethnographic present, in the mid-2010s. But the story begins much earlier.

Twenty Thousand Years of Collaborative Filtering

Joseph Konstan was giving a webinar. I was logged on from my windowless graduate student office at the University of California, Irvine, while Konstan, a lauded computer scientist at the University of Minnesota, lectured on the history of recommender systems.[13] Konstan had joined the GroupLens team in its early days, and in 2012, he was its head. But rather than starting his talk with the beginning of his career, Konstan took a longer view: "I'd like to briefly start back about twenty thousand years ago," he began. "You have a bunch of people living in a cave."

"They're all hungry all the time, and outside the cave, there's this plant growing with these bright red fruit on it," he continued. "The question is: Do you eat the fruit?" This primordial scene, according to Konstan, was the setting for an "early recommender system": rather than trying the fruit for ourselves, humans "evolved to take advantage of the learnings of others." Those who went ahead and tasted what turned out to be poisonous nightshade died, while those who waited and watched learned and survived. Thus, Konstan suggested, from our earliest days, humans have parsed the overwhelming variety of the world collectively. Recommendation was woven into our existence as a species by evolution itself.

Over the intervening millennia, Konstan continued, the basic collaborative scene prototyped in the cave was extended and complicated. From the bare necessities of survival, recommendation expanded to more elective and fine-grained concerns, like taste and efficiency. "Over time," Konstan explained, "we added science, we added technology, we added the concept of critics." The work of recommendation was professionalized, dividing the labor and risk of exploration "so that we don't all waste our time or money doing it." Critics could tell us which books were worth reading; scientists could tell us which theories about the world were worth believing. Today, Konstan argued, "we are all pretty comfortable and familiar with the idea that we take the opinions of others into account as we try to figure out what we're doing for ourselves."

Konstan's story traced a wide arc from the dawn of humankind, scrabbling for an evolutionary foothold, to the mundane present, where someone choosing what music to listen to might want a little help. As he had written with his GroupLens codirector John Riedl, "collaborative filtering is at the same time very new and very old" (Riedl and Konstan 2002, 1). The species history of humanity might be told, his lecture suggested, as a history of recommender systems, beginning with the very first time someone sought out another person's advice and ending up at today's algorithmic correlation detectors. Tying this grand story together was a particularly generic definition of what recommender systems were. As Konstan defined them in his online course, recommender systems were simply tools to "help people find things, when the process of finding the information you need to make choices might be a little bit challenging because there's too many choices, too many alternatives."

Overload, in this story, was not a consequence of the information age, but much older. Contemporary humans might be overwhelmed by media of our own creation, but even primordial man could be overwhelmed by the plenitude of the natural world and its mysteries. Overload was, it seemed, simply a consequence of living in a world with horizons broader than one's own. And algorithmic recommender systems were just the most recent development in a species-spanning history of recommendation, dating back to the origins of human sociality itself.

In his online course, Konstan suggested that recommendation might, in fact, be even older, beginning before the dawn of humankind: "Let me take you back first a few hundred thousand years to the emergence of recommender systems, as ants crawled around the face of the Earth." Ants wandered the planet looking for food, and when they found it, they left a "scent trail that the other ants soon follow. Those ants are exhibiting social navigation, a type of recommendation system."[14] Recommendation existed even "before we had concepts like language or writing," in the semiochemical patterning of ant trails—a formic recommender infrastructure that pointed to the coincidence of recommendation not only with humanity but potentially with life itself.[15]

The Myth of Overload

Appeals to human origins like Konstan's are surprisingly common features of discourse in academic computer science and the commercial software industry alike. Start-up founders tie their business plans to claims from evolutionary psychology; conference talks show indigenous people, framed as "primordial man," using contemporary information technologies. Yuval Noah Harari, a medievalist who has found great popular success in a turn to species-scale histories like *Sapiens* (2014) and *Homo Deus* (2016), has been described as "Silicon Valley's favorite historian" (Ungerleider 2017), tying visions of technical futures back to scenes from humanity's past.

Anthropologists are well positioned to critique the accuracy of such stories, which often drape themselves in anthropological garb, as the titles of Harari's books suggest. Michelle Rosaldo, for example, critiqued such appeals to origins in 1980: "the 'primitive' emerges in accounts like these as the bearer of primordial human need," but these vernacular anthropologies are typically stuck in a universalizing mode, inventing ancestors as a screen on which to project contemporary concerns, "the image of ourselves undressed" (392).

However, while these just-so stories often borrow a veneer of scientific authority from evolutionary psychology (see McKinnon 2005), they are not factual in any concrete sense. Konstan was not claiming that his allegory of the cave actually happened as he recounted it. Rather, something like it *must* have happened, given his understanding of how the world works. Overload is understood to be a necessary fact of existence, one that can be known from personal experience and readily extrapolated to any situation, however remote.

In other words, the story of the cave people is a myth. It has mythology's signature style: set in a primordial period outside of history, we find a tale about human origins and essences, which frames our ordinary experiences within a timeless reality. As Claude Lévi-Strauss (1983, 16) put it, myth "overcomes the contradiction between historical, enacted time and a permanent constant." Myths conjure the epic scale of existence to contain and explain the small scale of personal experience. They provide origin stories for "things that cannot possibly have origins" (Weiner 2009, 493)—like water, or the feeling of being overwhelmed—locating them beyond the contingencies of historical time.

In 1999, the library scientist Tonyia Tidline suggested that information overload, despite its prominence in academic and popular discourse, had never been rigorously documented. While it was often invoked as an obvious fact of the "information age," it was not clear what the problem was: Was it just a form of anxiety? Was it a lack of interest in making choices? Information overload, she argued, could be best understood not as a scientific fact but as a myth—an "overarching, prescriptive belief" (Tidline 1999, 486).

As the feminist technology scholar Anne Balsamo (1998, 227) has written, "myths are neither true nor false; rather, they are collective accounts of our collective life." To call information overload a myth is to recognize it not as a factual claim, but as a statement about the nature of the world we live in. Konstan's telling is just one instance of this myth: we have always been overwhelmed, whether by the scope of the world or by the cultural artifacts we've created to fill it. And as long as we have been us, we've depended on recommendation to mediate between the small scale of the individual and the large scale of the environment in which we live.

Although we don't find programmers reciting relevant myths while they work, as we do in conventional ethnographies of myth and technology (e.g., Malinowski 1935; Nahum-Claudel 2017), computing is no stranger to myth. There are stories about genius founding figures like Apple's Steve Jobs, who are cast away from their companies only to return and lead them from the brink of ruin to towering success.[16] Ontological games, like the Turing test, chess, or go, mark a tenuous boundary between humans and machines. Venture capitalists claim that software is "eating the world" (Andreessen 2011), like a Norse serpent, and tech workers return to the desert every year in search of profane release and entheogenic experience (Turner 2009). The celestial jukebox orbits in the heavens, waiting to be brought down to Earth. The world of science and engineering is less rational and disenchanted than it purports to be (Haraway 1988), and it is more entangled with the supposedly "irrational" world of myth than we might think (Schrempp 2012; see Stefik 1997; Davis 1998; Stahl 1999).

Mythological discourse is conventionally understood to be concerned with form over content—abstract types over concrete instances. Roland Barthes (1972, 143) has argued that myths' abstraction lets them function as "depoliticized speech": by tying together timeless cosmic orders and ordinary historical experience, myths naturalize the archetypes and structures they contain, giving historical contingencies "a natural and eternal justification, . . . a clarity which is not that of an explanation but that of a statement of fact." In computer science, abstraction is also a central practice and value, which identifies underlying coherence by disregarding details considered extraneous. To suggest that collaborative filtering and prehistoric ant trails are the same kind of thing requires just such an abstraction, shedding the many features that might distinguish them in favor of a timeless, underlying unity. Critics of computer science have, echoing Barthes, suggested that this commitment to abstraction has made the field "antipolitical"—aggressively dismissive of historical particularity (Malazita and Resetar 2019).

We can think of these myths as scaling devices. They establish the scope of discussion, indicating that we are not talking about minor acts of coding but about enduring problems of existence. If the ordinary work of programming seems boring—like staying put all day and typing—these stories reimagine telling computers what to do as transformative action on the largest possible scale. As the linguistic anthropologist Judith Irvine (2016, 228) argues, "scale-climbing" is an ideological operation: by claiming the broader view, people try to encompass one another within their own explanatory frameworks (see Gal and Irvine 1995). Epochal software stories set human species-being within a computational frame, recasting practically all social activities as precursors to their narrators' technological projects. David Golumbia, in *The Cultural Logic of Computation* (2009), has adapted a term from the philosophy of mind—"computationalism"—to describe this expansionist tendency in the rhetoric of computing, which enables software to alternately lay claim to the future and the past: new companies figure themselves as both innovators and inheritors of timeless truths.

Identifying these myths as myths is a first step toward reimagining our situation, making received wisdom contestable by reinstalling it in historical time (see Bowker 1994). We can locate overload in concrete situations, with all the particularities that abstraction scrapes away. But we can also analyze how the myth works, as a story that is intellectually productive and world-enframing for the people who tell it. In anthropological terms, we can take myths not as falsehoods to be disproved but as keys to their tellers' cosmology: their worldview, their sense of the order of things, their background theory of society and of existence more generally.

"Cosmology" may seem like an overly broad term, but I use it advisedly: overload serves as a frame not only for thinking about algorithmic recommendation narrowly but also for thinking about the world outside the recommender—before it in time, beyond it in space, and external to its explicit logics. It is part of a world-encompassing understanding that is much more consequential than the question of what song you should listen to next. This cosmology, as I describe here, is essentially informatic, taking the universe to be composed of informational flows and transformations, populated by information processors. In such a world, the contrasts between humans and computers—or taste and technology—that animate many critics of algorithmic recommendation don't make sense because the boundaries they defend do not seem to exist.

Western cosmologies are often expressed as grand social theories. Like other cosmological narratives, these frequently involve speculative stories about primordial humans—think of the fables undergirding Enlightenment political theory (Pateman 1988) or the role played by the myth of primitive barter in economics (Humphrey 1985). Feminist studies of science have worked to identify and critique what Sharon Traweek (1992, 430) calls "narrative leviathans"—"all-encompassing stories of cause and effect"—cosmological ideas expressed in myth that undergird science and its extension out into the rest of the social world. Such cosmologies are a mixture of explicitly stated theories and ambient, pervasive ways of acting and thinking.

Overloaded Subjects

The term "information overload" is commonly credited to the futurist consultant Alvin Toffler, who, in his 1970 book, *Future Shock*, made a dire forecast: as demands on their attention grew, fueled by new media technologies, people would "find their ability to think and act clearly impaired by the waves of information crashing into their senses" (354).[17] His book, which would later pick up the evocative subtitle "A Study of Mass Bewilderment," described the "shattering stress" (Toffler 1970, 2) of rapid social change in aphoristic McLuhanite style, warning that the future was coming quickly, promising to overwhelm human minds, with potentially disastrous consequences.

That same year, the psychologist Stanley Milgram published "The Experience of Living in Cities," describing how city dwellers adapted to the overwhelming scale of urban living—what he called "urban overload"—by narrowing their focus and ignoring the needs of others (Milgram 1970). But where Toffler pointed to the future, Milgram's work recalled a theory from the past, elaborated by the sociologist Georg Simmel in his 1903 essay "The Metropolis and Mental Life." There, Simmel ([1903] 1969, 48) argued that cities overwhelmed their inhabitants not only with their size but also with their internal variety—"the rapid crowding of changing images, the sharp discontinuity in the grasp of a single glance, and the unexpectedness of onrushing impressions." This "intensification of nervous stimulation" resulted in what Simmel saw as a distinctive kind of metropolitan personality—intellectual, calculating, and individualist—which helped the city dweller cope, "protecting him against the threatening currents and discrepancies of his external environment which would uproot him" (48).

Toffler and Milgram seem to reflect a Cold War cosmology dominated by anxieties about unmanageable scale—not only information overload but also population growth and nuclear annihilation (see Masco 2006, 17).[18] But Milgram's resonance with Simmel points to a longer history of overload, dating at least to the turn of the twentieth century. Many cultural critics have identified overload as a signature feature of modernity per se, inaugurated particularly in the metropolitan centers of late nineteenth-century Europe studied by Simmel, as people found themselves tumbled together at unprecedented scale, with one another, their machinery, and their media (e.g., Crary 1999; Killen 2006; Kracauer [1926] 1987).

Historians of early modern Europe point even further back, finding precursors to information overload in academic reactions to the explosion of books in the wake of the printing press (Rosenberg 2003; Ellison 2006; Blair 2010). In the mid-1500s, scholars worried about the "confusing and harmful abundance of books" (Blair 2003, 11). In the late seventeenth century, Gottfried Leibniz complained that the "horrible mass of books keeps growing"; a German bookseller at the end of the eighteenth century wrote that a "plague of books" threatened the national intellect (Wellmon 2012). Some accounts of the history of information overload reach back to antiquity, quoting the Roman stoic Seneca—"the abundance of books is distraction" (Blair 2010)—or the Bible: "of making many books there is no end, and much study is a weariness of the flesh" (Ecclesiastes 12:12 KJV).[19]

These accounts of overload all tie it to then-recent developments in media technology: from the printing press to television to on-demand music streaming services. At any moment, it seems, we can find people feeling overwhelmed and attributing that feeling to changing media technologies. And although these accounts often reference certain quantities of accumulated media, whether a plague of books or an ocean of CDs, their persistence suggests that the problem is something more than a limited human capacity finally being surpassed.[20] Thus, overload feels persistently new, like the future bearing down on the present, while being much older than it seems.

What can we make of the long history of overload's unrelenting novelty? If we treat these stories as instances of a myth and look for their shared structure, we might note that they are not just historical accounts of the state of media; they are stories about a scalar relationship between archives and individuals. Overload requires more than an overwhelming amount of stuff; it requires someone to feel overwhelmed. Scaling, as linguistic anthropologists might remind us, depends on social processes of comparison, which selectively objectify the entities compared (Carr and Lempert 2016). Libraries are rendered large and people rendered small through their comparison.

We might say that overload does not happen to people; it *makes* people, defined through a relationship with archives. While common stories about overload focus on the side of media abundance, we need to also look for the construction of the overloaded subject. Who is this person, and how are they defined in relation to the thing that overwhelms? What qualities, capacities, desires, and obligations do they have? What kinds of relations with archives are they expected to enter into?

In his history of the modern research university, Chad Wellmon (2015, 10) asks why scholars would have seen large libraries as a threat instead of a resource; he suggests that overload was a consequence of a "desire for universal knowledge" that had become part of scholarly identity. Early modern scholars were overwhelmed both by growing libraries and by emerging ideas about what a scholar should know. This "unsteady balance between desire and anxiety" (Rosenberg 2003, 1), the wish to know everything already, was a necessary component of overload. Without it, an overwhelming library was simply a library. In the case of Simmel's burdened metropolitan subject, the issue was the emergence of the objectively overwhelming metropolis and its counterpart: a particular kind of "modern" individual who was isolated, responsibilized, and attentive (see Crary 1999, 73–74).[21]

Wellmon argues that claims of overload are always accompanied by techniques meant to mitigate it—new indexing schemes for books, new ways of walking down city streets, or new filtering algorithms.[22] These techniques, like the social processes of comparison and scale making on which they depend, carry normative ideas about what is worth knowing, how people ought to engage with media, and how institutions should be organized (Wellmon 2015, 11). They are closely tied to emerging subjectivities: the scholar in the stacks, the flâneur on the street, or the listener using a streaming music service.

Returning to Ringo, we can find the user interpellated as a "music lover," living in a "world of music" that begs to be explored. What makes this world of music so overwhelming as to require technological help is not its size but the presumption that a listener wants to explore it—to not simply return to familiar listening material. Edward, a senior engineer at Whisper, captured that mix of desire and anxiety well when he told me, "I'm plagued by the idea that there's something I haven't heard yet." The problem is not only that Spotify offers more than thirty million songs but that people like Edward want to have listened to all of them.

The Cybernetics Moment

As we have seen, computer scientists are not shy about retrojecting new concepts into the past, and some historians have found the anachronistic use of "information overload" helpful for tracing historical continuities back centuries before the advent of modern computing. However, it was not until the mid-twentieth century that people could interpret their experiences of being overwhelmed in terms of "information" or "overload" in their modern senses. To historicize the idea of information overload, we need to look more closely at the notion of information itself and the beginnings of the "information age."

"Information," the media historian John Durham Peters (1988, 10) has written, "is a term that does not like history."[23] Like other scientific mega-concepts, and like myth, information is commonly taken to exist outside of historical time. Information exists, as a standard definition puts it, "independently of living beings in the structure, pattern, arrangement of matter and in the pattern of energy throughout the universe" (Bates 2006). Because information is pattern alone, it can move through time and space, across different substrates, without changing: the periodic flashing of a pulsar in distant space a thousand years ago; the electromagnetic waves it radiated across the galaxy that were captured by a radio telescope in Arecibo, Puerto Rico, in 1968; the drawing of those waves' intensities on a roll of paper by an electromechanical plotter; the india ink tracing of that plot by a draftswoman at Cornell University; the publication of that image in an astronomy dissertation; and its eventual reproduction on the cover of Joy Division's 1979 debut album *Unknown Pleasures* can all be described as the "same" information in different media (Christiansen 2015). Information is thus profoundly generic, and scale-vaulting narratives like the preceding sentence are one of the information age's signature rhetorical tricks, demonstrating how the diverse entities that appear to populate the universe might be brought together under a single logic.

But like other generic terms, information embodies particular ideas about what it means to be generic. As Marilyn Strathern (2014) has argued for other terms, like "relations," identifying the specificities of our generics is crucial anthropological work: these are the terms that people use when they try to speak without contextual baggage; the baggage they nevertheless carry is thus ideologically potent. We have already seen how computational myth making relies on genericized definitions of its terms, as a scale-climbing strategy. In Konstan's telling, a "recommender system" is not merely a kind of software program invented in the mid-1990s but an abstract class of filtering operations that reaches out through time and space to encompass the communicative practices of ant colonies or pre-linguistic humans.

Many historians trace the origins of the information age to the mid-century period that Ronald Kline (2015) calls the "cybernetics moment," which hosted a set of related "revolutions" across the natural and human sciences: the "quantitative revolution" (Burton 1963), the "systems revolution" (Ackoff 1974), the "communications revolution" (Haraway 1979), the "control revolution" (Beniger 1986), and the "cognitive revolution" (Miller 2003), among others. These interrelated transformations spread through an interdisciplinary "epistemic ecology" (Boyer 2013, 160) of postwar science that found a common language in information theory, a common metaphor in computing, and a common method in mathematical formalization (Aspray 1985). Most conspicuous among these disciplines were computer science and the new cognitive science, but these transformations could be found in fields ranging from molecular biology to cultural anthropology (Kay 1997; Seaver 2014).

Cybernetics, the relatively short-lived interdiscipline named by the MIT mathematician Norbert Wiener, played an influential role in this ecology, producing terminology and an analytic style that was widely picked up by people working in other fields (Bowker 1993). Cybernetics' signature idea was the comparability and continuity of animals and machines, understood as information-processing systems. This idea, according to scholars like Katherine Hayles (1999) and Paul Edwards (1996), facilitated the material and discursive production of cyborgs—hybrid entities at once animal and machine. If, at root, there was no essential distinction between animals and machines, then there was no necessary boundary between them either. They could be taken together as part of a more general system of communication and control.

The language of this system was information, as formalized by Claude Shannon in his "Mathematical Theory of Communication" (1948), published in *The Bell System Technical Journal* and derived from his work as a researcher for AT&T's Bell Telephone Laboratories.[24] Information, quantified in bits, was a statistical measure of a message's predictability: for Shannon, the less predictable a message was, the more information it contained. This sentence, for instance, governed by rules of English syntax and spelling, is fairly redundant; many of its letters can be deleted without harm to a reader's ability to understand it. An equally long string of random characters (say, a very secure password) contains more information, in Shannon's sense, because missing characters cannot be predicted from the ones left behind. Predictable messages are thus more compressible and were more resistant to damage—both concerns of tele-communications companies that seek to optimize their use of bandwidth and to reduce errors in transmission. Because information is a matter of pattern, measured in dimensionless bits, it does not matter if those messages are encoded in electricity traveling along a telephone line or in a cipher on a typewritten sheet of paper.

Many critics have drawn attention to the military origins of cybernetics and information theory—Wiener famously developed key cybernetic concepts while designing missile-targeting systems, and Shannon derived his communication theory while working on cryptography for the US military (Galison 1994). But as Jonathan Sterne has argued, the role of the telecommunication industry as sponsor and source of metaphorical language is also important to understanding how cybernetic common sense spread across the sciences and popular discourse (Sterne 2012).

Information theory worked from the perspective of the communication network itself, concerned only with the fact and shape of messages, not with their meaning. Warren Weaver (1949, 14), an ardent popularizer of Shannon's theory, described it like this in a 1949 issue of *Scientific American*: "An engineering communication theory is just like a very proper and discreet girl accepting your telegram. She pays no attention to the meaning, whether it be sad, or joyous, or embarrassing. But she must be prepared to deal with all that come to her desk." Using a revealingly gendered metaphor, Weaver figured communications infrastructures (and human secretaries) as mere conduits (Day 2000), passing along messages. Information theory was "nonsemantic"—a way of engaging with human communication that might bypass hoary questions of meaning. The collaborative filters that would be designed in the 1990s embraced this ethos as well, focusing on the shape of ratings patterns rather than the content of items to be recommended.

Finite Creatures in an Infinite World

Cybernetics was an analogy machine, facilitating a host of new comparisons between formerly diverse entities that had become figured as "systems" for information processing. For instance, in his popular book *Cybernetics*, Norbert Wiener (1948, 18) described how the human brain was, like the telephone system, vulnerable to "overload" that could cause it to "give way in a serious and catastrophic manner. This overload may take place in several ways: by an excess in the amount of traffic to be carried; by a physical removal of channels for the carrying of traffic; or by the excessive occupation of such channels by undesirable systems of traffic, such as circulating memories that have accumulated to the extent of becoming pathological worries. In all these cases, a point is reached—quite suddenly—when the normal traffic does not have space enough allotted to it, and we have a form of mental breakdown, very possibly amounting to insanity." According to Wiener, even the telephone network was vulnerable to this kind of "insanity," or a cascading series of failures resulting from a system's inability to keep up with the demands placed on it. What mattered to human overload was not the content of one's thoughts, but their quantity and the pattern of their circulation. Brains and telephone networks were the same kind of thing. Information overload rendered the familiar feeling of being overwhelmed as a technical problem—one that could be expressed formally, abstracted from affective responses, and afflicting systems large or small, human or otherwise.[25]

This was the framing taken up by the psychologist James Grier Miller in a 1960 article titled "Information Input Overload and Psychopathology." This article, which was perhaps the first to name "information overload" as such (Levine 2017), reported on five studies of overload conducted at different scales: neurons, brains, individuals, small face-to-face groups, and institutions. Thinking of these as a set of nested systems, Miller sought to measure their information-processing capacity: how many bits per second they could reliably pass on and what happened when that threshold was exceeded. By slowly increasing input rates—whether in the form of electrical impulses delivered to a cell or symbols presented to human subjects—Miller (1960, 697) identified these systems' "channel capacities," cataloging the "mechanisms of adjustment" they resorted to when overloaded. These mechanisms included skipping some inputs, making errors, and simply quitting the task or shutting down.

As the historian Nick Levine (2017, 33) has argued, Miller's experiment, part of a nascent cognitive science, "represented a reconceptualization of human beings and their organizations as communication channels whose capacity could be overwhelmed." The notion of information overload did not begin with people being overwhelmed by information technologies, but with an understanding of overwhelmed people *as* information technologies. The idea that the brain was a kind of computer outpaced the spread of computers themselves. Cybernetics facilitated the design of hybrid cyborg entities, as well as a more generic cyborg ontology: everything was an information-processing system, anything could be thus connected with anything else, and, in fact, everything already was so connected. People could be considered continuous with the communication networks they used; if both sides of the interface were information-processing systems, then the interface marked a moment of transduction between two different media for the same basic stuff, not a radical break. Miller eventually developed this line of work into his "living systems theory," which he laid out in a mammoth 1978 book, *Living Systems*: "All nature is a continuum. . . . From the ceaseless streaming of protoplasm to the many-vectored activities of supranational systems, there are continuous flows through living systems" (1025).

The "system" is another key contemporary generic, as the anthropologist of systems science Valerie Olson (2018, 31) has argued—a kind of conceptual technology to "make things and processes seem contiguous at scale." Olson names the tendency for scale jumping we have seen in this chapter "scalarity," a sensibility and rhetorical style that draws together apparently disparate-scaled entities in the service of generic, universalizing claims. Scalarity is both a recognizable aesthetic style and a cosmological precept: Olson gives the classic imagery of space travel—one small step for man, one giant leap for mankind—as a key example, one that analogizes human footsteps to human evolution. We might also think of my earlier description of pulsar radiation or the classic film *Powers of Ten*, which zooms in to the scale of atoms and out to the scale of galaxies; this style figures everything in the universe as essentially comparable and potentially contiguous.

Since the cybernetics moment, many of us have lived in what the anthropologist Abou Farman (2017) calls an "informatic cosmology"—a cosmos unified under the sign of information. Information theory is cosmological in both the anthropological sense—as a theory that specifies a worldview, a sense of the order of things, a background understanding of society and of the universe more generally—and in the now-conventional astronomical sense: professional cosmologists, as Farman describes, argue that the basic stuff of the universe, beneath matter and energy, may, in fact, be information. The portentous opening line of the philosopher Fred Dretske's 1981 *Knowledge and the Flow of Information*, which sought to align epistemology with cognitive science, captures this dual cosmological significance: "In the beginning there was information. The word came later" (vii). This vast cosmological scale was an extraordinary achievement for a theory whose original purpose was to make the telephone system more efficient.

In a universe of theoretically unbounded information flow, moments of limitation, halting, and error become anomalies to explain. Like James Grier Miller, cognitive scientists concerned themselves with exploring the limits of the human mind, conceived as an information-processing system (as in George Miller's famous 1956 article on "chunking"); the human being was, as the historian Hunter Heyck (2015, 83) put it in his book *Age of System*, "a finite creature in an infinite world." If information's scalarity facilitated expansive interscalar comparisons on the grounds that everything was essentially made of the same stuff, it also recast what had seemed to be differences of type as differences of scale: a human mind could be "plugged in" to a large communication network, but it might become overwhelmed by information flows exceeding its capacity, thus requiring filtering techniques for self-protection. Across disciplines undergoing "cognitive turns," key concepts were thus reinterpreted as filtering methods, which protected limited minds from overload. Cognitive anthropology, for instance, reconceptualized culture and classification as an adaptive technique for coping with an overwhelming world: "We classify because life in a world where nothing was the same would be intolerable. It is through naming and classification that the whole rich world of infinite variability shrinks to manipulable size and becomes bearable" (Tyler 1969, 7).

Through the latter half of the twentieth century, as Levine (2017) recounts, the primary areas of concern for research on information overload were work and consumption. Organizational theorists like James March and Herbert Simon reimagined corporations in terms of information flow and its limits (e.g., Cyert and March 1963; March and Simon 1958), while cyberneticists like Stafford Beer (1972) sought to design new organizational models that would optimize those flows and reduce the bottlenecks caused by, for instance, overload on the CEO (see reviews in Eppler and Mengis 2004; Edmunds and Morris 2000). Contemporaneously, research in consumer psychology investigated the effect of providing consumers with more information about their choices (e.g., Jacoby 1975), motivated by concerns that more options and information about them might prove demotivating to potential buyers of products.

Preferential Technics

At the 2013 meeting of the conference on Computer-Supported Cooperative Work—or CSCW—Paul Resnick and John Riedl, lead authors of the original GroupLens paper, re-presented it in a session titled "The Most Cited CSCW Paper Ever."[26] In character as their 1994 selves, to laughter from an overflowing crowd, they described the overload problem posed by online bulletin boards like Usenet. Resnick described in mock astonishment how a single Usenet group might generate one hundred megabytes of data in a day, which would quickly overwhelm the forty megabytes of memory in his computer (which, he joked, he had paid extra for). Usenet was certain to increase in popularity as new internet users came online, and this basic problem of memory would only worsen over time.

Many details of the original paper were played for laughs nearly twenty years later: Usenet had declined in popularity, eclipsed by blogs, email, and social media sites; computers had come to have thousands of times the memory of their predecessors. The original GroupLens paper had envisioned a system of distributed servers called "Better Bit Bureaus" that would collect user ratings and calculate recommendations for their clients, outside the control and influence of any specific platform.[27] This vision was almost completely abandoned as recommender systems grew in popularity—now, the proprietary systems run by companies are practically synonymous with algorithmic recommendation.

A striking feature of this early discourse on recommendation, which is largely absent today, is the focus on computational resources like memory and bandwidth. As Resnick's joke indicated, recommender systems were seen as an aid to overloaded computers as well as users. By preselecting relevant Usenet posts, rather than delivering them all, a recommender system could optimize information flow around the network. Shoshana Loeb (1992, 47), a researcher at one of the labs descended from Bell Telephone Laboratories, wrote in 1992: "The ability to anticipate the information delivery needs of network users may become an important enabling technology for scheduling and delivery optimization in future networks." The technical operation of information infrastructure could be optimized by thinking of users as part of the overall computational system, as elements to be modeled and anticipated.

This style of optimization through anticipation can be found more broadly in the information sciences, perhaps most acutely in the form of algorithmic compression that Jonathan Sterne (2012) calls "perceptual technics." In his history of the MP3 format, Sterne describes how models of human hearing—patterns of frequencies that are filtered out by typical human ears—were built into the infrastructure of audio circulation: the MP3 standard anticipates the filtering that a typical human's brain and ears will enact and performs it in advance, making audio files smaller, and thus easier to store and transmit. By encoding theories about hearing (and a normative hearing subject) into digital audio, companies could save computational resources and money, capitalizing on this anticipation. This intermingling of scientific models of perception, infrastructures of circulation and distribution, and the economic interests of corporations was distinctively cybernetic, effecting "a concordance of signals among computers, electrical components and auditory nerves" (Sterne 2006, 837). Perceptual technics made sense in a world where ears were essentially microphones; brains, computers; and hearing, a sort of filtering that might be distributed across a network and thereby optimized.

In the early visions of collaborative filtering, we can see recommender systems presented as a kind of *preferential technics*. Where MP3 encoding would save bandwidth and memory by prefiltering the frequencies a particular user wasn't likely to hear, collaborative filtering could optimize the network by cutting out the material that a user wasn't likely to like. Like perceptual technics, preferential technics blends the technical exigencies of circulation together with theories about the functioning of human recipients. Operating within a cybernetic cosmology that sees no essential difference between brains and computers, these systems optimize them together.

Preferential technics varies from perceptual technics in a few significant ways. It depends on social theories rather than biological ones: Sterne describes how the developers of the MP3 adapted findings from the science of psychoacoustics into their work. Recommender systems, by contrast, rely on ideas about the social nature of preference; these ideas, as we have already seen, are typically derived from the common sense of developers, not from the social sciences. And where perceptual technics posits a normative model of human hearing, rendering ears as pieces of predictable, fleshy machinery, preferential technics is usually premised on difference: a collaborative filter would be personalized, trimming back the set of Usenet posts in a way that varies across users. As we move through the next few chapters, we will see this differentiation progress: people like different things, they like things in different ways, the ways they like things may themselves differ over time.

Today, as Resnick's joke indicated, bandwidth constraints are largely considered a thing of the past, and recommender systems are no longer commonly framed as techniques for optimizing the bandwidth of a computer network. When people suggest that recommender systems are necessary to manage an overwhelming amount of information, they are not making a claim about digital computers. It would be technically easy, for instance, for Facebook to simply present every update from a user's friends in chronological order. The problem with this much-requested feature, Facebook suggests, is *human* bandwidth: users would be overwhelmed.[28]

But within an informatic cosmology, these problems are fundamentally the same kind of problem. Recall Peter's explanation of musical overload: filtering used to happen at a different point in the system, through the apparatus of publishing or the constraint of having to purchase individual albums. Now, that filtering has to happen somewhere else, and because human minds lack the computational resources to manage it all, recommender systems can do it for them. Where information theory was originally presented as a way to reduce strain on communication networks and to make them more efficient, recommender systems have moved the location of optimization from the network into the user's mind. This vision of user and network as part of a single system, which might be jointly optimized, is a legacy of the cybernetic moment and an ordinary feature of informatic cosmology.

Man Is the Query

The scattered groups of academic and industry researchers who worked on recommender systems through the 1990s eventually coalesced into a well-defined research community with a dedicated annual conference: RecSys, which was first held in 2007, hosted by the GroupLens researchers at the University of Minnesota and sponsored by the Association for Computing Machinery. RecSys would grow into an international conference and meeting place for recommender systems researchers, who worked on techniques to expand algorithmic recommendation beyond its origins in collaborative filtering.

In 2016, I sat under the sweeping arc of Kresge Auditorium at MIT, in the audience for a panel at RecSys Boston, titled "Past, Present, and Future." This was my third time at RecSys, having previously attended Silicon Valley 2014 and Dublin 2012, and the presenters were in a reflective mood, appraising the state of the field and imagining its potential futures.

Representing a group of European researchers, a man presented a vision of what recommender systems might be, "algorithms aside"— beyond the focus on technical detail typical of the conference. On the screen behind him, instead of the usual bullet-pointed slide deck, was a rapidly advancing montage of stock images, recalling the visual style of Godfrey Reggio's *Koyaanisqatsi*: crowds of people in cities and stadiums, elaborate root structures of trees, long-exposure images of highway traffic, bubble-chamber tracings from high-energy physics.[29] This interscalar jumble of images set the scene for a presentation of cosmological scope. The paper the talk drew on had twenty authors, from both academia and industry, and although the psychedelic style of its presentation was very unusual for a computer science conference, the talk embodied widely shared presuppositions about recommender systems' cosmology.

As Konstan had done, the paper positioned algorithmic recommender systems as simply one instance of a more general practice of decision-making support: "When we stand at a crossroads in life we often seek out those who are wiser or more experienced in order to decide what to do next" (Motajcsek et al. 2016, 217). What could recommender systems become, the authors wondered, if they were "not tied to technology" (215), freed from the technical paradigm of collaborative filtering that had been set two decades earlier? Looking up from their algorithms, they saw analogues to recommendation in moments of explicit advice seeking and decision-making—and, it seemed, everywhere else. "Life itself," they wrote, "is the original recommender system" (217)—the experience of being alive, encountering possibilities, having intuitions, making choices, all of it was something like a recommender system, distributed across the whole of the sensible and insensible world. If life itself is a recommender system, then it followed, they suggested in a suitably mythological register, that "man is the query" (219).

Although the paper suggested that it was approaching recommender systems "through the lens of life," we might instead say that it approached life through the lens of recommendation, finding recommender systems everywhere, until nothing was left outside them. This is an informatic cosmology in action: looking beyond the "technology" of computing, researchers see a world rendered computational.

This ability to find recommendation anywhere matters because it informs how people working on recommender systems respond to many common critiques. Take, for example, the typical response to arguments about the "filter bubble"—the idea that personalization technologies isolate users in self-reinforcing echo chambers, making it harder to find contradictory opinions or to engage with people unlike oneself (Pariser 2011). Empirical studies have generally failed to substantiate the filter-bubble hypothesis (see Bruns 2019), but the typical rebuttal from practitioners is theoretical, not empirical: the real filter bubble, I often heard, was the isolated small town, imagined to have poor access to the internet.[30] That is a filter bubble instantiated in physical space. In comparison to the potentially extreme and biased filtering effected by ordinary conditions of life on Earth, they argued, algorithmic recommendation could broaden horizons.

In an informatic cosmology, there is no "natural" unfiltered state, and recommender systems are everywhere, whether or not they have been named as such.[31] Like perceptual technics before it, preferential technics makes sense in a world of information flows and filters that exist across all possible scales: the structure of the music industry is one filter, while a person's individual preferences are another. Overload becomes a bandwidth problem, and overloaded subjects become the targets of technical solutions. Through this abstraction, the details of these various filters are elided: even if we agree that parochial upbringings and recommender systems are essentially both "filters," it does not follow that they filter in the same way. And indeed, we can see a difference in how these styles of filtering are presented, which brings us back to the centrality of information overload: The filtering imposed by geographical isolation is described as a bad thing, which unfairly constrains people. The filtering imposed by algorithmic recommendation, by contrast, appears as a form of care for overloaded subjects who, freed from the bad filters, find themselves in need of some good ones.

CHAPTER 2

Captivating Algorithms

The Hang-Around Factor

It is an overcast day in Northern California, and I am eating sushi with Mike. We sit down the street from his office at Willow, the personalized radio company where he has worked for the past fifteen years. Mike has bright blue eyes, an ersatz mohawk, and an unusually energetic affect, even by the Bay Area's gregarious standards. I have been living in San Francisco for the past few months, meeting with workers in their offices, bars, coffee shops, and climbing gyms.

Among the fleeting companies and careers that are common in the industry, Mike and Willow are notably long-lived. He joined the company as a college dropout, as Willow's first engineer. Over a decade later, Willow still exists, and he is its chief scientist. I ask him what a chief scientist for a streaming music company does, and he replies: "I'm responsible for making sure the music we play is awesome."

For his entire career, Mike has been responsible for Willow's playlisting algorithm—the recommender system that decides which song should play next on each of the service's millions of algorithmic radio stations. At first, he worked alone: "I was the algorithm guy—the only guy working on the algorithm—trying to figure out how to play music right." As Willow grew, so did the algorithm and Mike's job, tracing typical, parallel trajectories. "Now," he tells me, "I run teams of teams," each of which is responsible for a different part of Willow's recommendation infrastructure.

Willow has, since its inception around the turn of the century, prided itself on not using collaborative filtering, relying instead on data about the sound and style of the music it recommends. But like most of its peers, Willow has become more omnivorous in the data it collects, growing to encompass a broad range of data sources. Now, "the algorithm" is not one algorithm at all, but "dozens and dozens of algorithms," which parse various signals: What does a song sound like? What device is a user listening on? What has a user listened to in the past?

All those signals are orchestrated together into an "ensemble" by another algorithm, which is tuned to a listener's particular listening style. Some signals may matter more for one user than others. One listener may be adventurous while another may prefer familiar artists; one may interact with the interface constantly while another may rarely click. As Willow keeps track of these signals and how its users respond to recommendations, it learns how to balance the overall ensemble, optimizing its radio stations for each of its users.

It does this through nonstop testing. From his perspective as chief scientist, Mike describes Willow as a vast experimental apparatus. If Mike's team is considering a change to the way the overall system works, it can make the change for 1 percent of Willow's users and measure its effect: "Say we double the number of artists you hear every hour. What happens? Do you listen more or do you listen less? Do you like it? The answer is probably going to be: some people like it, and some people don't. Who are they? Why?" The results of these tests are aggregated into Willow's algorithmic ensemble, which grows increasingly complex and personalized over time. A design change that seems to work well for one part of the user base may be implemented for only that segment, if its members can be readily identified.

The ultimate measure of functionality, Mike explains to me, is "the hang-around factor"—what keeps listeners listening. When users skip songs or turn Willow off, this is a sign that something has gone wrong. Under his leadership, Mike boasts, "every single change that happens on Willow has been exactly measured for its listening and retentive impact."

Willow's recommender system is also experimental on a smaller scale: every recommended song is a little test, a probe meant to fill out a picture of what a given user likes. "Depending on where you are in your lifetime of interaction and experience with us," Mike tells me, "you get very different music experiences." For longtime users with lots of listening data, Willow can offer precisely personalized music selections that take into account deep listening histories, pushing into more obscure musical territory with confidence.

But new users pose a challenge: data-driven recommendation requires data, and new users don't have any. How can you recommend music to people you know almost nothing about? Researchers call this the "cold-start problem," and companies like Willow are aggressive in their efforts to identify new users' preferences and retain them as quickly as possible. So, while veteran users get recommendations from elaborately orchestrated algorithmic ensembles, new users get something a bit coarser. As Mike puts it: "If you're in your first week of listening to us, we're like, 'Fuck that! Play the hits!' Play the shit you know they're going to love to keep them coming back. Get them addicted. In the beginning, I'm just trying to get you hooked."

: :

Mike's account of Willow as an experimental apparatus, designed to capture users, is very typical of contemporary software companies. But it may seem like a dramatic reversal from the beneficent vision of algorithmic recommendation outlined in the previous chapter, where recommender systems were invented to help eager but overloaded individuals cope with the plenitude of the information age. What happened?

This chapter traces a paradigm shift in the purpose of algorithmic recommendation, from aiding overwhelmed users to enticing people into becoming users. To understand this shift, we need to locate algorithmic recommendation not within the timeless informatic cosmology described in chapter 1, but in the particular historical context where these systems were implemented—in actual companies, on live platforms, under new organizational pressures. In the technical, economic, and epistemic context of a changing software industry, recommender systems would come to be understood as a kind of trap, fine-tuned to capture the attention of users, who were their prey.

People like Mike routinely described their goals in traplike terms: they sought to capture market share or attention, they wanted to "hook" their users or at least to attract and retain them. Here, inspired by steady references to capture in the field, I draw on an unusual theoretical source to help me think through how recommender systems work in practice: the anthropology of animal trapping. This may seem at first to be an unnecessarily dramatic choice. An algorithmic radio station appears quite unlike a hidden, poison-tipped spear; when developers say they want to capture users, they are certainly not thinking of thorn-lined baskets or holes in the ground hidden by leaves. Trapping is conventionally associated with violent denials of agency and a kind of blunt (or sharp) technicality that lies far away from what we mean when we say "technology" today, as though it were synonymous with computers. Algorithms are usually imagined to be essentially immaterial abstract procedures, symbols of informatic modernity free from any coarse materiality of the spearing, snaring, or smashing sort. Traps are muddy and physical; algorithms are electric and logical, "made of sunshine, . . . all light and clean" (Haraway 1991, 153).

But one of anthropologists' many privileges is discursive mobility: we can take our interlocutors more and less literally than they take themselves, pursuing connections that they may not make. Placing collaborative filters alongside trip wires and trapdoors usefully takes the shine off recommender systems, reminding us that, after all, algorithmic systems are still technologies, products of ordinary human engineering. Turning to the anthropology of trapping proves useful for making sense of what recommender systems have become: devices for anticipating, attracting, and retaining users that embody theories about how their prey behave and that provide knowledge about behavior to the people who set them. In the anthropology of trapping, traps are understood to be sophisticated artifacts that function psychologically, not merely through the coercive application of physical force. Although, as we will see, a popular critique of algorithmic personalization as traplike has already emerged, my goal here is not polemic. The point of analyzing recommender systems as traps is not to say that they are bad but to recognize in them an entanglement of agencies in technical form. Traps offer models for thinking about technology beyond common dichotomies like the voluntary and the coerced, the mental and the material, or the cultural and the technical.

In what follows, I describe the emergence of a vernacular theory of captivation among the developers of recommender systems, which changed what it meant for a recommender to "work." This shift saw algorithmic recommendation transform from a technology designed to more accurately predict user ratings into one designed to retain users. Thinking with traps can help us see how epistemic and technical infrastructures come together to produce encompassing, hard-to-escape cultural worlds, at a moment when the richest companies in the world dedicate most of their resources to getting people hooked.

Captology

Hooked, it turned out, was also the title of a book by the Silicon Valley blogger and entrepreneur Nir Eyal (2014). Subtitled *How to Build Habit-Forming Products*, the book draws on behavioral economics and cognitive psychology to teach software start-ups how to get users to crave their products—to instinctually check their apps as a matter of habit rather than conscious choice.[1] Successful products, according to Eyal (2014, 3), beat their competitors by making themselves "first-to-mind": users "feel a pang of loneliness and before rational thought occurs, they are scrolling through their Facebook feeds." Achieving this goal requires thinking of users as instinctual minds, susceptible to subtle outside influences, not as customers choosing among various commodities. The purpose of his book, Eyal (2014, 2) writes, is to teach "not only what compels users to click, but what makes them tick." The book's cover depicts a cursor clicking on a human brain.

Eyal was not alone in advocating for such a mind-oriented approach to product design. During my fieldwork in the Bay Area in the early 2010s, the behavioral economist Dan Ariely hosted an annual summit, Startuponomics, which trained company founders in the basic tenets of behavioral economics, pitched as tactics for retaining employees or drawing users down the "product funnel" (i.e., turning them into paying customers or long-term users). Books featuring the intuitively counterintuitive lessons of behavioral economics and cognitive psychology more generally are routine best sellers in the United States.

Figures like Eyal would often trace these ideas back to behaviorist psychology and to B. F. Skinner's famous variable reinforcement experiments that induced "superstition in pigeons" (Ferster and Skinner 1957): caged birds, given a lever that released food, would learn to press it; if experimenters adjusted the lever to release food only intermittently, the pigeons would learn to press it incessantly. Replace the pigeons with people, build the right levers into your product, and you too might amass a user base of incessant lever pressers.

Comparisons to Skinner boxes soon became a common trope in critiques of the software industry, suggesting that such designs were essentially dehumanizing, treating users like laboratory animals to be manipulated and experimented on (e.g., Davidow 2013; Leslie 2016; Zuboff 2019). And yet these comparisons were first made by designers themselves, who saw in Skinner's reinforcement cycles a generalizable truth about behavior—a fact about the behavioral world that held true whether or not companies took advantage of it. They would often note in passing the potential for harm, but they would conclude, as Eyal (2014, 11) did, "If it can't be used for evil, it's not a superpower." While the ramifications of such designs on social networking sites appeared quite serious, the goal of getting people "addicted" to listening to music seemed relatively innocuous.[2]

One of the headwaters of this surge in behaviorist thinking in the software industry was B. J. Fogg's Persuasive Technology Lab at Stanford. Fogg founded the lab in 1998 to develop the field that would eventually be called "persuasive design," but that he first named "captology." The "capt" in captology stood for "computers as persuasive technologies" (Fogg 2003, 5), and the lab's mission, as described on its website, was to "research and design interactive technologies that motivate and influence users."[3] Many alumni of the lab and Fogg's regular courses at Stanford would go on to influential positions in Silicon Valley, among them a co-founder of the photo-sharing service Instagram and Nir Eyal himself. Although he too cited Skinner's precedent, Fogg's emphasis on "persuasion" offered a gentler vision of what such designs might entail, which he defined in terms meant to foreground human agency: persuasion was "a noncoercive attempt to change attitudes or behaviors," definitionally opposed to force or trickery (Fogg, Cuellar, and Danielson 2009, 134). Captology would focus on "voluntary change," requiring the active participation of the persuaded (Fogg 2003, 15).

While Skinner, in *Beyond Freedom and Dignity* (1971), famously disavowed the existence of free will, captologists relied on it as an ethical shield. Whatever powers Facebook may have, for instance, it cannot *force* anyone to do something through the computer interface—it can only persuade. This is, as the anthropologist Shreeharsh Kelkar (2020) has argued, a key ideological difference between classical behaviorism and the version of it practiced in the software industry: captology simultaneously claims for itself great and delimited power.[4] Practitioners respond to critiques by focusing on the voluntary nature of persuasion or emphasizing how it can be used for unquestionable social good. "Peace innovation" and "mobile health" are among the projects cataloged on the Persuasive Technology Lab's website.

Given the cultural salience of the Skinner box, the fact that "captology" sounds like it means "the study of capture" proved troublesome for Fogg, who has more recently favored the term "behavior design." But for my purposes here, that semantic blurring usefully calls to mind the relationship between behaviorist understandings of action and efforts to trap the entities thus understood. In the work of Skinner, Eyal, Ariely, and others, we always seem to find behaviorism entangled with physical and psychological techniques of capture: birds caught in cages become transfixed by schedules of reinforcement; users are hooked; employees are retained; potential customers are drawn into acquisition funnels.

In practice, captology does not depend on a firm distinction between persuasion and coercion—between voluntary choices and trickery. In fact, it is predicated on the idea that such distinctions are hard to draw, since apparently "free" choices can be shaped without our knowledge, and influence is everywhere. "Let's admit it," Eyal (2014, 164) writes, "we are all in the persuasion business." Some critics and practitioners have responded to this ethical muddle by trying to distinguish persuasion from coercion (e.g., Susser, Roessler, and Nissenbaum 2018), but the fact that a knotty ethical situation exists does not mean that we can untie it, and the idea that we might isolate properly "free" choice from this mess is as dubious as the idea that someone browsing the internet is ultimately making their own decisions. Captology "works" in practice—that is, people find it defensible and it has effects—because the distinction between persuasion and coercion is unclear.

I use the term "captology" to refer to this broadly behaviorist common sense in the software industry, which understands behavior as malleable and technology as a means to alter it.[5] We can find captological thinking in texts like *Hooked* or in workshops like Startuponomics, but these artifacts only make explicit and systematic what is elsewhere a tacit and ad hoc way of thinking. Though indebted to behaviorism, ordinary captological thinking is not necessarily faithful to it, nor is its ancestry always claimed. Instead, we find people like Mike declaring that they want to hook their users, imagining the object of their labor as an experimental apparatus that is at once a device for learning about users and a trap for retaining them. The center of contemporary captology is the vague and pervasive notion that for software to work, it has to captivate.

The Predictive Paradigm

There are many ways one might measure how well a recommender system works, but for most of the field's history, one metric has dominated all others: predictive accuracy. The recommender "problem," as it was formalized in early, paradigm-setting work on collaborative filtering took the shape of a matrix, with items along one side and users along the other (table 1). Filling the matrix were ratings that users had given to items. Because most items had not been rated by most users, this matrix was mostly empty, or "sparse." The goal of the recommender algorithm was to predict the ratings that would appear in the matrix's empty spaces. Items with high predicted ratings could be shown to the user as recommendations. If the predictions were accurate, then the system "worked."

Evaluation was thus a matter of comparing two matrixes: one with the predicted values and one with the actual values. There are also many ways to do this, but one, called root mean squared error—or RMSE—would become the paradigmatic measure of success in the field. If you learned how to build a simple recommender system in a computer science class, you would evaluate it using RMSE. If you presented a new collaborative filtering algorithm at the RecSys conference, you would measure its

TABLE 1: A simplified collaborative filtering matrix

	User A	User B	User C	User D	User E
Item 1	5	3		4	1
Item 2	4	2	4		3
Item 3		4	3	5	2
Item 4	4		3		
Item 5	1	4		2	5

improvement in terms of RMSE. If you developed a new evaluation metric, you would be obligated to compare it to RMSE. Root mean squared error was an integral part of the normal science of recommender systems research, which had coalesced in the mid-1990s and held strong into the 2010s.[6]

Here is how to calculate it. First, take the differences between all predicted and actual ratings: if we guessed that a user would rate an item 4 stars and they rated it 3, then our error is 1; if we guessed 2 stars and they rated it 5, our error is –3; if we guessed 3 and they rated it 1, our error is 2. Simply averaging these errors together will not suffice, because errors in opposite directions cancel each other out: for our examples here, the average error would be 0.[7] Because RMSE is a measure of error, lower values are better. An RMSE of 0 would indicate that all ratings were predicted perfectly.

The next step in calculating RMSE is to square all the errors. This makes everything positive, and it also amplifies larger differences: our 1-point error is still 1, but the negative 3-point error becomes 9. The basic premise is that small errors do not matter much to users, whereas large errors do: they might cross the midpoint of the scale. Predicting that users will slightly like an item when they actually like it a lot is less of a problem than predicting that users will like an item when they actually don't. Averaging these errors and then taking the square root of the result returns us to the scale of the original ratings and gives us RMSE: the root of the mean of the squared errors.

Researchers sometimes attributed RMSE's paradigmatic status to the Netflix Prize, a contest run by the online movie rental company from 2006 to 2009 that offered a $1 million award for the first algorithm that could beat its existing system's RMSE by 10 percent.[8] Netflix provided a data set of about one hundred million ratings, including anonymized user IDs, movie titles, release dates, and the date each rating was made. Competitors could use this data to train their algorithms, trying to predict the ratings in the set as precisely as possible.

Netflix withheld an even larger data set, on which competitors' algorithms could be evaluated, to see how well they worked on new data. Netflix's own CineMatch algorithm could predict the held-out ratings with an RMSE of 0.9514. By the end of the contest in 2009, the winning algorithm, submitted by a team named BellKor's Pragmatic Chaos, had achieved an RMSE of 0.8567 and established the state of the art for predictive accuracy in collaborative filtering.[9]

The Netflix Prize is often credited with raising the visibility of recommender systems research and with instigating the development of some of its key techniques (e.g., Funk 2006). Its prominence helped establish RMSE as a standard measure in the field. The first meeting of the RecSys conference, in 2007, featured presentations by many researchers who had been working on the Netflix Prize.

But the winning algorithm did not succeed by finding one particular technique that beat all others. Rather, as the contest went on, high-performing teams combined their efforts and models together into ensembles that essentially blended the outputs of a set of algorithms. BellKor's Pragmatic Chaos was a combination of teams named BellKor, Pragmatic Theory, and BigChaos. The second-place team, appropriately named the Ensemble, was an amalgam of twenty-three other teams.

After the Netflix Prize, it became common sense among recommender systems researchers that the best results were achieved by systems that blended together the outputs of many techniques, like the system Mike was building at Willow. "The more the merrier," as the winners of the prize reflected (Bell, Koren, and Volinsky 2010): even techniques that worked quite poorly in isolation might contribute slight improvements to an ensemble model. These large models were pragmatically driven, concerned with performance, not with developing a coherent theory about why they worked.[10] Different algorithms within an ensemble might be premised on distinct or even contradictory theories about what was going on in the data, but in the pursuit of lower RMSE, researchers threw everything they could at the problem.

Critics of algorithmic recommendation would point to the Netflix Prize as evidence of "how central the accuracy of the recommendation system is to such organisations" (Beer 2013, 64), displacing any concern for the effect these systems might have on the cultural worlds they modeled. But by the time Netflix awarded its prize in 2009, the predictive paradigm was already faltering, and the company never implemented the winning algorithm. As Netflix engineers often noted in their public presentations, the winning ensemble was unwieldy, complex, and computationally intensive, having been designed to reduce RMSE at all costs. But perhaps more significantly, the shape of Netflix's business had changed.

The tacit assumption of the predictive paradigm was that users would be more satisfied by a system that could more accurately predict their ratings. This assumption had not been subject to much internal critique in the early days of the research field—it seemed obvious enough, and it facilitated a single-minded engineering focus on reducing RMSE. While companies might try to implement or improve recommender systems in pursuit of customers, their approach was not yet captological in the way it would soon become: there was no model of user decision-making here, and basic research on recommendation proceeded independently of efforts to measure user retention.

When the Netflix Prize began, Netflix was a DVD rental company, mailing discs to its customers' homes. By the time the contest ended, it had become a video streaming service, playing on-demand in users' web browsers. That allowed the company to collect finer-grained data about what users actually watched: users could easily abandon a movie they didn't like, and Netflix would have a record of it. The work of predicting user ratings would become less important than measuring the effect that recommendations had on user behavior. The goal of the recommender was no longer to identify DVDs that people might like, but to keep people watching.

The Rise of Captivation Metrics

Netflix's transformation was symptomatic of a broader shift in internet business models. It reflected a set of changes in the economic, technical, and epistemic settings of recommender systems research and design. The research community's center of gravity was shifting from academia into industry, as companies employed researchers to work on their own data sets. Those data sets were rapidly growing, as the turn to streaming media offered unprecedented amounts of information about user interactions. And researchers in a field once dominated by RMSE were beginning to find faults in the assumptions underlying the predictive paradigm. These changes led to the rise of a set of measures that I call "captivation metrics," which would soon become the paradigmatic measures of recommender success.

In 2012, I attended a meeting of the RecSys conference in Dublin and sat in on a workshop exploring evaluation methods "beyond RMSE." The workshop had been co-organized by Netflix's head of algorithm engineering and research, Xavier Amatriain, who gave a familiar presentation about the history of the Netflix Prize and the eventual uselessness of the winning algorithm. The organizers' report summarized the mood of the event: "There seemed to be a general consensus on the inadequacy of RMSE as a proxy for user satisfaction" (Amatriain et al. 2012, iv). Two years later, the next time I attended RecSys, I saw Amatriain deliver a talk with a striking slide: an enormous, crossed-out "RMSE."

Within the research community, RMSE had encountered a series of crises that led to this public disavowal. First, improvements in RMSE had become harder and harder to achieve, stuck behind what some researchers called a "magic barrier" (Herlocker et al. 2004, 6). A common explanation for the magic barrier was, as one grad student told me, that people's preferences were "noisy." A recommender system could not predict a user's preferences any more precisely than those preferences were held, and it appeared that people did not, in fact, hold their preferences very precisely. In experiments where users were asked to rate items more than once, their ratings often varied widely over time (e.g., Amatriain, Pujol, and Oliver 2009).

Second, when researchers tried to measure "satisfaction" through other means, like surveys, they found that improvements in RMSE did not necessarily lead to increased user satisfaction (Knijnenburg et al. 2012; see also Pu et al. 2011). While researchers eked out minor improvements in RMSE, stories circulated claiming that user satisfaction might be more substantially improved by small interface changes, like adding the phrase "Recommended for you" above an algorithm's results.[11] As the title of one influential paper put it, "being accurate is not enough" (McNee, Riedl, and Konstan 2006). A single-minded focus on RMSE had led to the neglect of actual users.

Academic recommender systems research had been in the peculiar position of being a user-oriented field that required no contact with users. Many RecSys attendees would consider themselves researchers in human-computer interaction, but it was very common for work on algorithmic recommendation to focus narrowly on the mathematics of optimization. Accuracy metrics like RMSE had made it easy to imagine recommendation as a technical engineering problem, concerned with numerical adequacy instead of the "soft" concerns of interface design or user research.[12] (In one memorable conference talk I saw, a presentation about an algorithm for recommending hotels began, "If you're afraid of math, you can leave the room now.") For many of the researchers drawn to recommender systems, these questions of interface design were simply uninteresting; the idea that a solution to the crisis facing RMSE might lie in changing how a list of recommendations looked, or in talking with users, was untenable.

The changing infrastructure of the web offered a way out of this problem. Ever since the earliest collaborative filters, researchers had entertained the idea of using "implicit" ratings rather than explicit ones: for instance, treating the time a user spent reading an article as though it were a rating (Resnick et al. 1994, 182). Now, logs of user interactions were collected as a matter of course at most software companies, offering many kinds of data that could be interpreted as implicit ratings: stopping a video partway through, scrolling past recommended items in a list, or listening to songs multiple times could all be treated as data about user preferences, without requiring any explicit ratings. These data were plentiful, generated from any interaction a user had with a system, and they were usually treated as more truthful as well: if people might dissemble in their ratings, their behavior told the truth.[13] Netflix engineers would often note in their public talks that, while users rated critically acclaimed movies highly, they never really watched them; if the goal was to recommend movies that users would actually watch, then viewing history was a more reliable source of data than ratings. Activity logs, interpreted through a behaviorist lens, became a privileged source of information about users.

One of the reasons this kind of data had become readily available was a change in the way that software was made, updated, and maintained over the early 2000s. The "agile turn" (Gürses and Hoboken 2018) shortened development cycles and refigured the work of making software into a form of experimentation. Companies could release new versions of their software, accessible online, in weekly or even daily intervals, collecting large amounts of data about how it was used. As a result, most software was "permanently beta" (Neff and Stark 2002)—always changing and never solidifying into a final form. The experimentation Mike had described at Willow was part of this turn, which envisioned software as an apparatus for testing "market hypotheses" and exploring the world of potential users.

Under the predictive paradigm, evaluation typically happened "off line," using sets of ratings data that had already been collected. These new experimental systems, run by companies themselves, could be evaluated "online": it had become plausible to deliver a recommendation and measure how user behavior changed in response to it. By understanding users through their traces in interaction logs, the developers of recommender systems maintained their position in the technical "back end," avoiding any need to interact with users directly. After all, the truth was in behavior, not talk. And looking for signs of "satisfaction" in the logs, developers found it in measures of user retention: captivation metrics.

Where canonical error metrics like RMSE compared snapshots—a set of predicted ratings and a set of actual ratings—captivation metrics measured retention over time: from counts of daily or monthly active users, which indicated how many people use a service in a given day or month, to the evocatively named "dwell time," which measured the length of individual user sessions. Just as repeated listening could indicate preference for a song, so continued usage was taken to indicate satisfaction with a service. In a blog post describing their move "beyond the five stars" of explicit ratings, Netflix engineers wrote that they were focusing instead on "our members' enjoyment"—measured by how much time people spent watching videos and how long they remained paying subscribers (Amatriain and Basilico 2012).

A user seen through ratings data is a fuzzy portrait rendered in preferences; a user seen through activity logs is a ghostly presence who leaves traces over time. Retained users are, simply, bigger in the logs—they leave more traces, which provide more data for recommendations. Recall Mike's description of Willow's strategy to capture new users: they were confronted with recommendations designed to elicit interaction and increase their presence in the logs as quickly as possible.

These measures also satisfied a crucial constituency in industry: investors. In the contemporary software industry, captivation metrics are key indicators of a company's health and value (Graham 2012). Customer acquisition and retention are so important to start-ups and their investors that they are often prominently displayed on dashboard screens in offices, like a patient monitor in a hospital room. At Whisper, one such screen showed regular active user counts alongside technical information, like how quickly their servers were responding to requests.

As captological thinking spread around Silicon Valley, these technical changes offered a way to attend to users that appealed to engineers. This way of thinking was explicitly an effort to be "user-centered," bringing concerns about what users were actually like (and what they might actually want) back into engineering work. Appeals to user "satisfaction" hold a moral authority in the software industry, and they can be used to justify a wide range of technical choices (Van Couvering 2007).[14] But by the time I entered the field, captivation metrics were also a subject of moral ambivalence. It seemed commonsensical that users who spent more time on a service were more satisfied with it, but developers often found themselves describing their goals in terms of trapping and addiction. On the one hand, people like Mike would say, "We're trying to really make your musical life good, so in the long term you'll come back." On the other hand, the CEO of Netflix claimed that the company's main competition was not other video streaming services, but sleep, which limited the amount that users could watch (Kafka 2017).

Traps as Persuasive Technologies

A century earlier, in in the 1900 volume of *American Anthropologist*, Otis Mason published a survey of indigenous American animal traps. Mason (1900, 659) was curator of ethnology at the Smithsonian, and he had taken a special interest in the "ingenious mechanical combinations" that people around the world used to capture animals. These devices had captured many anthropological imaginations, and they populated the shelves of museums like the Smithsonian and the pages of ethnological reports.[15]

Early twentieth-century anthropological journals are dotted with brief descriptions of traps observed and collected around the world: conical Welsh eel traps made of sticks and baited with worms (Peate 1934), a bamboo rat trap from the Nicobar Islands (Mookerji 1939), pits dug along the Missouri river and baited with rabbits to trap birds of prey (Hrdlička 1916).[16] These mechanisms, extracted from the environments in which they worked, lent themselves to Victorian ethnological theorizing, serving as evidence for the diffusion of ideas across geographical regions or for the evolution of technical complexity.[17] Traps' diverse and variously elaborate mechanisms indexed a world of technical variety and change. "The trap," Mason (1900, 659) wrote, "teaches the whole lesson of invention."

That lesson, according to Mason, was to be found in the way that technologies evolved toward ever more automated action. A hunter might use a bow and arrow to shoot an animal, while a trapper could set an arrow trap, making the animal shoot itself. In this progression, Mason (1900, 660) argued, we can see how technologies extend the will of their makers: the arrow trap acts "as though it had reason"—as though "the thought of the hunter [was] locked up in its parts." This argument anticipated a common theme that would later emerge in science and technology studies: people can "delegate" their actions to technical objects (Latour 1992). Traps provide a vivid, almost diagrammatic example of how people extend their agency across time and space through technical means.

But as those later theorists would also argue, these technical extensions of agency "work" only to the extent that they anticipate their users, enticing them to do what their designers intended (Akrich 1992). In trapping, the "user" is, perversely enough, the animal to be trapped, and Mason's (1900, 657) definition of traps foregrounds the role played by animals in making them work: "A trap is an invention for the purpose of inducing animals to commit incarceration, self-arrest, or suicide." To get a trap to work requires not only technical ingenuity in the construction of mechanisms but also a thorough understanding of animal behavior.

The knowledge problem posed by trapping was so central to Mason's (1900, 659) understanding of traps that he framed his article as a "contribution to the history of empiricism"—as a record of ways that people had come to learn about the other beings that populated their world. Traps were not just practical devices, but a kind of experimental system, caught up with basic questions of knowledge. As Mason put it: "The trap itself is an invention in which are embodied most careful studies in animal mentation and habits—the hunter must know for each species its food, its likes and dislikes, its weaknesses and foibles. A trap in this connection is an ambuscade, a deceit, a temptation, an irresistible allurement: it is strategy" (659). We might imagine that traps are essentially crude material devices designed to inflict harm on animal bodies—"to inclose or impound or encage, or to seize by the head, horns, limbs, gills; to maim, wound, crush, slash, brain, impale, poison, and so on" (Mason 1900, 659–60). But for Mason, what made traps interesting was the fact that they had to orient themselves toward animals' *minds*, enticing them to play an active role in their own destruction.

Anachronistically, we can say that Mason figured traps as persuasive technologies—devices that influence behavior, according to the goals of their makers. There is no doubt that proponents of persuasive design like B. J. Fogg would object to such a characterization: trapping is clearly a form of trickery, and traps' violent ends are at odds with the idea that persuasion can be a force for self-improvement.[18] And yet in the anthropology of trapping that was to follow Mason, the psychological dynamics of trapping—how they carried forward the will of their designers and anticipated the behavior of their users—would take center stage, displacing the centrality of physical violence and coercion.

For Mason, understanding traps in primarily psychological terms turned them into sites of extraordinary drama. He narrated his traps like stories, describing their operation in both technical and poetic language: "The bear crouches between the logs, pulls the trigger, and releases the lever, which flies up and lets the ring that supports the fall slip off; then comes the tragedy" (Mason 1900, 673). Here, we encounter animals not as instinctive machines, but as tragic characters brought to untimely ends. Where behaviorists would eventually argue that humans were like animals because of their unthinking habits, Mason treated animals like humans because they were agents caught up in dramatic arcs beyond their control, susceptible to the designs of others. This is evident from his opening epigraph, which finds Decius Brutus boasting, in Shakespeare's *Julius Caesar*, how he will tempt the dictator to the scene of his eventual death:

> That unicorns may be betrayed with trees,
> And bears with glasses, elephants with holes,
> Lions with toils and men with flatteries, . . .
> Let me work;
> For I can give his humor the true bent,
> And I will bring him to the Capitol.
> (Quoted in Mason 1900, 657)

Like Mason, Brutus here treats mental and physical techniques of capture together—flattery is like the tree that catches a unicorn's horn, the mirror that entices a bear, or the net that ensnares a lion. With this opening, Mason inaugurated an enduring theme in the anthropology of trapping: if we attend closely to the process of entrapment, as it unfolds over time, we will find it hard to clearly distinguish persuasive from coercive, or mental from physical, techniques.

In 1996, the anthropologist Alfred Gell revived this theme in a celebrated essay on the anthropology of art in which he argued that we might think of artworks as a kind of "thought-trap" (37; see Boyer 1988). Where Mason highlighted the psychological complexity of technical devices, Gell sought to understand art as a kind of technology for producing psychological effects—what he had elsewhere called the "technology of enchantment," which included art, advertising, and magic (Gell 1988). Gell maintained that works of art, like conventional traps, carried forward the agency of their makers, aiming to ensnare their audiences' minds. "Every work of art that works is like this," he wrote, "a trap or a snare that impedes passage; and what is any art gallery but a place of capture[?]" (Gell 1996, 37).

Like Mason, Gell (1996, 29) analogized trapping to the unfolding of a Shakespearean drama. "It is hard not to see," he wrote, "in the drama of entrapment a mechanical analogue to the tragic sequence of hubris-nemesis-catastrophe." In Gell's telling, a curious chimpanzee, releasing a poisoned arrow while investigating a strange thread, is Faust; a hippopotamus, "lulled into a sense of false security by sheer bulk and majesty" before being speared, is Othello (29).

Although he seems to have worked in ignorance of Mason's article, Gell echoed his analysis. In both of their accounts of traps, agency is fluid and mobile, circulating among hunter, animal, and device in an unfolding process. Trapping is not simply the execution of human will but rather the interaction of a variety of intentional and automatic parts, brought together in the "nexus of intentionalities" that is a trap (Gell 1996, 29). And even more expansively than Mason, Gell blurred the line between physical and psychological capture: a gallery visitor transfixed by a painting and an animal enticed into a snare are, in his argument, instances of the same general dynamic.

Captivation and Its Critics

The term "captivation" usefully encompasses this broadened sense of capture, spanning rapt gallery audiences, deliberating consumers, and caged birds.[19] Today, captivation commonly refers to psychological phenomena, but in an older usage, the term referred to capture of both mind and body, without regard for the Cartesian dualism that would eventually treat these as entirely distinct concerns. Where persuasion is usually figured as mental and coercion material, an expansive usage of captivation helps us to suspend judgment and see how those concerns might blur together or intermingle. This way of thinking about capture extends my discussion of taste and technology from the introduction: it is analytically useful to draw into question the premise that psychological and technical phenomena are necessarily distinct, not to excuse technical overreach, but to reimagine what technological systems are like.

Nonetheless, to many people, a broadened understanding of trapping may seem like a stretch, crossing some essential boundary between psychological and physical capture. When I first presented the argument of this chapter to a room of research scientists at an industry lab, one of them came up to me afterward to render a common complaint: recommender systems are unlike animal traps in important ways, most notably in the fact that they do not seek to kill their users. A better analogy, he suggested, would be a kind of "behavioral" trap found in folk tales and on television: a jar of food or shiny objects, with a mouth too narrow for an animal's closed fist to pass through (TV Tropes, n.d.; Kimmel and Hyman 2014). In such a trap, he argued, the animal is caught because it can't—he corrected himself—because it *won't* let go of the bait. Thus, the animal's continued entrapment is in some sense its own fault, unlike an animal stuck in a cage. The folk tales about behavioral traps make the moral difference clear: greedy creatures pay the price for their pursuit of excess. In these cases the trapper is, as it were, off the hook.

Anthropological theorizing about traps lives in the space of my questioner's slippage, between the irresistible compulsion of "can't" and the conscious choice of "won't." Even when distinguishing between them seems like it should be easy or important, the difference is often unclear. In the case of animal traps, one might argue that animal minds are primarily instinctual, already machinelike, and that this sets animal traps apart from persuasive designs aimed at humans. But we do not need to pass such a judgment on the mental life of animals just for the sake of setting humans apart—humans also find themselves caught between automaticity and autonomy in a world of devices that play in the gap.

Consider, for instance, persuasive technologies like the slot machine. The anthropologist Natasha Dow Schüll (2012) has described how these devices are designed to lure gamblers into compulsive use—into what they call the "machine zone," where they sit and spend money for hours, sometimes even wearing diapers so that they do not have to leave their seats to use the toilet. Schüll (2012, 105) quotes from an online forum for gambling addicts: "When I gamble, I feel like a rat in a trap." Like a jar of pickles or a recommender system, slot machines do not physically compel people to stay put; and yet they achieve that effect, sometimes to such an extent that they are deemed worthy of government regulation and therapeutic intervention. But even here, so-called behavioral addictions are controversial among experts, and mental captivation is often attributed to the weakness of the captured, at least until it can be rendered in physical terms: once gambling addiction is medicalized and understood as a matter of chemical processes in the brain, it transforms from "won't" into "can't," shifting agency from the addict to the machine (Schüll 2012, 189–233).

So, it is perhaps unsurprising that as a popular critique of persuasive design has grown, critics have taken up the language of traps and slot machines to suggest that technology, not users, is responsible for negative social consequences. I have already described the popular analogies to Skinner boxes and laboratory experiments; in *New York Times* editorials with titles like "You Are Now Remotely Controlled," we find arguments that the software industry is trying "to conjure the helplessness, resignation and confusion that paralyze their prey" (Zuboff 2020). Advocacy organizations like Time Well Spent have been founded to "reclaim our minds from being hijacked by technology" (Thompson 2017), sometimes drawing specifically on Schüll's writing about slot machines to describe the perils of social media. These critics of captology take issue with its power and scope, but they agree with its basic premises: persuasive technology works, and it works so well that we should think of it not as gentle persuasion but as coercive force. In fact, many of the current popular critics of captology, like Tristan Harris, a cofounder of Time Well Spent and a former Google product manager, have backgrounds in the field that they now vocally critique (Irani and Chowdhury 2019).

These critiques make clear that we should not understand persuasive technologies as merely persuasive, as though they pose requests that people can easily decline. But we should also be wary of the way that these critics ascribe omnipotence to these technologies, as though a recommender system might be designed to reliably command certain behaviors. (In the illustrations that accompany such critiques, hands holding marionette strings figure prominently.) Although ordinary understandings of traps take them as materially coercive devices, the anthropology of trapping opens them up, providing a way to think about the entanglement of persuasion and coercion in technical form.

From Representation to Interaction

Under the predictive paradigm, users were represented as collections of ratings. Recommendation had been abstracted into the task of minimizing the difference between two pictures of users' taste—the predicted ratings and the actual ratings. A striking feature of these evaluations was that they generally involved "predicting" events that had already happened. Competitors in the Netflix Prize did not have to predict new ratings from old ones; they sought to guess a set of randomly withheld ratings that overlapped in time with the ratings they knew about. With rare exceptions, these techniques figured a user's preferences as essentially stable over time.[20]

Critics often point to this style of retroactive prediction as evidence of machine learning's essential conservatism (McQuillan 2015; Chun 2018). Projecting past data into the future may foreclose on the possibility of transformation; it depends on the idea that things will not (radically) change. The media theorist Alex Galloway (2004, 115) has described collaborative filtering as "a synchronic logic injected into a social relation"—everything happens at once when the unfolding sociality of preference is flattened into a matrix. What recommender systems researchers see as a technique for broadening users' horizons by introducing them to new materials, critics see as stultifying, always comparing users with one another inside a frame that cannot meaningfully change. As Galloway writes, "While any given user may experience a broadening of his or her personal tastes, the pool at large becomes less and less internally diverse" (114).

But with the rise of captivation metrics, the logic behind these systems changed. Instead of predicting explicit ratings, developers began to anticipate implicit ones, and more importantly, they no longer had to be *right*. Recommender systems had become part of a larger data collection apparatus, which sought to learn what users were like, to captivate them. Any recommendation, provoking any response, could provide data about a user, which could be used to tweak how the system worked. In machine-learning systems, as the political theorist Louise Amoore (2020) has argued, errors are essential to function—they are how "learning" happens in the first place.

It is tempting to read traps, as Gell (1996, 27) suggests, "as texts on animal behavior," which tell us what their prey are like. A large net strung between trees captures deer who try to run quickly through, while a small net left on the ground and scattered with seeds will capture a bird who walks over it; "the rat that likes to poke around in narrow spaces has just such an attractive cavity prepared for its last, fateful foray into the dark" (27). By this logic, a trap that doesn't work is a bad text, which first fails to capture its object representationally and consequently fails to capture it physically.

But the shape of a trap reflects a process of learning: torn nets, empty baskets, and abandoned playlists suggest changes in design. Traps are simultaneously devices for acting in and learning about the world. As the anthropologist Alberto Corsín Jiménez (2016) argues, traps are "epistemic interfaces between worlds"—they are devices by which predator and prey learn about each other, because traps do not always work. Over time, traps come to materialize particular understandings of prey behavior, and while we might read them as texts, we need to recall that texts have authors, and trap makers are embedded in cultural contexts that facilitate certain kinds of learning. Any time users interact with a contemporary recommender system, even if the system is currently working with an "incorrect" model, they are contributing to that model's improvement.

An Infrastructure Is a Trap in Slow Motion

As captology spreads, critics have bemoaned how algorithmic recommendation has become inescapable for contemporary users of the internet. The digital dystopian TV series *Black Mirror*, for instance, uses trapping as a leitmotif, allegorizing the ends of mental captivation in extreme physical form: characters find themselves caught in screen-covered rooms or isolated in worlds where everyone else is stuck rapt to their smartphones, and any effort to escape causes the trap to ratchet tighter (Bien-Kahn 2016). As the series' director describes it, "every single character in all of those stories is trapped from the very first frame and then never gets out" (Bien-Kahn 2016).[21] How can we be free, these critics ask, when the very setting for social action becomes a trap?

Corsín Jiménez and Chloe Nahum-Claudel (2019, 385) have described a kind of trapping that they call the "landscape trap," which expands the structure of captivation well beyond individual devices. Kalahari hunters, for instance, slowly add brush to the terrain around their camp, narrowing the routes along which antelope travel and producing a "trap ecosystem" that efficiently drives prey into their rope snares (Lee 1979; Silberbauer 1981; quoted in Corsín Jiménez and Nahum-Claudel 2019, 395). Practices like these transform environments into what the ethnoarchaeologist Alejandro Haber calls "landscapes of anticipation," rendering the setting for social action into a kind of distributed trap (Haber 2009, 427, quoted in Corsín Jiménez and Nahum-Claudel 2019, 395). If the tragedy of entrapment begins when prey first, unwittingly, interact with a trap, then landscape traps produce environments in which prey is already effectively caught.

Where early collaborative filters might be analogized to simple traps, tucked into the corners of websites in an ecology dominated by other actors, more recent recommender systems have expanded to the scope of the landscape trap. No longer are recommendations isolated to clearly defined features of a few streaming media platforms. Now, on services like Netflix, "everything is a recommendation," from the items shown on the home screen to the images used to represent them (Amatriain and Basilico 2012; Mullaney 2015). Across much of the web, most of what a user sees will have been algorithmically filtered, and most of what a user does will feed in to those algorithms' designs. Recommender systems have settled deep into the infrastructure of online life, to such an extent that they are practically unavoidable.

Unlike the "natural" landscapes in which conventional traps are set, there is no illusion that online environments are untouched by human designs. Yet the expansion of recommender systems across the "ambient media environment" (Roberts and Koliska 2014) has been cause for alarm. Building on my thinking with landscape traps, the internet researcher Nancy Baym and colleagues have suggested that an alternative definition of the term, drawn from ecology, might be more apt (Baym, Wagman, and Persaud 2020). There, "landscape traps" have referred to disordered ecologies—dead ends into which ecosystems might inadvertently evolve and become stuck (Lindenmayer et al. 2011). The rise of platforms like Facebook, which have enclosed people's online experience to such an extent that they cannot imagine living without them, might be a landscape trap in this sense: an unhappy dead end for the ecology of online life.

Returning to the time structure of trapping makes the continuity between traps and infrastructures more visible: an infrastructure is a trap in slow motion. Slowed down and spread out, we can see how these landscape traps are agents of what Corsín Jiménez (2018, 54) calls "environmentalization," making worlds for the entities they enclose. Like infrastructures, traps organize and support certain kinds of behavior; they orchestrate activity; and in expanded spatiotemporal frames, they support life while simultaneously constraining it. Facebook users and Kalahari antelope live in terrains shaped by others, in the extended temporality of the landscape trap.

To be caught at this speed is not to be dead. Rather, it is to be enclosed, known, and subject to manipulation. In other theoretical registers, this is akin to Deleuze's (1992) "control" or Foucault's (1991) "governmentality," comparisons that critics of algorithmic recommendation routinely make to describe the kind of power that such systems exercise (e.g., Cheney-Lippold 2011; Rouvroy and Berns 2013). These styles of enclosure are no less sinister for being less than absolute. But to be caught at this speed is also to be hosted—to be provided with conditions for existence that facilitate activity while constraining it (Swancutt 2012; Derrida 2000). Captivation, as Rey Chow and Julian Rohrhuber have argued, is "an experience that exceeds an ex post facto analysis of power relations" (Chow 2012, 48). In other words, there is more to trapping than the unilateral application of technical force. Not only do traps require the agency of their prey to function; the experience of captivation itself can be a form of conviviality, experienced as pleasurable by transfixed audiences.

This expansive anthropological approach to trapping offers an alternative to the popular liberal critique of persuasive design as a form of trapping: traps are ubiquitous, and they are not necessarily bad. As Corsín Jiménez (2018, 56) argues, "Traps are predatory, but they are also productive," not reducible to a simple moral tale about the wickedness of capture. Beyond the trap we can see, there is not a state of traplessness, free from any enclosure or the designs of others. If infrastructures are already traps—arrangements of techniques and epistemic frames that are designed to entice and hold anticipated agents—then the alternatives to the traps we know are the traps we are not yet aware of, infrastructures that host our living and thinking, in which we are already caught. When contemporary critics of captology imagine an escape from the machinery of persuasive design, for instance, they usually remain trapped in captology's behaviorist frame, reliant on the same world-making epistemic and technical infrastructures they nominally militate against.

This understanding of trapping suggests one more comparison with the anthropological record, which makes the mutual benefit and sociotechnical nature of capture more evident: pastoralism, which finds humans tending to animals that are not absolutely enclosed but rather tended to. As Tim Ingold (1974, 525) writes in his ethnography of Sámi reindeer pastoralists in northern Finland: "Much of the knowledge concerning the behaviour of wild deer, used by hunters to trap the deer by deceit, is used by pastoralists to different ends: to achieve, in effect, a relationship of control through symbiosis." Sámi pastoralists track the reindeer through winter and summer migrations, modulating their environment enough to keep them around: they provide emergency food, they light fires that keep mosquitoes away, they entice them into temporary, ever-changing enclosures. While Ingold emphasizes the pastoralists' control over the herd, later scholars of pastoralism note that this "control is rarely complete" and rather is "an ongoing exchange with the self-determined behaviour and preferences" of the pastoralist's herd (Reinert and Benjaminsen 2015, 9). Pastoral enclosure is a kind of nonlethal, ongoing relationship aimed at growing the number of creatures enclosed through the careful social organization of animal and environment, in forms analogous to other landscape traps.[22]

Like reindeer pastoralists, the makers of recommender systems do not want to annihilate their prey. They want to keep them around and grow their numbers, through the artful production of captivating environments that at once limit and facilitate life.[23] They do not just set a snare and lie in wait; they play an active, ongoing role, tending to the infrastructures through which they influence and learn about their users. "For the pastoralist, capital lies in the herd" (Ingold 1974, 526).

CHAPTER 3

What Are Listeners Like?

The Girl in Headphones

Around 2010, if you read about music online, you would have seen her. On music blogs or the home pages of streaming services, a woman stood alone, her eyes closed or staring into the distance (fig. 3). She wore a pair of large headphones and pressed them tight against her ears, transported by the music coming through them. She was, in a word, captivated.

The "girl in headphones," as my interlocutors would come to call her, was not any specific person, but a familiar advertising trope in the digital music industry. If recommender systems were traps, this was an image of their prey: anticipated and transfixed. The various women who filled this position represented the pleasures of captivation, showing how one might actually enjoy being enticed into using a streaming service.

The girl in headphones also embodied an age-old vision of feminized, receptive listening subjects—a woman overcome, to be looked at without herself looking.[1] Among the engineers I spent most of my time with, the girl had come to be seen as a tired, sexist trope, and her persistence was blamed on out-of-touch marketing departments that ironically lacked the cultural sensitivity of the engineers. Spotting the girl amid the churning sea of music start-up marketing materials had become something of a game. Hype Machine, an online music aggregator, ran a contest to see which of its users could collect the most examples of what it described as a "tireless cliché."[2] At industry conferences, when the girl inevitably appeared on screen, my friends from the field would nudge one another to attention, point, and laugh; on social media, they would share screenshots of her recurring appearances.

While the girl in headphones reflected the problematic sexual politics of advertising, she also posed a problem of more direct concern to recommender system developers. Although this was one of the most

FIGURE 3. The girl in headphones, on the home page of the streaming service Rdio

recognizable images of music listeners, apparently showing the captivating power of algorithmic recommendation, it was not what listening usually looked like. The typical listener of music recommendation did not experience a rapturous abandonment of the self, but something much more mundane: background music, to be listened to while sending email at the office or working out at the gym. The girl in headphones had been pulled out of the world around her; actual listeners were usually embedded in particular contexts.

Not long after the lunch where Mike had told me about how Willow sought to hook its users, he told me a story to boast about the company's data savviness. Like many streaming services, Willow offered its users "focus" playlists, designed to be played in the background while they worked. One week, Mike explained, the metrics on one of these focus playlists suddenly dropped—people were stopping the music at an unusually high rate. This triggered a hunt for explanations, which eventually singled out one particular track that seemed to be driving users to turn the music off. Upon listening to it, it became clear that what set this song apart from the others was that it contained a vocal track, while the other music on the playlist was instrumental. What had happened, Mike guessed, was that the voice had brought the music into listeners' conscious attention, spurring them to turn it off. With the track removed, the metrics went back up, and the music faded back below the threshold of listener awareness.

Although developers frequently spoke about capturing listener attention, there was something off about the image of engrossment presented by the girl in headphones. She presented a vision of captivation much like

Alfred Gell's account of gallery visitors in the previous chapter; but listeners could be caught much more subtly than this. Capturing attention in practice often meant encircling it and then fading away from conscious awareness, producing situations in which listeners would keep listening, no matter what else they might be doing.

Achieving this goal required more than finding patterns in ratings like a collaborative filter or optimizing engagement metrics: it required an explicit theory of listeners, their behavior, and their variation.

: :

The previous two chapters described two dominant visions of the listener in algorithmic recommendation: the first was eager but overloaded, seeking help to manage an overwhelming array of choices; the second was an elusive potential user, whom developers had to tempt into use. This chapter describes how these apparently disparate understandings of users coexist in the design of contemporary algorithmic recommendation. Today, the imagined users of recommender systems are understood as highly variable: they may be eager or elusive, with preferences that shift over time. Accounting for this variability has become a central task for the makers of music recommendation. If these traps are going to work, then they need to anticipate the variety of their prey.

Historically, the dominant model of listener variability in the music industry has been demographic, organizing styles of music and styles of listening in terms of age, gender, and race. But since the origins of algorithmic recommendation, developers have pitched their systems as postdemographic—as tools that allow users to transcend dominant social categories and enter into new, emergent communities. So, although the history of recommender systems is a history of ever-broadening data sources, the makers of music recommendation actively avoid using signals that they consider explicitly demographic as inputs. But because social categories like race and gender continue to shape how music is made, circulated, and received, there are no data sources completely independent of their influence. Thus, dominant social categories persist, frequently in latent form, in the new social imaginaries of developers.

As we might expect from the discussion of trapping, these ways of understanding listener variability are closely tied to technical infrastructures, which bring more and new kinds of data into the machinery of recommendation. More log data provides new opportunities to profile users according to their interaction styles; more sensor data from devices like smartphones provides a way to model a listener's "context." While they pursue the open plan, trying to facilitate exploration and growth, the makers of music recommendation persistently find themselves pigeonholing listeners into categories that they then seek to relativize. By tracing these efforts to profile users without pinning them down, we can see how knowledge about listeners is entangled with infrastructures of data collection.

Unboxing

For the first generation of recommender system developers in the mid-1990s, the fact that algorithmic recommendation worked on ratings data alone, with no reference to user demographics, was one of the technology's great strengths. Instead of anticipating a user's preferences on the basis of race, gender, or age, a recommender system could draw on the user's "actual" preferences, rendered as ratings or behavior. As John Riedl, head of the GroupLens group at Minnesota, said in an interview with the *New Yorker*: "What you tell us about what you like is far more predictive of what you will like in the future than anything else we've tried. . . . It seems almost dumb to say it, but you tell that to marketers sometimes and they look at you puzzled" (Gladwell 1999, 54).

"Marketers" proved a useful foil to define algorithmic recommendation against, although early recommender systems researchers had little direct experience with that industry. When I spoke with Riedl in 2012, he told me that the encounter with marketing had come as a surprise to his team of computer scientists. "We were mostly in ignorance of marketing" during the early development of collaborative filtering, he told me, and academic publications in the field had typically framed their work as an elaboration of technical work on information retrieval, not market research. But as people like himself spun companies out of their research groups and tried to sell their technology, they found themselves interpellated by potential clients as a new kind of marketing firm.[3]

The company Riedl had spun out of GroupLens, together with Joseph Konstan, was called Net Perceptions, and it counted among its first customers the new online bookseller Amazon.com. Riedl and Konstan wrote a book together, *Word of Mouse: The Marketing Power of Collaborative Filtering* (2002), which embraced the marketing frame and pitched collaborative filters as a breakthrough technology for businesses moving their companies online in the wake of the first dot-com boom. In a chapter titled "Box Products, Not People," Riedl and Konstan (2002, 109, 112) warned that "the urge to poll and classify is intoxicating"—but "simple demographics don't begin to tell the story of individuals." Conventional market segments produced a society "lumped into cells, not a melting pot": "We're black inner-city youth, upper-class middle-aged WASP, conservative southern landowner, working poor, etc. These boundaries are increasingly difficult to extricate ourselves from, no matter how much we protest" (110). "Think," they wrote, "about how much more people would step outside their demographic groups if they were not only permitted to, but *encouraged* to" (Riedl and Konstan 2002, 113). Collaborative filters, by moving from demographic attributes to data that was "directly" about user preference, were potentially liberatory, helping people discover interests that they may never have discovered otherwise.

Collaborative filtering shared this postdemographic framing with the World Wide Web itself. Online advocates envisioned that virtual communities of anonymous users would obviate demography, allowing individuals to pursue their own distinctive interests and rendering social categories like race and gender irrelevant. This ideology has been subjected to substantial, continuous critique: not only are supposedly "color-blind" online spaces substantially shaped by race (see, e.g., Nelson and Tu 2001; Kolko et al. 2000), but this discourse figures race (and gender) as burdens carried by people who are not white and not men, which might be relieved by a new form of classification that claims to be agnostic about them (Nakamura 2000). So, while discussing efforts to be "postdemographic," there is no reason to assume that these efforts are successful or even desirable.

Nonetheless, contemporary developers of recommender systems maintain this rejection of demographic data. In a 2018 press tour, for instance, Netflix executives described how the service orients itself toward a set of roughly two thousand data-derived "taste communities" because "demographics are not a good indicator of what people like to watch" (Lynch 2018). I often heard researchers remark that efforts to incorporate demographic data did not improve the functioning of experimental systems. To the extent that demographics mattered, their effect should already be evident in behavioral data. If demographic profiling confirmed the results derived from behavioral data, then it was redundant; if it diverged, then it was a source of potential error, predicated on an unseemly essentialism. As the sociologist Alondra Nelson (2002, 1) wrote the same year that *Word of Mouse* was published: according to the dominant ideology of digital technology, "race is a liability . . . either negligible or evidence of negligence."

But the fact that recommender systems do not use explicitly demographic data does not mean that they are uninfluenced by race, gender, or other dominant social categories. As scholars have argued about "postidentity" claims in many domains, powerful social categories often re-emerge from systems premised on their unimportance, in modulated or hard-to-contest forms (McRobbie 2004; Daniels 2015; Cheney-Lippold 2017; Cohn 2019). Not only is the ability to be "postidentity" marked as white and male (see James 2017), but in a social setting where these categories have broad influence, *all* data about people and their behaviors are "demographic" to a certain extent (Barocas and Selbst 2016; Benjamin 2019). Users' listening histories may not explicitly include data about their race, for instance, but the music they listen to is shaped by the social fact of race—in the structure of the music industry and in broader patterns of listening.

"Racial profiling" often served as a shorthand for the kind of demography-aware targeting that recommender systems were meant to avoid, designating an approach that was self-evidently bad. In their book, Riedl and Konstan (2002, 112) wrote, "Racial profiling and profiling your customers both spring from the same lazy, prejudiced philosophy." When confronted with the basic sociological fact that music production and consumption were racially marked, my interlocutors nevertheless sought to avoid any kind of procedure that might be considered racial profiling. Given their willingness to entertain many other sorts of data that might be linked only tenuously to listening behavior—from the weather to the device a user listened on—the insistent avoidance of race was striking.[4]

The cover of *Word of Mouse* featured a conspicuously diverse crowd, waving from inside a computer screen. But this crowd's real diversity, the book suggested, was not found in their visible variety, but in their preferences, which collaborative filtering could finally recognize and cater to. As the anthropologist Marilyn Strathern (1992, 9) wrote, while the first collaborative filters were being designed, "free-ranging access, such apparent freedom of choice, in the end turns the sense of plurality into an artefact of access or choice itself." The kind of diversity envisioned in *Word of Mouse* did not precede large catalogs of material to be recommended, but was rather realized in them.

Lean Forward, Lean Back

With demography (nominally) pushed to the side, developers were still concerned with collective forms of variation. People were not absolutely unique—if they were, algorithmic recommendation could never work—but what tied them together?

In 2011, I was interviewing Peter, a senior engineer at Whisper. In one

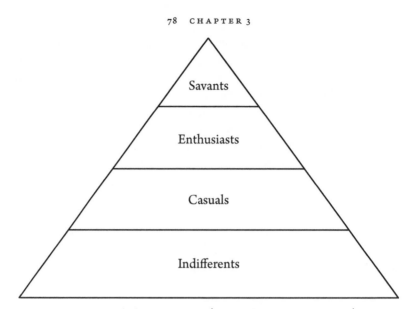

FIGURE 4. The listener pyramid (redrawn from Jennings 2007, 46)

of the start-up's meeting rooms, he told me that the biggest challenge for recommender system design at the time was the fact that listeners were not all alike. Not only did people have preferences for different styles of music; they had different styles of musical preference.

"There's a pyramid of listeners," Peter told me (fig. 4). At the base of the pyramid—the largest group—were people he called "musically indifferent": they did not particularly care for music, and they did not want to put any effort into finding music to listen to. Peter also described these listeners as "the Starbucks crowd"—back when the coffee retailer sold CDs at the checkout stand, these would be the people buying and listening to them, because they were readily available.[5] He estimated that these musically indifferent people made up about 40 percent of the population. Moving up through the pyramid, decreasing in size and increasing in avidity, he passed through "casual" and "enthusiast" listeners, before arriving at the smallest group, at the top: "musical savants." The name indicated the status ascribed to these listeners, who were extremely avid and knowledgeable—whose "whole identity is wrapped up in music." Later, Peter would describe savants as people who "live for music"—they "do the bar quizzes and all that stuff," eagerly pursuing both new music and information about it.

The challenge, as Peter put it, was that all these listeners wanted different things out of a recommender system. Savants might be interested in something to aid their browsing, to introduce them to more obscure music; casuals might just want some music to play inoffensively in the background, without much effort. "In any of these four sectors," Peter told me, "it's a different ball game in how you want to engage them." What worked for one group would likely fail for another. Recommender systems, and the overall user experience surrounding them, might need to be personalized to users' listening styles as well as their favorite music.

When we spoke in 2011, Peter couldn't recall where he had first seen the pyramid. But over the next few years, I kept encountering it, casually mentioned by PhD students in interviews or shown on the slides of conference presentations. I eventually traced it to a book, titled *Net, Blogs, and Rock 'n' Roll*, published by music industry consultant David Jennings in 2007. Jennings had taken the data for the pyramid from a market research study called Project Phoenix, conducted by UK media conglomerate EMAP in the early 2000s. Project Phoenix, as the name suggested, had been intended to help revitalize an apparently dying music industry, gathering data about the changing listening habits of people in the United Kingdom.

In his book, Jennings (2007, 31) was circumspect about the generalizability of the Project Phoenix categories: "They represent a snapshot in a particular country—the UK—at a particular time. Such categories are always evolving." However, he continued, "Whether or not the subgroups are empirically watertight does not matter . . . the main point here is simply the *existence* of different groups" (32). The takeaway, for Jennings, was not that listeners could be distinguished in precisely these ways, but rather that they could be distinguished at all: "Music listeners are not an undifferentiated mass" (32). But as the pyramid traveled, people like Peter used it to think with, reconciling it with their own intuitions about music listening. Jennings's qualifications fell away, and the pyramid became reshaped into a commonsense fact about musical audiences. While people like Peter might be able to point to the fact that the pyramid originated from a study, they were not concerned with assessing that study's validity or methodology; the pyramid traveled thanks to its intuitive appeal, not as a result of its scientific standing.

I use the term "avidity" to capture the set of loosely related ideas about musical enthusiasm, cultural status, and knowledge represented by the pyramid. Avidity did not necessarily correspond to any particular genres or artists—in theory one could be an avid fan of any sort of music. In this, it was roughly analogous to "omnivorousness" in the sociology of taste (Peterson and Kern 1996): listeners distinguished themselves not by their favorite genres, but by their attitudes toward the cultural field itself. And avidity commonly functioned as a vernacular equivalent to omnivorousness: savant listeners were generally considered more exploratory and diverse in their listening than their less avid counterparts.[6]

In practice, the four levels of the pyramid often collapsed into a binary distinction: avid listeners were "lean-forward," fiddling with settings, actively engaging with the interface, browsing, and skipping songs, and less avid listeners were "lean-back," looking to start the music and then leave it alone. These ideal types were commonly used to describe the ethos of an entire music listening platform: the algorithmic radio streams produced by a company like Pandora Radio were essentially lean-back, while the MP3s cataloged by Hype Machine were lean-forward, encouraging enthusiasts to browse in pursuit of obscure new music. On-demand streaming services like Spotify or Rdio, with their large catalogs, boasted features aimed at both kinds of use: listeners could start algorithmic radio stations and lean back, or they could lean forward and browse through the catalog, guided by algorithmically selected "related artists" and other such classifications.

Although avidity was abstracted away from the details of musical genre or listener demography, it often absorbed and came to stand for other kinds of difference. This was most obvious in the discussion of exemplary listener types: Mike, the head of engineering at Willow, explained to me that teenage girls who wanted to hear the same pop music on repeat needed a style of recommendation that was different from erudite jazz listeners (here he shifted to masculine pronouns) who were more likely to be open to exploration. The underlying recommender infrastructure might have no data about a user's gender, and if a gender were imputed to a user, it was likely to be used for selling advertisements, not recommending music; however, in conversations among the people working on these systems, user gender (and gendered understandings of musical genres, like pop; see, e.g., Cook 2001; James 2013) often stood in for lean-forward or lean-back tendencies. Thus, from one's first choice of what to play, a platform could begin to profile a given user in terms of avidity.

If the girl in headphones represented one archetypal feminized listening subject, the lean-back listener represented another. The musicologist Christina Baade (2018) argues that background listening has long been cast as the feminized alternative to a masculine attentive listening, locating contemporary "lean-back" services in a history that includes mid-century "tap listeners"—a term used at the BBC to refer to women who left the radio running, as though it were a faucet, in the background while working at home (Baade 2012).[7] Critiques of background listening (most typically directed at the Muzak corporation and its derivatives; e.g., Anderson 2015) generally repeat the implicit sexism of earlier critiques of mass culture, associating it with a docile, feminized listening audience.

When people like Peter invoked overload as the reason for recommendation, they typically described a lean-forward listener: someone eager to explore who found themselves overwhelmed by the amount of music to choose from. Lean-back listeners, in contrast, were the elusive prey of captological recommender systems that were fine-tuned to draw them in. While it had once been common to imagine the user of a recommender system as a "music lover" (as Ringo had put it), the largest market opportunity was found among indifferent listeners. "If you're looking for the big bucks," Peter told me, then a recommender system had to work for the musically indifferent.

Music and Data Geeks

The figure of the indifferent listener posed two problems for algorithmic recommendation. The first problem, as Peter described it, was that they were less willing to interact with a system, thus providing less of the data on which data-driven recommendation depends. While a lean-forward listener might make a hundred interactions in a listening session, handpicking every song, a lean-back listener might want to interact only once—for instance, to pick a "seed" artist for an algorithmic radio station. The second problem was that this attitude made these listeners quite unlike the people who built these systems, who almost universally identified as passionate about music and thus, in the framework of the pyramid, as "savants."[8] Where the target user was an indifferent Starbucks listener, engineers tended to be, echoing the name of one Dublin infomediary company, "music and data geeks."

On the last day of RecSys 2014, I was drinking in the hotel bar with a few of my longtime contacts in the field. Some of them had recently made the transition from academia to industry, and this was their first year representing commercial employers at the conference. They were arguing about the differences between themselves and their users. Oliver, a PhD computer scientist who described himself as a "data plumber" for the major music streaming service I call Wavelet, claimed that engineers generally had obscure taste in music. This made it hard for them to evaluate the experience of an average user, who was more likely to want popular music. Thus, while he would complain about the quality of Wavelet's recommendations for himself, his complaints might in fact indicate that Wavelet worked well for the typical user. "It's hard to recom-

mend shitty music to people who want shitty music," he said, expressing the burden of a music recommendation developer caught between
two competing evaluative schemes: his own idea about what made music
"good" and what he recognized as the proper criteria for evaluating a recommender system. This was a common cause for complaint and source
of humor among engineers; when told that Whisper's algorithmic radio
station based on the popular artist Taylor Swift was bad, Michael, one of
Whisper's radio developers, declaimed, "Well, with a seed artist like that,
what do you expect?!"

Across the table in the hotel bar, Seth, a research scientist at Willow,
described the obligations of a music recommender in terms that were
common across the industry: "We're not tastemakers," he said. A recommender system should give people what they want, even if it offends developers' sensibilities. While Seth understood the cultural intermediaries
of the traditional music industry—the DJs, booking agents, record store
clerks, and so on—as actively shaping the flow of music (see Negus 1995;
Powers 2012), he felt an obligation to get out of the way. This idea is conventional across the "platforms" of Silicon Valley, which present themselves as neutral conduits and supports for information, even when they
shape its flow through algorithmic filtering (Gillespie 2010).

Despite that commitment to neutrality, Seth attributed the success of
his new employer to the savant status of the company culture: "everyone
in the company is really fucking cool," he said. Within a longer history
of knowledge work in Silicon Valley, such claims are not at all unusual
(Turner 2010). As the literary scholar Alan Liu (2004, 77–78) wrote in
The Laws of Cool, referring to the ubiquity of "coolness" as a corporate
descriptor during the first dot-com boom: "Cool is an attitude or pose
from within the belly of the beast, an effort to make one's very mode of
inhabiting a cubicle express what in the 1960s would have been an 'alternative lifestyle.'" It was this "coolness"—a self-aware distancing from ordinary taste—that made it seem plausible to developers that they might
be objective about others' preferences.

In addition to the kind of "cool" typical to knowledge work, the employees of music streaming services were also "cool" in their adjacency to
the music industry: popular artists might drop by the office and perform
at lunch, and knowledge of obscure or marginalized genres was prized.
During my fieldwork I met DJs, noise artists, experimental composers,
and former professional musicians who had all ended up working as software engineers. As in the more conventional music industries, a "passion
for music" was essentially obligatory for employees of music streaming

companies, regardless of whether a given role was considered "creative" (Bennett 2018). The acquisition of cultural capital represented by avidity was crucial to getting the job (see Koppman 2016).

In my interviews with technical employees of these companies, most recounted a long-standing and avid interest in music—as fans or performers—and many could not imagine moving on to jobs in other domains. After years of making software for insurance companies or banks, they saw working on music as the best possible occupation. Music streaming services often present the musical enthusiasm of their employees as evidence that they properly care for music—that they are not outside interlopers from "tech," but legitimate and passionate cultural stewards.[9] On rare occasions, an interviewee might confide in me that they were less into music than their coworkers, suggesting that this set them apart from the overall company "culture," which presumed musical avidity as a unifying characteristic. Such people usually worked in roles that were already marginalized within office hierarchies: system administrators who maintained a company's local computers, or office managers who were responsible for the logistics of space and scheduling (see Bennett 2018b). These employees were not indifferent to music, and by ordinary standards were probably quite avid listeners. Only within the context of company culture, with regular live performances, employee bands, and constant discussion of new genres and obscure musical edge cases did they seem less enthusiastic.

By 2014, the idea that software companies depended on their internal "culture" for success had become commonplace in Silicon Valley (Chesky 2014). Such invocations of "culture" were characteristically vague, referring to something like a shared ethos or a set of values when they did not refer to the material amenities like foosball tables or free snacks that made offices "fun" (English-Lueck and Avery 2017; Chen 2019). The notion of culture fit—the idea that employees should be hired not only for their relevant skills but also for their more subjective compatibility with a corporate disposition—had become an object of critique within broader arguments about workplace diversity (e.g., Tiku 2013). Culture fit was a homogenizing force: workplaces that hired people who were like the people already there tended to hire more young, white men, and this homogeneity is generally considered a central cause of the biased outcomes perpetuated by software systems (Noble and Roberts 2019).

For companies building music recommenders, the defining feature of corporate cultural fit was musical avidity. As Seth put it, it was crucial that his coworkers were cool: "you can't risk polluting the culture." The boundary between the interior of the company and the people outside of it had to be carefully managed to ensure that the people there were avid enough to do their jobs well. This, too, perpetuated demographic homogeneity—not under the more common Silicon Valley cover of technical expertise and meritocracy, but in relation to musical enthusiasm. Like other geeks, music geeks are stereotypically white and male (see Eglash 2002). Although the people employed by these companies, particularly in technical roles, were predominantly white, relatively young, English-speaking men, they cast the key difference between themselves and outsiders—between engineers and users—in terms of avidity, not demography.

We Have Science Here

Many critiques of Silicon Valley suggest that start-ups avoid thinking about alterity by simply making products for themselves. As one author put it in the *New Yorker*: "the hottest tech start-ups are solving all the problems of being twenty years old, with cash on hand, because that's who thinks them up" (Packer 2013). When that software is not something like a laundry pickup service, but comes to be pervasive social infrastructure, like a search engine or social networking site, the problem manifests as unanticipated consequences visited upon already-marginalized users. Thus, companies implement "real name" policies that put victims of stalking or abuse at risk (boyd 2012), persistent social network profiles that stymie those making gender or other transitions (Haimson et al. 2015), facial recognition systems that cannot see nonwhite faces (Phillips 2011; Buolamwini and Gebru 2018), and speech recognition systems that cannot hear women's voices (Margolis and Fisher 2002). These are some of the problems that can emerge from a combination of demographic homogeneity and what critical technology scholars have called the "I-methodology" (Oudshoorn, Rommes, and Stienstra 2004), whereby developers simply imagine themselves as users.

These critiques were quite familiar among the makers of music recommendation, though set in terms of avidity rather than demography. Engineers frequently reminded me and one another that, as enthusiasts, they could not simply imagine themselves in users' shoes or pretend that their desires for features were widely shared. Although people continued to rely on their own judgment in the countless "sniff tests" and informal evaluations of functionality that marked the working day, the idea that they might know what users wanted or needed was regularly brought into focus as a problematic tendency to be resisted. Rather than imagining oneself as the user, one had to imagine the user as someone unlike the self.

To return briefly to the trapping metaphor, these engineers found themselves in a position like the Siberian Yukaghir hunters depicted by the anthropologist Rane Willerslev: "Trapping," Willerslev (2007, 91) explains, "involves a kind of mental projection by which the hunter seeks to place himself imaginatively within the character of the animal, matching that which is unique about it." But these projections are unreliable, and "perspectivism among Yukaghirs is not really about moving from one point of view to another. Rather, it is about not surrendering to a single point of view. It is concerned with action in between identities, in that double negative field" (110).

Like Yukaghir "soul hunters," the developers of recommender systems find themselves in the middle of a double negation: they should not think like themselves, but they cannot think like their users. For many of my interlocutors, this double negation was managed by references to "science"—to infrastructures of data collection that seemed to offer recourse to an objective outside position. By renewing their focus on data, avid music fans might be able to understand indifferent listeners.

On a cross-country video call in summer 2013, Tom, a Whisper product manager responsible for "audience understanding," described to me his company's data collection efforts: "We don't interview users," he said. Instead, he told me, they used aggregated listening data, which reflected actual listening behavior rather than claimed listening behavior.[10] "We think we have real science here," he said. Science, in this case, referred to the kind of knowledge that could be derived from activity logs—not from direct engagement with users. The stores of listening data accumulating on their servers were privileged sources of information about users, granting "technical" employees the power to explain and interpret how users behaved and what they wanted, without having to rely on dedicated user researchers. Not only was this a legitimated source of knowledge about users directly under engineers' control—it was also figured as more reliable than the kind of knowledge that might be gained through other means. This data, Tom suggested, reflected how people *actually* behaved, unlike what they might tell an interviewer. He would refer to the listening activity aggregated in Whisper's logs as a user's "musical identity."

In the early 2010s, many infomediary companies, like Whisper, employed no dedicated user researchers at all; at larger companies that did employ user researchers, they were typically remote from the recommender systems teams, working on issues like interface design. The availability of log data and the technical expertise required to parse it meant that engineers had become newly empowered to produce authoritative accounts of user tendencies on their own.[11] As I described in the previous chapter, recommender systems researchers occupied a peculiar niche: they were user oriented in a way that many other subfields of computer science were not, but they generally avoided "soft" forms of qualitative user research that might provide data about how their systems were received (Knijnenburg and Willemsen 2015). As one of the organizers of RecSys 2014 noted in an introductory presentation, most of the papers presented that year were oriented toward technical methods, with "surprisingly few papers addressing issues of user experience."

Since the end of my fieldwork, there have been more efforts to integrate qualitative user research with the data gathered through logs (e.g., Garcia-Gathright et al. 2018), but these user researchers have also been enrolled as interpreters of interactional data, finding patterns that are often rendered as "personas," or idealized user types. When I caught up with Nate, a researcher at the streaming service Wonder, in 2019, he told me how the user research team had produced a set of nine personas, who were given names and illustrated on posters stuck around the office, meant to remind employees whom they were making software for. These fictional composite users represented a range of demographic and interactional types, but as Nate recounted to me, people on his team typically referred to only two of the nine personas—the two that roughly corresponded to lean-back and lean-forward listeners.[12] In turn, those personas were the target users for Wonder's paid service (which allowed choosing songs on demand) and its free service (which limited the amount of user interaction, requiring a relatively hands-off listening style). In this, we can see a straightforward way that technical infrastructures shape understanding: listener types are defined not in their own terms but in how they interact with a system—or even more narrowly, in terms of preexisting software features.

One Listener Is Many Listeners

The idea that data collected through online interaction is fundamentally more truthful and reliable than self-reporting is a matter of common sense in recommendation—as we've seen from Tom and from John Riedl—and it is also a very common object of humanistic critique. The media theorist José van Dijck (2014, 201) calls it "dataism": "belief in a new gold standard of knowledge about human behavior," grounded in "a belief in the objectivity of quantification and in the potential of tracking all kinds of human behavior and sociality through online data" (see Kitchin and Lauriault 2014; Crawford 2013).

The presumed stability of profiles like the ones Tom had helped design is also a frequent target of popular critique from users who feel that they have been pigeonholed or misapprehended. Parents, for instance, complain that their recommendations are full of kids' music as a result of playing music for their children.

Ironically, a similar problem had manifested for the employees of Whisper, who often listened to music that they did not like as part of their jobs. They would joke that testing a new playlisting algorithm had thrown off their recommendations; when I helped the quality assurance team assess their "similar artists" measure, I found my own recommendations temporarily full of suggestions that had picked up on what appeared to be my newfound interest in the music of Enrique Iglesias. Eventually, many of these workers would create secondary accounts to use for work, to avoid such misrecognitions.

Academic critics typically identify these problems as the result of data's failure to grasp context (e.g., boyd and Crawford 2012, 9). While Tom might gather together a user's listening history, he could not know the situations that had generated it: maybe a parent was playing music for a child, or maybe a Whisper employee was testing a new feature. These contexts change the significance of events like playing through a whole song in ways that cannot be easily captured in the logs.

The makers of music recommendation had a number of responses to critiques like these. First, they would suggest that anomalous listening events would eventually be obscured by more durable tendencies in a user's listening. But second, Tom would ask, Why should recommending kids' music to people who listened to kids' music be considered an error? Although he used the language of "musical identity" to describe the taste profiles he produced, he argued that there was no reason a taste profile had to be coherent.

"One listener is really many listeners," Tom told me, and Whisper would soon start analyzing listening data to produce what the company called "clusters," which represented the various styles of music a person listened to. One user might listen to death metal, smooth jazz, and progressive trance house, and a good recommender should recommend music from all three styles—not music that somehow synthesized them all together. Such variety might indicate that multiple users shared an account, but they could just as easily reflect a listener whose tastes varied from moment to moment.

And just as someone's genre preferences might vary across time, so too could their listening styles. The dominance of lean-back and lean-forward listeners as ideal types sometimes struck the makers of music recommendation as another unseemly essentialism that personalization might unravel. Perhaps, they suggested, lean-back and lean-forward were not really kinds of people, but kinds of situation. A person might be lean-back while working out or driving a car but lean-forward while choosing something to listen to once they got home. Even the most avid music listener could move through lean-back situations.

Understanding these varying situations was crucial to making appropriate recommendations—to recommending workout music at the gym or focus music at the office—but it was especially important for making sense of user interactions. If a user was in a lean-back context, like driving a car or going for a run, then a recommender should play it safe and not recommend risky music that might require the user to hit the skip button. The less avid the listener and the more lean-back the situation, the more important context became in determining what a listener might want to listen to.

In 2012, the music technology trade blog *Hypebot* suggested that the industry would soon see the rise of what it called "context culture": a "freaky, but inevitable" trend toward contextually sensitive software (Hoffman 2012). Academic researchers in human-computer interaction had long been interested in creating "context-aware computing" (Schilit, Adams, and Want 1994), but the growing popularity of smartphones—which housed a variety of sensors that might provide data about a user's context—made it much easier to integrate new kinds of data into the architecture of algorithmic recommendation (Adomavicius and Tuzhilin 2015). Accelerometers might indicate whether a person was driving or walking; GPS receivers could show where someone was. Linked to calendars or social media accounts, music streaming services might begin to address their recommendations to people in different situations. As another commentator put it: "If the first streaming music revolution was about access, the second one is about context" (Van Buskirk 2012).

Peter had been experimenting with this data, building prototypes for a kind of recommender system he called No Interface, which would play music without requiring any user interaction at all. The No Interface ideal existed as a kind of limit point for algorithmic recommendation, where everything about a music streaming service was reduced to nothing, except for the recommender at the center. His goal, as he wrote on his blog, was to "capture the attention of indifferent listeners," and embodied in this trap's design was a model of listeners uninterested in interaction—or perhaps moving through lean-back situations.

Peter elaborated on the basic idea of implicit ratings encountered in the previous chapter: "When listeners change the volume, when they skip songs, when they search or stop listening, they tell us about their taste." Any number of signals, not only the choice of what to play, might be considered evidence of taste, to be gathered together into an ensemble where they might incrementally improve captivation metrics. But more than that, one's listening could be correlated with any of the data one's smartphone could collect. "My phone knows that I'm late for a meeting. Maybe it knows the favorite songs of the people I'm meeting with," Peter wrote.

If No Interface was a trap for lean-back listeners, its goal was more like a pastoral enclosure than the transfixion represented by the girl in headphones—a continuous soundtrack for the day, following a listener through a series of moments. Where Tom's taste profiles were built from collections of artists, genres, and songs, rendering a user's "musical identity" out of listening history, the listener envisioned in Peter's No Interface project was something more. This user was a member of various statistical distributions, waiting for interactions to actualize an identity out of the potentials predicted by certain known features.

Context Cultures

Like their critics, these data miners had come to place great importance on context. But they seemed to disagree with their critics about what "context" meant. Among researchers in context-aware recommendation, "context" usually referred to any data beyond the users, items, and ratings that constituted a basic collaborative filter. Most commonly, this meant adding information about time and location to a given interaction: if someone listened to high-energy techno music at the same place and time every week, then a system could associate that music with that place and time. Perhaps this person was listening at the gym, but that didn't matter; recognizing the fact of the pattern was good enough. Critics from the social sciences, however, understood context as "a subtle reckoning" (boyd and Crawford 2012, 10)—the sort of thing people could do only from within specific situations.

The human-computer interaction researcher Paul Dourish (2004) has identified these two approaches to context as "representational" and "interactional." In the representational mode, context is taken to be a stable container for activities: one's context can be described as an accumulation of data points such as location, weather, the people nearby, or the time of day. This is the prevailing attitude within most computing research, Dourish argues. It fits well with the information theoretic understanding of the world described in chapter 1: context is "anything outside the signal," as one engineer told me. To make sense of context is to represent it, to bring that container's qualities within the calculating domain of software systems.

The interactional mode, by contrast, is a legacy of phenomenology: contexts are not objective containers but relational properties occasioned through activity. This attitude toward context is shared by many linguistic anthropologists (e.g., Duranti and Goodwin 1992), who understand contexts as essentially created by people while they interact with one another and go about their lives. So, a GPS signal may indicate that someone is physically at the office, but their "context" is more transient and elusive than their location: talking to a coworker about politics, someone may invoke the nation or city; emailing a relative may locate that person within an extended family; taking a call from a romantic partner, someone may be drawn into an emotional context that a GPS receiver has no hope of identifying. In this understanding, context is emergent, not objective.

These two modes of understanding context, Dourish argues, are incompatible with each other. Social scientists aiming to understand context or to critique others for not understanding context are usually working in the interactional mode, while computer scientists tend to the representational.[13] There is, it seems, no signal that might be added to a computational model that could answer the criticism that it takes things out of context. What the developers of recommender systems see as contextualizing, a humanistic critic might see as deracinating: is the location of your smartphone a context, or is it data in need of contextualization? "Essentially," Dourish (2004, 22) writes, "the sociological critique is that the kind of thing that can be modeled . . . is not the kind of thing that context is."

The question of what context is, and how we can know it, has vexed anthropological critics since at least the 1980s, as they sought to clarify and pursue the mission of an anthropology that understands human life in context. The problem, as Roy Dilley (1999, 15) wrote in *The Problem of Context*, is that "interpretation in context requires the pre-interpretation of the relevant context, that in turn informs the subsequent interpretation." In other words, when we say that a user interaction can be understood only "in context," we set up a situation where we have to decide what the relevant context is; this requires an act of interpretation in the first place—a choice among the countless things that might count as context. Interpretation depends on interpretation—a classic problem of hermeneutics, as Dilley noted—and there is no ultimate criterion we might use to know which context matters.

To elaborate, let's say we wanted to contextualize a play event: a user has listened to the entirety of Britney Spears's chart-topping 2004 single "Toxic." An ethnographer witnessing the scene might be privy to context unavailable to the recommender system. Once the ethnographer begins looking for context, it starts to accumulate: the listener might be located in a social context (relaxing with roommates), a cultural context (nostalgic for the mid-2000s), an economic context (unemployed), a geological context (listening during the unfolding devastation of the Anthropocene), or a biological context (avoiding the pandemic spreading outside the apartment), and so on, ad infinitum. Any of these contexts could be "thickened" in a number of ways, mixed with the others, and extended across scales. Because an exhaustive catalog of context is impossible, a contextual analysis inevitably involves choices about what counts and where the work of contextualization should stop (Strathern 1996).

These choices do not derive simply from the decision to consider context, but from the contexts and goals of the contextualizer: software engineers pursue different contextual goals than anthropologists do, as do office managers, activists, and venture capitalists. These approaches to context are also shaped by the methods used to apprehend it. Ethnographers, with their field notes, participant observation, and thick description, produce context in one way, while smartphones packed with sensors produce it in another. These various forms of context "are not self-evident aspects of reality that are pre-given or to be taken-for-granted, in the sense of being understood as existing prior to analysis. They are part of the analysis and interpretation itself" (Dilley 2002, 449).[14]

Repurposing the term from *Hypebot*, we might think about these approaches to context as different "context cultures," which prioritize different relations and styles of connection as "context." Arguments for the importance of context are, in this frame, better understood as arguments *about* context: what should we accept and seek out as relevant for the work of interpretation? The answer to this question is, appropriately enough, context-specific. For the developers of recommender systems, their answer emerged within the data-centric world of contemporary software. But informed by the interactional approach, we can look at practices of "contexting" (Asdal and Moser 2012): how contexts are constructed by the people who invoke them, even when those people are being representationalists.

Widening Contexts

As Peter continued his No Interface work, he moved in a surprising direction: Thanks to a corporate partnership, Whisper had collected demographic data about many of its listeners, from social media profiles linked to their accounts. Using this data, Peter calculated the most "distinctive" music listened to by various groups of people—not the most popular, but music that was frequently listened to by one group and infrequently listened to by others. Some artists were more commonly listened to by women, or people in their thirties, or residents of Vermont. If a brand-new user was located in Vermont, then playing them music distinctively liked by residents of Vermont might yield a slightly higher rate of success than playing something at random. If the only data a recommender system had about a user was demographic information from a social media profile, then demographic patterns in listening might provide a temporary solution to the cold-start problem, until more interaction data became available.

This reappearance of demography surprised me: most of the people I spoke with continued to insist that, in general, the elimination of demographic profiling was one of algorithmic recommendation's key benefits. But in the absence of other data, demography had come to seem viable in a very peculiar form: not as an essential quality of a listener but as a kind of maybe-relevant context, analogous to the fact of being at the gym or listening in the evening. Demographic information became palatable when understood as context instead of essence, where it could be used to draw indifferent users into correlations with one another, locating them within a web of partial statistical connections.

:   :

At the 2016 RecSys conference in Boston, I watched a team of European researchers make a familiar argument for the significance of context in more extreme terms. While recommender systems researchers had become accustomed to the idea that contextual data might be added into existing systems as an extra signal, on top of conventional data like ratings or listening time, this team argued that the field should go further into a "contextual turn" (Pagano et al. 2016). Rather than being merely context aware, algorithmic recommendation should become context *driven*, bringing contextual signals from the margins to the center of recommender systems. "People have more in common with other people in the same situation," they argued, "than they do with past versions of themselves" (Pagano et al. 2016, 249).

This claim split apart two of the founding ideas of algorithmic recommendation. On one side were claims like John Riedl's from the beginning of this chapter: the best way to know what someone was going to like in the future was to see what they liked in the past. On the other side was the idea described in the original GroupLens paper and implicit in Ringo: recommender systems worked because people resembled each other. If older versions of recommendation might be critiqued for reifying individuals as static desiring subjects, with stable latent preferences, these new techniques appealed to the partible person. Users' taste, and maybe even identity, might vary according to the situations they found themselves in.

The contextual turn depended, as the presenters recognized, on "huge amounts of data generated by users" (Pagano et al. 2016, 249). While this may seem ordinary in the contemporary context of ever-growing digital surveillance, it is striking for its inversion of the early themes of collaborative filtering. What made early recommender systems seem so "magical" was how little data they needed to work. By contrast, these contextual systems have grown to accommodate an ever-widening set of data sources.

Critics have analyzed such practices as a phenomenon of surveillance capitalism, gathering together more and more data about people into centralized profiles that can be used not only for apparently innocuous purposes like recommending music but also for more nefarious ones that might restrict a person's life choices or subject individuals to greater scrutiny from the state. Peter, for instance, was concerned that a music streaming service asking for a user's location data might seem "creepy," but he noted that people already shared their location for many other sorts of personal purposes and thought that the idea might eventually become normalized.

Yet the team presenting at RecSys argued that on the other side of the contextual turn lay a future where context-driven recommendation might in fact protect user privacy: if people shared more in common with others in the same situation than with themselves in the past, then a contextually driven recommender could do away with persistent user profiles altogether, replacing them instead with a series of contextual models. This was a form of recommendation that might be adequate to what they called "continuous cold start," where it was not only new users who lacked a history of interactional data but everyone, and the machinery of algorithmic recommendation had to be turned inside out, profiling everything but the unitary user.

Given the history of data collection in the software industry to date, there is little reason to expect that such a privacy-preserving future will actually be realized. But this vision of context usefully traces out the trajectory of thinking about what listeners are like in music recommendation. From the avid "music lovers" of Ringo, with stable preferences, known and revealed through ratings, we move to the lean-back listeners of Willow, who revealed their taste only through implicit signals and were always at risk of turning the music off. As the ideal imagined listener has become less avid and more fragmented—and as more forms of data have become available for integration into recommenders—we find forms of recommendation that turn the early ideals of collaborative filtering on their head.

Instead of autonomous individuals seeking out unknown pleasures, we have systems designed to profile users as members of emergent collectivities, defined not by demographics (at least not explicitly), but by whatever data is ready to hand, locating people in newly constructed and dynamic groups. At some times, they evince the flaws of behaviorism—mistaking measurements for the thing being measured, neglecting the contextual specificities that make one click different from another. At other times, they evince the flaws of demographic market segmentation—overestimating the coherence of predefined groups of people.

Throughout this evolution, the meaning of taste has shifted as well: within the architecture of recommendation, it has transformed from a collection of stated preferences, to something tacit and behavioral, to a diffuse and intricate form of collective patterning. Taste in contemporary music recommenders is enacted as many things at once, through the use of many kinds of data. These kinds of data foreground different aspects of users as relevant to their preferences, tying theories of taste together with technical infrastructures. The development of preferential technics is marked by these mutualities and feedback loops, through which some understandings are reinforced at the expense of others and integrated into circulatory infrastructures. The question of what listeners are like finds many answers in the machinery of music recommendation.

CHAPTER 4

Hearing and Counting

Music Is a Signal

On the train into town, with my suitcase between my legs, I begin to suspect that I am sitting next to a graduate student. Seth, it turns out, has actually just finished his PhD—in electrical engineering, at a US university. He's in Portugal, like I am, to attend ISMIR, the annual meeting of the International Society for Music Information Retrieval. ISMIR is a meeting place for researchers in computer science, library science, musicology, and a handful of other disciplines, all of whom study music as a kind of information.

The field is small but broad, and the research presented at ISMIR covers a wide range of topics. Every year, there are a few "symbolic" papers, usually from the more traditional musicologists, which present methods for computationally analyzing scores. There are papers that introduce new data sets, like a large collection of playlists or a corpus of songs labeled with information about their instrumentation. Some researchers focus on the details of machine learning, while others are interested in applying the field's techniques to musical traditions like Turkish makam or South Indian Carnatic music. Every year I attend ISMIR, more and more of the work presented there is aimed toward use in recommender systems.

Seth works on music emotion recognition: his graduate research aimed to computationally model the moods latent in musical sound, so that a computer might be able to tell whether a given song sounds happy or sad. If this seems strange to find in an electrical engineering program, he assures me that it is not. Music emotion recognition is ultimately concerned with signal processing, a core interest of electrical engineers, he says. When it is captured by microphones or sent to speakers, music exists as a continuous stream of electricity. Signal processing aims to derive information from that stream, finding meaningful patterns in it. Those patterns may be simple, like the periodic fluctuation that marks a certain pitch, or they may be complex, like the aggregations of frequencies that Seth is trying to map to moods.

Diego, a graduate student from Uruguay, speaks up from across the car, where he has been listening to our conversation. He also works in signal processing, and he has come to ISMIR to present his work analyzing recordings of improvised performances; he wants to infer the implicit rules that improvisers follow, looking for telltale patterns in the audio signal. (Later, once I check into my hotel, I write in my notebook that "inferring the implicit rules of improvisation" could describe what anthropologists do as well, albeit from very different source materials.)

A graduate student myself, I rehearse the usual explanation of my own research interests: How do the people who make recommender systems think about what they do? Seth and Diego are both skeptical that music recommendation could ever really work. Although many of the presenters at ISMIR are developing techniques for classifying and organizing music, these graduate students think that the idea of musical similarity, on which recommendation depends, is too vague to be scientifically evaluated. There are simply too many ways for music to be similar.

But, Seth continues, if you *were* going to do it, it would be "natural" to start by analyzing musical sound, or "content." After all, he suggests, "You do content analysis, I do content analysis, when we listen to music and decide what we like." Taste, he seems to be arguing, is not primarily a social phenomenon but the result of listening, which he describes as a kind of signal processing that takes place in the head. Listening transforms sound into preference, using the information latent in musical signals.[1]

The next time I see Seth after the conference, it will be two years later, and he will have joined the research team at Willow, working to improve the recommender systems he was once skeptical of. There, he will help develop the company's machine-listening infrastructure, trying to train computers to model the kind of signal processing he believed we were already doing in our own heads.

: :

For most of music recommendation's history, the sound of music has been surprisingly marginal to the recommending of it. As we have seen, from Ringo onward, algorithmic recommendation has largely ignored the content of what it recommends, modeling taste as a pattern of interactions between users and items—which could just as easily be recipes or hotels as songs. Content analysis is, by contrast, domain-specific. To analyze music requires different techniques from those of analyzing movies or newspaper articles. It requires a theory of hearing. Analyzing content also requires much more computational power than conventional collaborative filtering, dealing with whole audio files instead of singular data points. As a result, most music recommenders have ignored the quality of music that most people—from experts like Seth to ordinary listeners—assume is central to musical taste: how it sounds.

But since the beginnings of algorithmic recommendation, there have been researchers who shared Seth's intuition—who thought that musical sound must matter and sought techniques for analyzing it. With the growth of budgets, data sets, and computational power, adding sound into the mix of signals used for recommendation has come to seem more plausible. Today, most of the large ensemble models used for music recommendation include, in some way, a representation of sound, mixed in with the other data sources we've encountered so far.

This chapter is about how people like Seth think about listening, in relation to the basic problems of recommendation. This thinking happens within the same informatic cosmology I described in chapter 1: As another graduate student told me at ISMIR, "Music is a signal, like anything else." To treat music as a signal means to treat it as a series of numbers laden with patterns that humans parse when we listen and that computers might learn to mathematically recognize. While everything may be signal, music seems to be especially so: the idea that music, listening, and mathematics share some deep, essential connection is widespread in the social worlds of tech workers. As a result, automated content analysis has attracted much more attention in music, contrasted with other popular domains of recommendation, like movies. There is a long history within Western science of understanding listening as essentially a form of embodied signal processing (see Sterne and Rodgers 2011).

Humanistic scholars are generally skeptical of claims like these, which seem to reduce the richness of audible experience to numbers. When anthropologists write about sound, for instance, we usually write about the body. Steven Feld (1996, 97) gives an exemplary statement of anthropological interest in sound: "Sound, hearing, and voice mark a special bodily nexus for sensation and emotion because of their coordination of brain, nervous system, head, ear, chest, muscles, respiration, and breathing. . . . Hearing and voicing link the felt sensations of sound and balance to those of physical and emotional presence." Feld (2015, 12) argues for attention to acoustemology—to "sound as a way of knowing," which is contrasted with scientific approaches to studying sound. To know through sound is to know in an embodied, emplaced, and relational way. Similarly, calls for a "sounded anthropology" have urged attention to embodiment, to the emplacement of listening, and to the affective experience of being a listening subject (Samuels et al. 2010; see Lippman 2020).

But what can an anthropology of sound premised on embodiment and physical experience say to the graduate student researcher who confesses, "For me, music exists when it's digitized"—who imagines a universe where everything is number and signal, and music is an electrical pattern coursing through speakers and ears? We could, of course, tell him that he is wrong. Music is much more than a signal, connected in fleshy ways to the actual lives of people who make it and hear it.[2] As avid music listeners themselves, most of these people would probably agree. This approach, however, would not help us understand why people like Seth and his ISMIR colleagues continue to find it reasonable to analyze music as a signal. More importantly, it would stop us from examining in more detail how they themselves listen. Like anyone else, they use their ears and feel sound in their bodies; they experience music in places, as physical and emotional presence. They do this not only in their nonworking lives but also during their professional engagement with music, which requires them to mediate between ways of thinking about sound that can seem contradictory.

Although people like Seth embody many of the stereotypes of scientific approaches to sound—they understand it as essentially informatic and numerical—this attitude does not lead to the abandonment of acoustemology or the complete rationalization of music as a mathematical problem (cf. Born 1995). Rather, the equivalence between music and math has surprising consequences for how the people at ISMIR and my other field sites interact with, describe, and come to know both sound and the numbers produced to represent it.

What I encountered in the field was the stubborn persistence of acoustemological practices—of scientists and engineers listening to their work, even when they think they are not supposed to. This is not just a quantitative reduction but the entanglement of hearing with counting. The presumed equivalence between listening and frequency analysis that Seth proposed on the train does not only change how people approach listening—it changes how they understand numbers as well. By listening to their work, the developers of machine-listening systems enter into relationships with them that change how they and computers attend to sound.

Many critics and practitioners have suggested that music recommendation might be improved by focusing on "music itself"—that is, how it sounds. This chapter demonstrates how that suggestion is less straight-forward than it seems: sonic data are shaped by ideas about listening and music, and the ordinary listening practices of engineers are folded into the supposedly inhuman listening done by computers.

A Variegated Crowd of Intersecting Wave Systems

I am standing in the cloister of a Portuguese monastery listening to Nate, a graduate student from New York. It is the third day of ISMIR, and we are chatting during the coffee break between panels. Nate, like Seth and Diego, works on signal processing, and he too will eventually end up working for one of the major streaming services, as an engineer at Wonder.

The monastery has been converted to a conference center. Its court-yard is covered by a white metal roof and lighting rig, the ground a vast parquet floor. I struggle to hear Nate over the din of the coffee break, as dozens of voices ricochet off the hard, smooth surfaces before reaching my eardrums. Researchers have a name for this: the "cocktail party prob-lem." How do people manage to pick out the voice they want to hear from all the others?

Human ears are remarkably good at solving the cocktail party prob-lem, picking out individual sound sources from complexly sounded en-vironments. But computers—like ears as they age—often struggle to separate signal from noise. Among the people who present their work at ISMIR, many are concerned with tasks like these: "source separation" aims to identify which frequencies in a recording come from which in-struments; "melody extraction" tries to determine which series of pitches constitutes a song's melodic line.

Nate is explaining his philosophy of musical signal processing to me. "It's all just frequencies at different time scales," he says. At one scale are pitches—an A vibrates the air 440 times per second. At another scale, tempo—a song advances at some number of beats per minute. Melody, rhythm, and meter repeat on their own timescales, and higher up we find song structure: verse and chorus repeating over the course of a few min-utes. To listen to music, as Nate understands it, is to perceive these vari-ous layers of repetition.

Nate's theory of music as a collection of repetitions at various scales fits well with his interest in machine learning, which is essentially a field committed to pattern finding. But it also reflects a deeper tradition in the science of sound, dating back through most of the recorded history of music and mathematics (Crombie 1990, 363–78). A key location in that history was nineteenth-century Germany, where the polymath Hermann von Helmholtz elaborated an influential model of the ear as a kind of frequency analyzer, which would shape dominant understandings of what it means to listen through to the present (Steege 2012; see Jackson 2006; Hui 2013).[3]

In the winter of 1857 Helmholtz presented a lecture in Bonn, "The Physiological Causes of Harmony in Music." In his lecture, which touched on the connections between music, physics, and the anatomy of the ear, he gave an unusual description of a concert: "From the mouths of the male singers proceed waves of six to twelve feet in length; from the lips of the female singers dart shorter waves, from eighteen to thirty-six inches long. The rustling of silken skirts excites little curls in the air, each instrument in the orchestra emits its peculiar waves, and all these systems expand spherically from their respective centers, dart through one another, are reflected from the walls of the room and thus rush backwards and forwards, until they succumb to the greater force of newly generated tones" (Helmholtz 1995, 57–58). In Helmholtz's (1995, 57) account, the world is awash in vibration and resonance; it is "a variegated crowd of intersecting wave systems." Not only music, but the whole audible world is full of repeating waves, everywhere.

Hearing, according to Helmholtz (1995, 58), was the privileged sense for disaggregating that crowd into its constituent parts: "Although this spectacle is veiled from the material eye, we have another bodily organ, the ear, specially adapted to reveal it to us. This analyzes the interdigitation of the waves, . . . separates the several tones which compose it, and distinguishes the voices of men and women—even of individuals—the peculiar qualities of tone given out by each instrument, the rustling of the dresses, the footfalls of the walkers, and so on." While the physiological details of Helmholtz's "resonance model" of hearing would eventually be contested, his basic account of listening remains a matter of disciplinary common sense for the people at ISMIR. The world is full of waves, which enter the ear all mixed together. Listening is a kind of physiological calculation, which filters these waves apart, reconstructing their various sources. The cocktail party problem is, in this account, the basic condition for hearing; as we saw in chapter 1, the world is overwhelming and filtering is a basic precondition for acting within it.

Where Helmholtz blurred the line between sensation and calculation, he also tangled together sonic and social distinctions. In his evocative concert scene, ears do not only decompose complex waves into their component frequencies—they distinguish between instruments, genders, music, and noise. The ability to distinguish among tones and the ability to distinguish among social categories are linked for Helmholtz in the biomechanics of the ear, and he hints at the possibility that the resonance between math, music, ears, and sound might extend even beyond them, to the social scene of sonic action. Hearing is simultaneously biological, numerical, and sociocultural: it resonates with stiff hairs in the ear, the mathematics of sine waves, and the vibrating entities that populate the world.

"Mathematics and music!," Helmholtz exclaimed. "The most glaring possible opposites of human thought! and yet connected, mutually sustained! It is as if they would demonstrate the hidden consensus of all the actions of our mind" (Helmholtz 1995, 46–47). Nate confides in me that his theory of music is really a theory of everything—of perception in a world of interscalar patterning.

I think of how different the courtyard must have sounded when this was still a Benedictine monastery: hushed whispers along the arcades instead of the lively chatter of an annual meeting echoing across a large, enclosed hall. Our conversation fades out as they tend to at conferences, dissipating back into the crowd of people looking for old friends and new coffee.

The Cepstral Domain

The next day, I am sitting in a session on "Audio Classification." The four presenters offer new techniques for content analysis, which promise to enhance computers' ability to parse musical signals. The basic problem is that digital music files are large, even when they've already been compressed: a typical MP3 file might store audio data as a sequence of 44,100 numbers per second; these numbers represent the waveform, telling speakers how to vibrate and transduce a signal into the air, where it can be heard. To analyze large quantities of audio like the ISMIR researchers want, these sets of numbers have to be reduced to a manageable size.

This is usually done using "feature representations"—quantitative summaries of sonic patterns that represent the salient features of a recording. A typical feature representation might reduce audio data down to about 650 numbers per second, analyzing and condensing the "raw" data of the original recording.[4] For most of ISMIR's thirteen-year history, there have been researchers carefully engineering these transformations to capture details they consider musically important. These "low-level" representations are intended to be used as input for algorithms that perform many of the field's signature tasks, like identifying instruments or musical structure.

But since the first ISMIR meeting in 2000, the dominant feature representation has remained one created for nonmusical purposes: mel-frequency cepstral coefficients, or MFCCs, which were originally developed for speech recognition in the 1970s (Mermelstein 1976). As one of the papers presented at the first ISMIR meeting described them, MFCCs are "short-term spectral based features" (Logan 2000, 1), meaning that they describe short segments of sound in terms of the audio frequencies that make them up. The procedure for generating them is a series of transformations "motivated by perceptual or computational considerations" (Logan 2000, 1)—that is to say, MFCCs are a feature representation that adjusts both to the peculiarities of human hearing in the ear and brain (or "psychoacoustics") and to the particular efficiencies of computers. They are part of the heritage of cybernetics and an instance of the perceptual technics discussed in chapter 1. They blend together ideas about information processing in humans and computers, under the assumption that there is some fundamental unity that connects them.

Walking through the steps that produce MFCCs will make their interleaving of human and machine capacities more evident. We start with an audio signal, which is first divided into short (usually about twenty millisecond) windows. The audio signal is in the "time domain"—it is a series of numbers that corresponds to the shape of the sound wave, over time. While waveforms are a popular way to represent audio signals among the general public (Walker 2011), they are considered essentially uninformative at ISMIR.

So, time domain data is transformed into the "frequency domain," using a technique called Fourier analysis—this is the mathematical operation that Helmholtz suggested ears implement in vivo. Transforming a signal from the time domain to the frequency domain is a way to reveal patterns that would not be obviously apparent in a complex waveform. For example, if our recording contained a chord composed of three pure tones, it would look like a rather bumpy wave in the time domain. In the frequency domain, where the vertical axis represents specific frequencies, we would see three bright spots corresponding to our three tones. By repeating this over a series of sampling windows, we could see how the frequencies present in the recording change over time, generating an image called a spectrogram. Spectrograms are the preferred way to visualize music at ISMIR. Across the conference hall, I see someone wearing a lab T-shirt that reads "The time domain is for losers" on the back, above a stylized three-dimensional spectrogram.

Next, we adjust the intensities logarithmically to account for how ears work: human hearing does not register signal strength directly as loudness—small variations among quiet sounds are more perceptible than small variations among loud ones. Similarly, audio frequency and perceived pitch are not directly equivalent either: using the "mel scale," which models this variation in human hearing, we arrive at a version of the spectrogram that has been adjusted for the peculiarities of typical human ears (Umesh et al. 1999).

Spectrograms "look like" music to most ISMIR researchers, who sometimes lamented that applying computer vision techniques to these images, as though they were pictures, often worked just as well as using audio-specific machine-listening techniques. But researchers are interested in even higher-order patterns than those readily visible on a spectrogram. Most naturally occurring sound sources produce identifiable clusters of frequencies; the same note on a violin or a trumpet will contain distinctive frequency patterns that reflect those instruments' distinct timbres. These patterns are easily audible, but not so easy to see on a spectrogram. To see them, we can apply another Fourier transformation to the spectral data. This brings us to the "cepstral domain"—an anagram of "spectral." One presenter at ISMIR jokes that they are always taking the "FFT [fast Fourier transform] of the FFT of the FFT of the FFT," in pursuit of ever-higher-order patterns. Where a bright spot in the spectrogram indicates a repeating pattern in the waveform, a bright spot in the cepstrum indicates a pattern in the spectrogram.

The resulting numbers are the mel-frequency cepstral coefficients, typically about thirteen numbers per twenty milliseconds of sound. We can see in the process of their construction how they fold together theories of human perception (the mel scale, the logarithmic adjustment of intensity) into the basic materials on which machine-listening systems work. Like the MP3s that Sterne analyzed in his work on perceptual technics, MFCCs are a technique for optimizing computational resources by preemptively "listening" to signals, reducing their size according to a model of human hearing. But unlike MP3s, MFCCs are not designed to be listened to by human ears. They are so reduced that they cannot be played back through speakers; they are destined for a kind of listening that happens only in software. In theory, at least.

Resynthesis

The widespread use of MFCCs in the ISMIR community has made them a target for scrutiny. Three of the papers in this panel on classification offer new feature representations meant to capture aspects of musical signals that their authors claim MFCCs neglect. One presenter suggests that, because MFCCs were developed for speech recognition, they do not capture musically salient features like pitch. Another argues that, because MFCCs are usually calculated from such small slices of time, they miss musical structures that develop over longer timescales. They present their own feature representations, designed with particular tasks in mind, and compare their performance to MFCCs.

The current presenter is attempting a task that requires the algorithm to correctly tag a large set of songs with labels like "rock," "piano," "electronica," or "exciting." He shows how well the classifier performs when using MFCCs versus his own new feature representation—unsurprisingly, his feature representation outperforms the MFCCs. But he does not stop with quantitative evidence. Like the two presenters before him, he demonstrates the differences between feature representations with a sonic illustration.

Although MFCCs cannot be played back as sound "directly," it is possible to make them audible by "resynthesizing" them—fleshing out their skeletal numbers, usually by adding white noise to the signal, once it has been retrieved from the cepstral domain (Moussallam, Liutkus, and Daudet 2015). This is, effectively, a sonification of sonic data.[5] The presenter has done this to a clip of Carole King's 1971 song "You've Got a Friend," which he plays over the conference hall's speakers after playing the original for comparison. The opening piano notes sound like cavernous drumbeats, and King's barely recognizable voice hisses tunelessly over them. It sounds terrifying, as though every time King opens her mouth to sing, a rush of noise pours out. The audience laughs. When he plays his own feature representation, of course, it sounds much closer to the original—like a low-quality MP3 rather than an ominous message from the cepstral domain.

During the question-and-answer period after the panel, an audience member points out that, technically speaking, it shouldn't matter what these representations sound like to human ears. It is possible that MFCCs numerically contain information that is simply not audible to humans through the white-noise resynthesis process. The real test of a representation's adequacy, he argues, should be how it performs in computational tasks.[6] What a representation sounds like when turned back into sound is essentially irrelevant to a computer's ability to make sense of it. The presenter who had orchestrated Carole King's wicked metamorphosis agrees but suggests that "the point was to hear what was lost in the transformation"—to illustrate, rather than conclusively demonstrate, how well a representation works.

∷

The persistence of these listening practices was thus something of a puzzle: Why would music information scientists keep producing sonifications that they themselves did not consider scientifically legitimate? If an audio analysis system did not necessarily have to listen like a human in order to work, then why did these human listening practices persist?

The equivalence between ears and frequency analyzers laid out by Helmholtz offers one answer to this question. Although we commonly speak of quantification as a kind of "reduction" (e.g., Merry 2016) and think of technologies as simplified models, the link between sensation and quantification does not only go one way, in which all phenomena are reducible to numbers. Rather, that assumed equivalence, which we find in Helmholtz, but also in the cybernetic tradition, goes both ways: ears are like frequency analyzers, but frequency analyzers are also like ears. As the media scholar John Durham Peters (2004, 189) has written, "human-machine mimesis is mutual." The idea that technical analogies change how people understand their bodies and their senses is a familiar one in media studies: eyes come to seem like cameras, brains like computers, ears like microphones. But because we assume that engineers are always in pursuit of reduction, we have tended to pay less attention to the other direction of the analogy, which finds technical artifacts imbued with less-than-rational characteristics.

Quantification can be understood as a kind of transduction (Helmreich 2007)—a technosocial interface between numeric and acoustic domains. Like other forms of transduction, quantification is frequently simplified, naturalized, and taken as straightforward. Disputes over feature representations give lie to the idea that there is some simple, obvious way to move between sounds and numbers; this is a contested site of translation, where transductive options abound. Researchers argue about these options by drawing on both numerical and perceptual justifications, not abandoning listening once numbers have been produced.

And like other transducers, quantification works in both directions. Understanding the functions of algorithms and ears as analogous, machine-listening researchers hold them together. It becomes important to them not only to prove their math but also to hear it. Scientific ideals that dictate the purity of methodically produced numbers conflict with the analogical thinking that linked hearing to counting in the first place. Although numbers proliferate in computer audition, the evaluative capacities of the human ear are still in play. If hearing is something you can count, then counting is also something you can hear.

We find in machine listening another case to add to work on the anthropology of number as an "inventive frontier" (Guyer, Khan, and Obarrio 2010). This work contests the common humanistic critique of quantification as solely a force for rationalization and disenchantment. Instead, when we look at the use of numbers in practice, we often find irrationality, strangeness, and creativity—qualities that the production of quantitative data is supposed to dispense with, according to critics and advocates alike. By resisting our disciplinary assumptions about what hearing and counting are like, we are better equipped to observe the peculiarities of their entanglement.

The Semantic Gap

There are hints during the conference that things are about to change. One of the presentations is advocating for an approach to analyzing audio called "feature learning": instead of engineering a representation like MFCCs to be used as input for various tasks, a machine-listening system might work directly from audio data, learning a feature representation that works best for whatever task it has been put to. Given a set of recordings that have been tagged with genre labels, for instance, a machine-learning system could find a correlation between patterns in the audio and those labels, without relying on the mediation of a precalculated feature representation like MFCCs.

Feature learning is possible only because the large amounts of computing power and data it requires have started to become available to researchers. In my conversation with Nate, I learn that he has just finished an internship at a large software company known for such techniques, and he is convinced that feature learning is the future. He derisively calls feature representations like MFCCs "handcrafted," suggesting that they are archaic and ready to be replaced.

Two years after the conference in Portugal, I am sitting in Madison Square Garden with Tomas. Tomas is a researcher in deep learning, and "Madison Square Garden" is what Spotify calls the biggest meeting room in its New York offices. Every month, this room hosts a local music hackathon, which brings together thirty or forty people from the area to work on their music technology side projects. Scattered at tables around the large room, people are getting to work: a group of high schoolers is trying to use motion sensors to generate music from dance moves; someone is trying to turn a web browser into a synthesizer; tech company employees are demonstrating new software features; local grad students are working on their research.

At my table, Tomas is showing off his latest project: a neural network that he has trained to hear the differences between musical subgenres. I first met Tomas at another hackathon the previous year, and at this one, I easily spot him from across the room: his long red hair and wardrobe consisting mostly of metal band T-shirts set him apart. Tomas is an avid fan of a subgenre of metal called "djent"—named onomatopoetically for its signature sound, a precise, unison guitar-driven chugging. Djent is a kind of "technical" metal: rhythmically intricate, often in an unusual meter, and defined by skill and technique. Identifying it (not to mention appreciating it) poses a challenge to computers and non–metal fans alike.

But metalheads are notorious taxonomizers, and when I look online, I find fans of djent bands like the Swedish group Meshuggah arguing at length about whether the band is properly technical post-thrash, math metal, groove metal, progressive metal, or metalcore. Music information scientists like Tomas are also enthusiastic about taxonomy, and automatic genre detection is one of the field's long-standing unsolved problems. It turns out that training a computer to identify musical genres from their sound alone is very hard to do.

I offer Tomas a social scientific explanation for why this might be. Genre, as many sociologists and musicologists have argued, is primarily a matter of scenes, not sound. The sociologist Jennifer Lena (2012, 6), for instance, defines genres as "systems of orientations, expectations, and conventions that bind together industry, performers, critics, and fans in making what they identify as a distinctive sort of music." Djent is defined not by the *djent*, but by the community of people like Tomas, who come together on web forums or at concerts and make the genre cohere. If this is what genre is, then it is unsurprising that algorithms working only from audio data would make mistakes that appall true fans. Often, their mistakes are obvious even to untrained ears like mine: many systems seem to fixate on minor sonic similarities that short-circuit across genres, claiming connections between apparently unrelated styles of music.

But Tomas is insistent: if he can hear the difference between djent and metalcore, then in principle computers should be able to, as well. Like most of the people we have encountered so far, Tomas presumes that brains and computers—and human and machine listening—are essentially comparable. The challenge, as he understands it, is not that certain aspects of music are simply unavailable to computers but that researchers have yet to determine what a computer needs to know in order to perform like a human listener.

This problem, I learned, is called the "semantic gap": there is a distance between the information encoded into an audio file and the meaning that an enculturated human mind can interpret from it. While I was ready to accept this as an insuperable barrier, Tomas argued that it was only a matter of time before the problem was solved. With the right data and the right algorithm, it should be possible for a computer to jump over the semantic gap.

Learning to Listen

Tomas has spent the past few months as an intern at the streaming music service Wonder, which has given him access to the data he thinks he needs to close the semantic gap. On one side, audio data for the million most popular songs on the service; on the other, data about the listening behavior of Wonder's users, which indicates which songs are listened to by the same people.[7]

What Tomas has done is to bring these data sets together, training a neural network to identify correlations between them. So, instead of relying on a feature representation that foregrounds specific musical or acoustic qualities—as someone presenting at ISMIR until recently might have done—his network should learn which differences in the audio correspond with differences in listening behavior. The goal is a machine-listening system with a "cultural" sensibility—one that does not have to invent genre distinctions from audio alone but can be informed by the distinctions latent in human listening practices.

Neural networks are a machine-learning technique that has recently exploded in popularity, although their basic principles date back many decades. They are inspired by an informatic understanding of the brain: a neural network is composed of nodes, or "neurons," which receive bits of data, perform small mathematical operations on them and then pass the transformed input on to other nodes. These nodes are organized in a series of "layers," which perform functions like summarizing the output of a previous layer or recognizing a specific kind of pattern in it. While the basic operations performed by individual nodes are usually simple, their quantity and interconnectedness produce systems that can be quite complex.

For our purposes here, we can think of neural networks as essentially very complicated formulas for taking input data and transforming it into something else—like turning a sample of audio data into a label indicating its genre. The details of these formulas are determined by training them on data sets like Tomas has done.

"Pick a number between 0 and 2,047," Tomas instructs me. These numbers correspond to the nodes in a layer of his neural network. Any song processed by the network will pass through this set of 2,048 points, with varying levels of "activation" at each neuron. The idea, Tomas explains, is that the layers of his neural net perform an iterating series of classifications, which aggregate the results of earlier layers. He has not specified what these layers should do, but in the process of training the network with his data, it has "learned" an optimal set of classifications, which get more precise in each successive layer.

It is possible, for any given node in the network, to generate a list of the songs that are most strongly associated with it. These songs, Tomas suggests, offer us a way to understand what a node has learned to listen for in the audio data. He has been listening to his system, trying to identify what its layers have learned to do, and he suggests that this particular layer's nodes correspond to subgenres.

I pick a number, and the computer generates a playlist of songs. Tomas plays a sample from the middle of the first track for me. He identifies it as metalcore. He plays another track from the list and draws my attention to some of metalcore's distinctive features, which are shared by the two samples: there is a rapid-fire drum pattern common to much metal, known as a "blast beat"; there is a singing style that sounds to me like plaintive shrieking; there is a particular guitar tone. Then he plays snippets from a few more tracks, and we continue to note the similarities in their sound, imagining what features of the audio the computer is "listening" to.

Tomas has tried to label the fifty or so most active nodes in this layer, generating playlists to demonstrate what his system can do, and he plays some back for me. I hear Chinese pop, Christian rock, female comedians. The effect is uncanny. It sounds like the computer has learned to listen with a culturally trained ear. Christian rock, for instance, is a common example given for why audio-only classifications are doomed to fail: it sounds like most other kinds of rock, and without understanding the lyrics or knowing about the bands' backgrounds, it is hard to tell it apart. But Christian rock attracts a distinctive set of listeners, and Tomas's system seems to have picked this up, separating it out from other rock music. One playlist is composed exclusively of electronic dance music by a single producer—Armin van Buuren, whose signature tone plagiarizes itself across dozens of tracks. Tomas jokes that this quantity of similar-sounding recordings has resulted in a genre unto itself.

It is an astonishing experience, and later that night I write in my field notes: "I'm wondering if this is the weekend I lose my incredulity: this thing seems like it *works*." I had cultivated a studied indifference to functionality—a good social analyst of technology, I knew, was supposed to treat "successful" and "unsuccessful" technologies symmetrically (Bloor 1976). It should not matter whether the technologies in question seemed to work or not; after all, I knew that the designation of technologies as "functional" was itself a social process. But this abstract commitment was much easier to maintain when algorithms regularly failed in obvious ways. This system, which seemed to have achieved an incredible performance, threw my cynicism off balance. How was it possible that this black box had learned to listen like a person?

From Interpretability to Interpretation

A few weeks after my chat with Tomas, I am sitting in the Whisper offices after hours, hanging out with some of the company's audio engineers. Tomas has opened up his system to public use, and we are playing around with it. We can input a song, like Janet Jackson's 1986 hit "Nasty," and the network will return a playlist of tracks that it deems acoustically similar. We recognize in them the distinctively 1980s sound of a gated snare drum—an enormously reverberant clap, cut short. We suspect that this is what the system has learned to hear, although there is no way to know for sure.

Neural networks are the archetypes of algorithmic opacity: their internal complexity and the way they are trained mean that it can be very challenging to provide a straightforward account of why they return the results that they do. Some researchers do not consider this a problem: if neural nets perform well at their tasks, then the fact that humans have a hard time grasping their logic does not really matter. But for many inside and outside of machine learning, this "uninterpretability" is a serious problem. When systems make mistakes or behave in unexpected ways, it can be hard to understand why; systems working in high-stakes domains like medicine or law may not be trusted without an account of how they work. Critics have argued that algorithms like these use opacity to hide their biases from public scrutiny, exerting damaging power in domains ranging from mortgage approval and parole decisions to popular music charts or the state of public discourse (e.g., Pasquale 2015; Noble 2018).

Neural networks seem to pose this problem in an intensified way, because they are not only opaque to outsiders who lack the access or technical expertise to make sense of them—they can be opaque even to the people who build and maintain them. While, in principle, it is possible to trace the calculations that produce any one result, this does not provide an explanation for why a system has learned the specific parameters of those calculations. This kind of opacity is profound: maybe no one can understand how the system works, at least not directly. The sheer scale exceeds human capacities (Burrell 2016).[8] This problem has spurred a lively subfield of machine-learning research into interpretability, which seeks techniques for designing or analyzing systems to make them amenable to human interpretation (Doshi-Velez and Kim 2017).

Reading through the literature on interpretability in machine learning, it is striking to note how rarely the term "interpretation" appears. The central concern in this work is how to make systems interpretable, without much concern for interpretation as a process. When interpretation does appear, it is usually defined something like this: "the process of giving explanations to humans" (Doshi-Velez and Kim 2017). Where "interpretation" is rare, "explanation" is extremely common. In all this talk about interpretability, no one ever really interprets anything. People don't spend any uncertain period of time figuring something out—they just communicate their already formed interpretations to others, in the form of explanations. It often seems in the literature that interpretability researchers are identifying themselves with their systems: they are not the destination for these explanations; as they often claim in their papers, these explanations are unnecessary from a technical point of view and useful only as a response to human demands.

But even practitioners like Tomas rely on interpretation as they work. At the table in New York and in the office at Whisper, we interpreted, seeking identifiable patterns in the machine's outputs that served as confirmation that the machine was working. Our interpretations were not conclusive explanations, but tentative, social efforts to make sense of phenomena.

Interpretation has long been a central concern for anthropologists, and the key feature of anthropological interpretation is that it unfolds within a particular frame of reference. People in different cultures make sense of the world differently because they draw on a set of associations, relative hierarchies, and so on that they've learned while growing up. More narrowly, people who occupy different positions within a society—like having a gender, a caste, or a job—will have more particular variations in their interpretive processes. This means that interpretation is essentially contestable—different people will make sense of the same thing in different ways. Because interpretation takes work, unfolds over time, and is highly sensitive to context, it is also necessarily incomplete: there is always something else you might take into account or another angle you might consider.

Just as "interpretation" rarely appears in the machine-learning literature on interpretability, "interpretability" rarely appears in the writing of interpretive anthropologists. In Clifford Geertz's canonical book *The Interpretation of Cultures*, it appears once, in an essay on religion. Geertz (1973, 100) writes: "There are at least three points where chaos—a tumult of events which lack not just interpretations but *interpretability*— threatens to break in upon man: at the limits of his analytic capacities, at the limits of his powers of endurance, and at the limits of his moral insight. Bafflement, suffering, and a sense of intractable ethical paradox are all, if they become intense enough or are sustained long enough, radical challenges to the proposition that life is comprehensible." Here, we find Geertz making a claim that resonates with concerns about neural networks: the absence of interpretability is associated with overwhelming scale.[9] But in Geertz's telling, uninterpretability is one of the most extreme situations a person can encounter, a sign of true chaos, not mere uncertainty. Unless they are under extreme duress, people will grasp for any interpretation they can imagine rather than letting an anomaly remain anomalous. It takes a lot to stop humans from interpreting things.

Algorithmic Acoustemology

While exploring nodes with Tomas, we hit upon an anomaly. One of the playlists seemed to contain two genres at once: choral music and smooth jazz. I got to work interpreting, trying to hear what obscure sonic connection there might be between these two musical styles. Tomas stopped me, offering an explanation I couldn't have considered: this node was "multimodal," he said, activating for two clearly distinct styles. He reasoned that, in a later layer of the network, these two styles would be sorted apart from each other. This was not an interpretation I had known possible, and Tomas's ability to reason in this way stemmed from his own familiarity with how neural networks behave. The copresence of multiple genres became interpretable to him, and then to me, thanks to a particular theoretical frame.

The interpretability of notoriously uninterpretable neural nets, then, was a local achievement, a consequence of our preexisting knowledge and frames of reference. Ironically, situations that seem at first to be uninterpretable produce a wild efflorescence of interpretive work. Interpretation is not an activity tied to interpretable situations—it is the opposite. When an output is interpretable, it feels like it requires no interpretation at all—everything just fits together, harmonizes, and Tomas and I look at each other and smile, pleased by the apparent coordination of his, my, and the computer's perception. Only as things move toward seeming uninterpretability does the work of interpretation become obvious.

Our interpretation of his system's functionality was essentially acoustemological: It could not be guaranteed by the fact that music is math and neural nets find patterns, and therefore their results must be right. Rather, it was only through listening—and listening together—that the system came to be understood as working. This is something like the classic constructivist argument about interpretive flexibility and closure (e.g., Pinch and Bijker 1984). We could say that interpretability and success go hand in hand: the neural net is "done," ready to serve as a black box for outsiders like me, only once Tomas and the computer have stabilized their interpretations.

During the demonstration, I can only adjust my own attention, trying to listen as Tomas does. Tomas, however, has participated in many iterations of this game while building and tuning the network. After all, the neural net did not appear fully formed; it is the sum of a great many technical choices. There was no purportedly objective way to set up the neural net for training—only a set of heuristics and best practices. Tomas explained his choice of layers with reference to earlier work in deep learning: by using a sort of layer called "convolutional," he anticipated that successive layers would learn to identify musical qualities at different scales. As he developed the system, by listening to the tracks most strongly associated with particular nodes and trying to identify what they shared in common, he refined his design and developed an understanding of what his network's various layers had learned to do. In addition to playlists representing subgenres, he made others to demonstrate nodes that he thought corresponded to certain timbres or dominant pitches.

Tomas regularly tweaked his system and listened to it, trying to bring interpretations into alignment in a feedback loop of which his own trained attention was a crucial part. His attention was enculturated—he had a particular training in machine learning and a particular sensitivity to subgenres of metal that shaped what he found significant and plausible. His idea that the computer should be able to recognize djent, like he could, guided his understanding of what a computer could notice. The neural network bears the traces of his involvement. His own perception is "in the loop," so to speak, and we could argue that "the neural network" does not end at the computational nodes but extends to include Tomas's own mind.

: :

Practices of listening to computational products kept popping up throughout my fieldwork, beyond the presentations at ISMIR or the demonstrations of Tomas's neural network: interviewees at technology companies in San Francisco told me about how they listened to the playlists generated by software they wrote to see if the system "worked," and they learned to recognize the signature playlisting styles of major algorithmic radio companies; the people who sat next to me during my internship checked the work of classifying algorithms by listening to the songs they had sorted; and at weekend hackathons, where amateur and professional coders built prototype software, their performance was constantly assessed through headphones. Listening, literally and metaphorically, had become a central element in the feedback cycle of software production.

This interpretive work—the importance of human perception and judgment within algorithmic procedures—is a key element in cultural influence on algorithmic systems. Before being incorporated into a user-facing recommender system, audio feature representations are tuned to human hearing, through both the quantitative evaluation of algorithms informed by research on hearing and through the literal listening practices of their creators. These listening practices do not stop once the audio data is piped into the recommender: outputs are listened to and evaluated and systems are changed as a result. The tuning of an algorithmic system is more like the tuning of a musical instrument than one might think, requiring the tuner to listen to outputs and adjust them until they come into line with culturally informed expectations.

Understanding this listening acoustemologically offers some implications for how we think about the design of computational systems for analyzing music. As listeners trying to identify patterns in the output of opaque software, "insider" engineers and "outsider" users are more similar than often imagined. In any moderately complex algorithmic system, engineers have no objective or immediate way to see how an output was produced. There is no visual immediacy here—like outsiders, they range their attention over outputs and attune themselves to patterns. The primary difference between engineers and users, then, may be not in what they are able to see but in how they have learned to listen.

Algorithms are interpreted, evaluated, and valued over time, through sensory processes that are necessarily interactive, lacking clear distinctions between perceiving subjects and perceived objects, in line with Feld's account of acoustemology. In the course of training the neural net, the neural net has trained Tomas. He is tuned to the frequencies of chugging guitar riffs and to the metapatterns of neural network design. These listenings feed back into the workings of the algorithm, as it is built. Trained, interpretive listening is central to the production of algorithmic systems that are often understood in the visualist language of "black boxes."

Interpretability is a consequence, rather than a cause, of shared attunement. To build an algorithmic system is to stabilize listenings among members of teams and technical components. As a result, the terms by which people interpret their work—how they've learned to listen— become part of the apparatus of machine listening. And in music recommendation more broadly, the spot-checking listening practices of developers weave their own acoustemological reasoning into the functioning of algorithmic systems. We cannot "open" the black box of a machine-learning system's code and find these practices sitting there in legible form. Instead, we may have to listen to them, interpreting their outputs like their creators do. Black boxes don't always sound the way they look.

CHAPTER 5

Space Is the Place

The World of Music

"We are now at the dawn of the age of infinitely connected music," the data alchemist announced from beneath the Space Needle.

Glenn McDonald had chosen his title himself, preferring "alchemy," with its esoteric associations, over the now-ordinary "data science." His job, as he described it from the stage, was "to use math and typing and computers to help people understand and discover music." McDonald practiced his alchemy for the music streaming service Spotify, where he worked to transmute the base stuff of big data—logs of listener interactions, bits of digital audio files, and whatever else he could get his hands on—into valuable gold: products that might attract and retain paying customers. The mysterious power of McDonald's alchemy lay in the way that ordinary data, if processed correctly, appeared to transform from thin interactional traces into thick cultural significance.

It was 2014, and McDonald was presenting at the Pop Conference, an annual gathering of music critics and academics held in a crumpled, Frank Gehry–designed heap of a building in the center of Seattle. I was on the other side of the country, and I followed along online.

That year, the conference's theme was "Music and Mobility," and McDonald started his talk by narrating his personal musical journey, playing samples as he went. "When I was a kid," he began, "you discovered music by holding still and waiting." As a child at home, he listened to the folk music his parents played on the stereo. But as he grew up, his listening expanded: the car radio offered heavy metal and new wave; the internet revealed a world of new and obscure genres to explore. Where once he had been stuck in place, a passive observer of music that happened to go by, he would eventually measure the progress of his life by his ever-broadening musical horizons. McDonald had managed to turn this passion into a profession, working to help others explore what he called "the world of music," which on-demand streaming services had made more accessible than ever before.

Elsewhere, McDonald (2013) would describe the world of music as though it were a landscape: "Follow any path, no matter how unlikely and untrodden it appears, and you'll find a hidden valley with a hundred bands who've lived there for years, reconstructing the music world in methodically- and idiosyncratically-altered miniature, as in Australian hip-hop, Hungarian pop, microhouse or Viking metal." Travelers through the world of music would find familiarity and surprise—sounds they never would have imagined and songs they adored. McDonald marveled at this new ability to hear music from around the world, from Scotland, Australia, or Malawi. "The perfect music for you may come from the other side of the planet," he said, but this was not a problem: "in music, we have the teleporter." On-demand streaming provided a kind of musical mobility, which allowed listeners to travel across the world of music instantaneously.

However, he suggested, repeating the common refrain, the scale of this world could be overwhelming and hard to navigate. "For this new world to actually be appreciable," McDonald said, "we have to find ways to map this space and then build machines to take you through it along interesting paths." The recommender systems offered by companies like Spotify were the machines. McDonald's recent work had focused on the maps, or as he described them in another talk: a "kind of thin layer of vaguely intelligible order over the writhing, surging, insatiably expanding information-space-beast of all the world's music."

: :

Although his language may have been unusually poetic, McDonald was expressing an understanding of musical variety that is widely shared among the makers of music recommendation: Music exists in a kind of space. That space is, in one sense, fairly ordinary—like a landscape that you might walk through, encountering new things as you go. But in another sense, this space is deeply weird: behind the valleys and hills, there is a writhing, surging beast, constantly growing and tying points in the space together, infinitely connected. The music space can seem as natural as the mountains visible from the top of the Space Needle; but it can also seem like the man-made topological jumble at its base. It is organic and intuitive; it is technological and chaotic.

Spatial metaphors provide a dominant language for thinking about difference among the makers of music recommendation, as they do in machine learning and among Euro-American cultures more generally. Within these contexts, it is easy to imagine certain, similar things as gathered *over here*, while other, different things cluster *over there*. In conversations with engineers, it is very common to find the music space summoned into existence through gestures, which envelop the speakers in an imaginary environment populated by brief pinches in the air and organized by waves of the hand. One genre is on your left, another on your right. On whiteboards and windows scattered around the office, you might find the music space rendered in two dimensions, containing an array of points that cluster and spread across the plane.

In the music space, music that is similar is nearby. If you find yourself within such a space, you should be surrounded by music that you like. To find more of it, you need only to look around you and move. In the music space, genres are like regions, playlists are like pathways, and tastes are like drifting, archipelagic territories. Your new favorite song may lie just over the horizon.

But despite their familiarity, spaces like these are strange: similarities can be found anywhere, and points that seemed far apart might suddenly become adjacent. If you ask, you will learn that all of these spatial representations are mere reductions of something much more complex, of a space comprising not two or three dimensions but potentially thousands of them. This is McDonald's information-space-beast, a mathematical abstraction that stretches human spatial intuitions past their breaking point.

Spaces like these, generically called "similarity spaces," are the symbolic terrain on which most machine learning works. To classify data points or recommend items, machine-learning systems typically locate them in spaces, gather them into clusters, measure distances among them, and draw boundaries between them. Machine learning, as the cultural theorist Adrian Mackenzie (2017, 63) has argued, "renders all differences as distances and directions of movement." So while the music space is in one sense an informal metaphor (the landscape of musical variation) in another sense it is a highly technical formal object (the mathematical substrate of algorithmic recommendation).

Spatial understandings of data travel through technical infrastructures and everyday conversation; they are at once a form of metaphorical expression and a concrete computational practice. In other words, "space" here is both a formalism—a restricted, technical concept that facilitates precision through abstraction—and what the anthropologist Stefan Helmreich (2016, 468) calls an informalism—a less disciplined metaphor that travels alongside formal techniques. In practice, it is often hard or impossible to separate technical specificity from its metaphorical accompaniment.[1] When the makers of music recommendation speak of space, they speak at once figuratively and technically.

For many critics, this "geometric rationality" (Blanke 2018) of machine learning makes it anathema to "culture" per se: it quantifies qualities, rationalizes passions, and plucks cultural objects from their everyday social contexts to relocate them in the sterile isolation of a computational grid. Mainstream cultural anthropology, for instance, has long defined itself in opposition to formalisms like these, which seem to lack the thickness, sensitivity, or adequacy to lived experience that we seek through ethnography.[2] As the political theorists Louise Amoore and Volha Piotukh (2015, 361) suggest, such analytics "reduce heterogeneous forms of life and data to homogenous spaces of calculation."

To use the geographer Henri Lefebvre's (1992) terms, similarity spaces are clear examples of "abstract space"—a kind of representational space in which everything is measurable and quantified, controlled by central authorities in the service of capital. The media theorist Robert Prey (2015, 16), applying Lefebvre's framework to streaming music, suggests that people like McDonald—"data analysts, programmers and engineers"— are primarily concerned with the abstract, conceived space of calculation and measurement. Conceived space, in Lefebvrian thought, is parasitic on social, lived space, which Prey associates with the listeners who resist and reinterpret the work of technologists. The spread of abstract space under capitalism portends, in this framework, "the devastating conquest of the lived by the conceived" (Wilson 2013).

But for the people who work with it, the music space does not feel like a sterile grid, even at its most mathematical. The makers of music recommendation do not limit themselves to the refined abstractions of conceived space. Over the course of their training, they learn to experience the music space as ordinary and inhabitable, despite its underlying strangeness. The music space is as intuitive as a landscape to be walked across and as alien as a complex, highly dimensional object of engineering. To use an often-problematized distinction from cultural geography, they treat "space" like "place," as though the abstract, homogeneous grid were a kind of livable local environment.[3]

In this chapter, I trace how these two meanings of space diverge and come together in the spatial sense making of people building recommender systems. Similarity spaces are the result of many decisions; they are by no means "natural," and people like McDonald are aware that the choices they make can profoundly rearrange them. Yet spatial metaphorizing, moving across speech, gesture, illustration, and computation, helps make the patterns in cultural data feel real. A confusion between maps and territories—between malleable representations and objective terrains—is productive for people who are at once interested in creating objective knowledge and concerned with accounting for their own subjective influence on the process. These spatial understandings alter the meaning of musical concepts like genre or social phenomena like taste, rendering them as forms of clustering.

The Proximate and the Similar

In 2012, I sat in on an undergraduate course in recommender systems design, meant to introduce students to the basics of machine learning. Recommender systems are common topics in introductory machine-learning classes—they demonstrate a popular, familiar application of the technology, and they provide outputs that are easy to interpret and evaluate. For anthropologists with little technical background, introductory courses are useful not only for picking up technical language but also for seeing how students are introduced to a field's signature habits of thought. Key among these habits in machine learning is a tendency to understand data itself as intrinsically spatial.

We sit in the computer lab, where the instructor has given us a sample data set: a standard collaborative filtering matrix, containing the ratings that a group of imaginary users has assigned to a group of real movies. He explains the basic goal of collaborative filtering: we want to predict the ratings that will appear in the blank spaces of the matrix. We are going to analyze our data using a technique called matrix factorization, although we don't yet know what that means. We load the data into a computer program, select "Matrix Factorization" from a drop-down menu, and let the software do the work for us.

After a moment, the computer returns the output we are interested in: a pair of tables, one containing users, the other, movies (tables 2 and 3). Each user and each movie are assigned two numbers labeled "Dimension 1" and "Dimension 2." These numbers reflect statistical patterns in the data, extracted by matrix factorization—they "summarize" the ratings, the instructor explains. On the screen, he displays simplified versions of the tables and points at the first row: "We've represented Alice with two numbers, so I can make a two-dimensional plot, and I can locate Alice."

Proceeding through both tables, we fill a space with people and movies, treating the pairs of numbers we generated as though they were coordinates (fig. 5). The result is a similarity space, derived from the original ratings data. Distances in this space indicate similarity but also

TABLE 2: A table of users in two dimensions, derived by matrix factorization

	Dimension 1	Dimension 2
Alice	0.47	−0.30
Bob	−0.44	0.23
Mary	0.70	−0.06
Sue	0.31	0.93

TABLE 3: A table of movies in two dimensions, derived by matrix factorization

	Terminator	Die Hard	Twins	Eat Pray Love	Pretty Woman
Dimension 1	−0.44	−0.57	0.06	0.38	0.57
Dimension 2	0.58	−0.66	0.26	0.18	−0.36

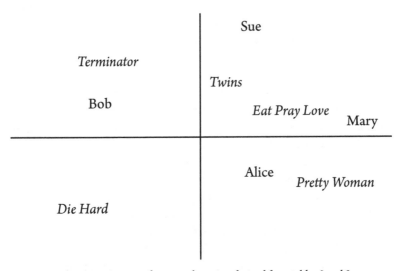

FIGURE 5. A space of users and movies, derived from tables 2 and 3

affinity: Mary is more like Alice than Bob, and she will probably like *Eat Pray Love* more than *Die Hard*. In the canonical syntax of algorithmic recommendation—"users like you liked items like this"—each "like" is a distance in this space. Here, we can identify "neighborhoods" of users and movies, interpreting their distribution as reflecting "latent factors" in the data. To be similar is to be nearby, and to be different is to be some measurable distance away.

We might imagine that there is nothing intrinsically spatial about our data, which reflect a few ratings of a few movies. But in machine learning, data is always already spatial: if we have numbers, we have coordinates, and if we don't have numbers, we can get them, turning something like a button press into a 1 or 0. One of the things novices learn as they become familiar with machine learning is to move seamlessly between encountering data in numerical tables and envisioning that data as distributed in space. Getting data, whatever its origins, into space—often called "embedding"—is a crucial task in making data amenable to machine learning. But this transformation from tabular data to meaningful space, which might strike us as remarkable, is "largely taken for granted" (Mackenzie 2017, 67) in machine learning, as though the two are effectively synonymous, the space already existing in latent form within the data.[4]

The instructor asks us to look for patterns in the space, and the students find one: the movies seem to have separated by genre. Romances are on one side, while action movies are on the other. A student asks how the algorithm knew about genre, when the input only contained ratings data. "It seems like magic, I know," the instructor replies. "Magically, we've measured two secret things about these movies." Those two secrets are the two dimensions of our space, although we could have instructed the computer to generate more of them. Our horizontal dimension appears to correspond to genre, as though information about the movies' genres were hidden in the data, waiting to be revealed. The significance of the vertical dimension is less obvious, although the instructor suggests that it may reflect how "serious" the movies are.

What made matrix factorization "magical," like McDonald's alchemy, was its ability to uncover such cultural secrets from data that appeared to be about something else. We were being instructed not only in the fundamental spatiality of data but in what the sociologist of science Catelijne Coopmans (2014) has called "artful revelation"—the rhetorical use of visualization to make manifest hidden patterns in data. Revelations like the one performed in class are a common way to claim authority for data analytic practices. Coordinate spaces are often presented as ways to make data intuitively understandable by people—an easy means to see, rather than to calculate, the similarities among a set of data points. The geographers Martin Dodge and Rob Kitchin (2001, 30) call images like these "spatializations," to distinguish them from proper "maps," which they reserve for visualizations that have geographical referents. But, as we will see, this distinction is not a significant one for most people working in machine learning. Spatializations effectively summarize differences along various axes into singular, readily comparable distances, appealing to intuitions about the relationship between distance and similarity. When visualized, these spaces are almost always described as "maps."

The magic of matrix factorization was in our heads as much as it was in the computer: without our prior knowledge of the movies in question, we would have been unable to interpret the pattern; if the arrangement of the points did not resonate with our preconceptions about the structure of the cultural world, then we might worry that we had made a mistake. We were learning to validate our work in two ways: not only through the kind of technical correctness guaranteed by software but also by applying our own cultural intuitions. As we saw in the previous chapter, checking results against prior interpretive frames is a crucial step in building machine-learning systems. Our intuitions confirmed the math, the math, our intuitions. And as usual, interpretation leaves room for multiplicity and contestation. An interpreter more familiar with the movies in question could have argued that the horizontal dimension we saw as representing genre indicated whether a movie starred Julia Roberts, while the vertical one corresponded to Arnold Schwarzenegger.

Pedagogical examples are chosen (or constructed) precisely to be readily interpretable—to provide students with the pleasure of recognition we felt in the computer lab. They are designed to draw students into the worlds they enact. Movie ratings work well for teaching because students can draw on their pre-existing cultural knowledge to interpret their results. That moment of recognition—where the student sees genre emerge from interactional data—is key to matrix factorization's magical appearance. If we were working with other data commonly subjected to machine learning—credit scores or medical imagery, for instance—we could not draw on our intuitions so readily.

The instructor's example had been designed to resemble one of the most widely circulated figures in the recommender systems research community, created by the winners of the Netflix Prize to illustrate their winning technique (fig. 6). It was during the Netflix Prize that matrix factorization emerged as a dominant technique for analyzing collaborative filtering data, and the article containing this figure, titled "Matrix Factorization Meets the Neighborhood," described how to do what we had just done, locating users and items in a shared space and then identifying "neighborhoods"—or clusters of similar entities—within it.

In the Netflix Prize figure, the dimension that we had associated with genre in the classroom was interpreted in terms of gender, with its two poles labeled "geared toward males" and "geared toward females." Gendered axes are very common in didactic illustrations like these, despite the fact that, as discussed earlier, recommender systems do not com-

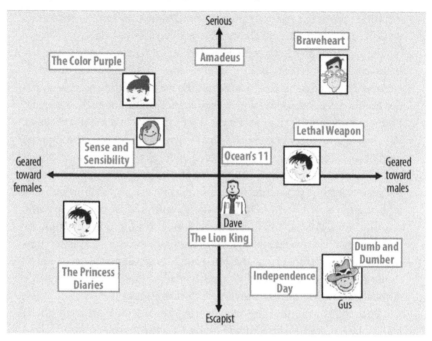

FIGURE 6. Movies and users distributed across a latent factor space
(Koren, Bell, and Volinsky 2009, 44)

monly rely on demographic data. There are two plausible explanations
for this: If users' ratings reflect the gendered structure of cultural production, then it makes sense that gender would manifest as a pattern in the
data. Conversely, we might look to the researchers themselves, who interpreted the dimension and applied the label; if they understood gender
to be a key organizing category, then they would be inclined to recognize
it in their data.[5]

In the Netflix Prize figure, we can see a typical effort, recalling the
discussion in chapter 3, to de-essentialize demographic categories that
nonetheless keeps them central: movies are merely "geared toward" men
or women, and faces that appear male and female are distributed across
the space, presenting a vision of gender that is rooted not in essences, but
in choices and tendencies, spread across a spectrum that is still defined
by the gender binary.[6]

Over time, a system's output might diverge from labels applied by people (as would happen if our genre dimension turned out to be a Julia Roberts dimension), and it was not uncommon for dimensions to be labeled
"uninterpretable"—to not embody any obvious cultural category. Such
uninterpretable dimensions could still be used for recommendations, as

they reflected some underlying pattern in the data, regardless of whether they were legible to humans. But as discussed in the previous chapter, apparently uninterpretable dimensions remained a source of anxiety: it was always possible that they were evidence of some kind of error, which might be hard to identify.

Here we find a gap between the work of mathematical calculation and human interpretation. Matrix factorization is unconcerned with the intrinsic qualities of items to be recommended, while the people who use it rely on their own cultural knowledge—unavailable to the system—to confirm that it works. So, despite the fact that gender and genre are technically excluded from the data of collaborative filtering, these concepts reappear in the process of building systems, used as evidence that they work.

Cursed Dimensionality

From the discussion so far, concerns about cultural space may seem to be a matter of how visualizations are generated and interpreted. The recognition of expected cultural patterns—in the output of matrix factorization or in a genre map—is central to the verification of these systems. But what distinguishes the spaces of algorithmic recommendation in use from those in the classroom is that no one needs to continue interpreting them or labeling their dimensions for them to "work."

As I was often reminded, the computer is indifferent to these labels: to identify clusters, calculate distances, and generate recommendations, there is no need to define what a given dimension means. So far as the mechanics of recommendation are concerned, it does not matter whether a dimension is labeled as gender or genre: the basic calculations of proximity and similarity that go into making recommendations remain the same. In practice, human-readable labels appear in a narrow set of circumstances: in pedagogical settings, like the classroom where we were being enrolled into the world of recommender systems design; in illustrative figures, where researchers try to communicate the functionality of their systems to one another; and during the construction of machine learning systems in industry, where people like Tomas in the previous chapter find it useful to interpret what their software is learning.[7]

Among practitioners, concerns about labeling are marginal to what they see as a deeper spatial issue: the properties of highly dimensional space. While visualizations are typically limited to two dimensions for the sake of human visibility, the similarity spaces of machine learning are not limited in this way. It is not uncommon to hear researchers discuss data with hundreds, thousands, or millions of dimensions. While such data sets pose no special challenge to computers, they quickly escape human spatial sensibilities. There is no way for people to see such highly dimensional spaces "directly"—that is, to see them in the way we can see a two-dimensional space represented on a flat page. To be seen, such spaces must be transformed.[8]

But these highly dimensional spaces are not made to be seen, at least not by human eyes. Like the audio feature representations described in the previous chapter, their audience is algorithmic. The purpose of treating data as spatial is not primarily to facilitate human intuition; in fact, highly dimensional spaces are notoriously counterintuitive, posing threats like the "curse of dimensionality," which refers to the peculiar qualities of highly dimensional spaces that set them apart from their physical analogues.

The curse of dimensionality is often explained with reference to a supermarket: if you manage a store and want related products to be stocked near each other, you have a limited set of possible arrangements. In one dimension, it is as though your store has a single shelf, on which items can sit side by side. Diapers might be stocked between baby wipes and rash ointment. In two dimensions, there are multiple rows of shelves, so related products can go above and below, as well: on top of the diapers, bottles; below, pacifiers. Counting the shelves across the aisle as a third dimension gives room for swaddling blankets and teething rings, but onesies and rattles have to sit farther away. With every new dimension, we add another way for items to be nearby; if we had enough dimensions, then everything could be next to everything else, in one dimension or another.

This means that, as dimensions proliferate, our three-dimensional intuitions about distance start to break apart. If engineers do not heed this warning, then the algorithms they design to produce and analyze similarity spaces run into trouble, as the points they seek to classify seem to clump together, as though there were too much similarity in the world to pick anything apart. This is the curse of dimensionality: as axes of difference multiply, so do potential connections.[9]

A grad student told me a joke that captured the impossibility of developing an intuition for machine learning's highly dimensional spaces, attributed to one of the field's most senior figures, Geoffrey Hinton: "How do you deal with a fourteen-dimensional space? To deal with a fourteen-dimensional space, visualize a three-dimensional space and say 'fourteen' to yourself very loudly. Everyone does it."

So, in the classroom, after establishing a basic understanding of data as intrinsically and intuitively spatial, instructors "advocate returning often to equations" (Mackenzie 2017, 65), which offer the only technically legitimated way to interface with these high-dimensional mathematical objects. The coexistence of formal and informal modes of engagement is key to machine-learning pedagogy: students build intuitions from low-dimensional spaces, which they then extrapolate to high-dimensional spaces while also learning that such extrapolations are suspect. In instructional materials, machine-learning techniques that typically operate on highly dimensional data are illustrated in flat, two-dimensional form; in conversation, similarity spaces that may have thousands of dimensions when implemented in a computer are gestured in three-dimensional space. As Hinton's joke indicates, the simultaneous use and disavowal of ordinary spatial intuition is commonplace. The math guarantees one form of correctness; the intuition about proximities in physical space guarantees another.

Cultural Space

Across campus, in the School of Social Sciences, I was learning about taste from a different direction, as a graduate student in anthropology.

The dual character of space—both intuitive and technical—that I have pointed out in computer science is not unique to it but can be found in social scientific uses of analytic space as well. In a graduate methods class, I was instructed in a technique that anthropologists had adapted from psychology in the 1970s, called "multidimensional scaling"—a computational method for analyzing data about cultural domains that generates spatial plots of similarity, not unlike the similarity spaces of machine learning.

For example, in one typical study, the anthropologist Michael Burton (1972) visualized the "semantic dimensions of occupation names," using data that had been collected from fifty-four Harvard students. The students were given cards with occupation names on them and instructed to sort the cards into piles according to their similarity. The more often occupations were sorted into the same pile, the more similar they were taken to be. A multidimensional scaling algorithm could transform this coarse data about the similarity of concepts or objects into a quantified, computational representation of continuous space (fig. 7). Clusters of points in this space might represent categories reflected in the students' piles; lines through the space might indicate important dimensions along which the sorted items were understood to vary, just like the dimensions derived from matrix factorization.[10]

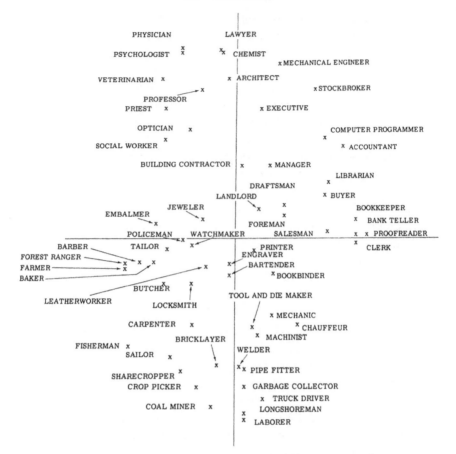

FIGURE 7. Two-dimensional scaling of occupation terms (Burton 1972, 63). Courtesy of the Center for Advanced Studies in the Behavioral Sciences, Stanford University.

At the time, I was regularly driving to visit Adam, a graduate student in computer science who was working on machine-learning techniques for measuring musical similarity at a California university. During one of my visits, I was surprised to learn that Adam had written one of his qualifying exam papers on multidimensional scaling, tracing a lineage back from contemporary machine learning to the same ancestors I had learned about in my own methods class. Eager to find more points of connection, I showed him the some of the famous figures from Bourdieu's *Distinction* (1984)—created using another spatializing technique, correspondence analysis—to see if he could recognize or interpret them. "I haven't seen these before, but they make sense, and that guy is trying to intimidate people," he told me. Compared to the figures common in machine learning, Bourdieu's were quite dense and idiosyncratic, but their basic spatial premises were shared. Correspondence analysis was an ancestor of the collaborative filtering methods I had learned about in the undergraduate classroom (see Desrosières 2012), and I came to realize that my social scientific training had more in common with machine learning than I expected.

In sociology, Bourdieu (along with other figures like Harrison White) took what had been a minor, unsystematized tendency in theoretical discourse—the ordinary spatial metaphorizing we have been discussing—and elaborated it into a master metaphor that eventually overtook much of sociology's theoretical language and analytical practice. Bourdieu (1985, 724), for instance, theorized the "social field" as "a multi-dimensional space of positions such that every actual position can be defined in terms of a multi-dimensional system of coordinates." That social field could be mapped by spatializing techniques like correspondence analysis, which he argued were uniquely adequate to the relational, evolving nature of society. Bourdieu's famous forms of capital were theoretical concepts derived from the interpretation of dimensions—latent factors in the organization of social space.

In a review of this spatializing tendency in social theory, the sociologist Ilana Silber (1995, 348) argued that spatial metaphors offered "a specific combination of concreteness and abstraction" that was appealing to social theorists looking to make theory that felt both rigorous and realistic. Thinking about sociocultural life as spatial was intuitive, but it also facilitated a kind of mathematization that aspired to the authority of the natural sciences: "Situated somewhere between models imported from the scientific disciplines and everyday life and language, spatial metaphors appear to displace constructs and metaphors emblematic of positivist or systemic theoretical trends now considered obsolete, while also reflecting the prevalent distrust of any kind of encompassing, totalistic image or paradigm" (Silber 1995, 348). The apparent givenness of space offered a way to escape prior theoretical frameworks through simultaneous recourse to the pragmatics of social action (the idea that people do things within the ordinary envelope of a vernacular "space") and to the mathematical language of the natural sciences. Because they depend so much on commonsense understandings of what space is and how it relates to similarity, they appear theoretically unburdened; because they are mathematized, they appear scientific.

As the ethnomethodologist Michael Lynch (1988, 229) has written of other scientific representations, "mathematical analysis and natural phenomena do not so much *correspond* as do they *merge* indistinguishably on the ground" of such figures (emphasis in original; see Morgan 2020). As another sociologist elaborating on multidimensional scaling models wrote in the 1990s, these spaces "look like what they represent" (Mohr 1998, 364), as though we finally could make good maps of that ever-elusive object, culture. But this claim to iconicity is not literally true: there is no obvious referent to which such maps might be adequate. Yet the sense of reality engendered by these spaces is so strong that they enable their wielders to sidestep significant dichotomies: between representation and reality, the formal and the informal, or the subjective and the objective. Bourdieu can speak of the social field as though it were the actual environment of social action and not just an algorithmic output; recommender systems researchers can move seamlessly between mathematical manipulations of abstract space and embodied imaginations of travel through it.[11]

A Tour of a Map of the Music Genre Space

Back in Seattle, Glenn McDonald was about to demonstrate one of his data alchemical productions: an interactive map of musical genres, derived from his employer's data, which he had evocatively named "Every Noise at Once." Playing audio samples as he went, McDonald took his audience on "one bouncy, erratic circumnavigation of the world of music"—a wide-ranging, para-ethnomusicological ramble through the world of possible listening represented on his map.

The roughly 1,100 genres shown on the map had emerged from a system largely of McDonald's own devising. Rather than classifying music into a top-down hierarchy of genres—where subgenres branch off from major genres and every artist has a proper location—McDonald's system classified music inductively, drawing on patterns in collective listening history and the other data that fed into his employer's artist similarity scores. Artists that were often listened to by the same people, or that were often described online with the same words, would find themselves grouped together, much like the users and movies I encountered in the classroom. Thus, the Norwegian symphonic black metal group Dimmu Borgir ended up clustered with their Scandinavian metal compatriots Gorgoroth and the American symphonic black metal band Wykked Wytch, while the American pop artist Britney Spears ended up with her ex-boyfriend Justin Timberlake in dance pop and the cast of the movie *High School Musical* in teen pop. The map was ever-shifting as the underlying data changed, and artists might appear in multiple genres across the map.

The location of genres on the map was determined not by listening histories, but by audio analysis: McDonald calculated the typical acoustic features of music within each cluster, arraying them in space along two auditory dimensions. "The calibration is fuzzy," he wrote on the company blog, "but in general down is more organic, up is more mechanical and electric; left is denser and more atmospheric, right is spikier and bouncier" (McDonald 2013). A third acoustic dimension manifested in the varying colors of the genre names, although McDonald intentionally did not explain what it was.

This procedure created a constantly shifting blob of genre names that, when I first encountered it online, roughly resembled a map of Madagascar. In the spiky and electric northeast sat many varieties of house music—deep tech house, minimal tech house, acid house, Chicago house. Traveling south along the eastern coast (or, toward the "more organic" end of the island, on its "bouncier" side), one passed through a few global dance musics—Brazilian baile funk, Angolan kuduro, Caribbean reggaeton—before coming upon a deeply set bay dotted with national hip-hop variants (the analogous location in Madagascar is called Antongil Bay): Canadian hip-hop, Russian hip-hop, hip-hop Quebecois. Continuing south along Madagascar's Highway 5, more "world music" genres appeared—Ghanaian highlife, Mexican norteño, Senegalese mbalax, Malagasy folk (the latter featuring Madagascar's own Rakotozafy, a renowned player of Malagasy zithers).

In the spiky, organic southeast, the map broke apart, with a coastline of jazz- and blues-related genres looking out onto an archipelago of spoken-word recordings with labels like "poetry," "guidance," "oratory," and "drama." The dense and atmospheric western coast was dominated by various rock styles, from black sludge in the south to dark hardcore in the north. The two coasts were separated by a dense ridge of pop genres—ranging from Japanese Shibuya-kei to French yé-yé. From the bottom of the island extended a classical promontory, sedimented from an eclectic set of labels: "opera," "Carnatic," "polyphony," "concert piano."

Identifying and naming these emergent clusters was part of McDonald's job, and as with the latent factors of matrix factorization, this work depended on his own interpretation. Sometimes, a label seemed obvious, and a cluster of artists appeared to correspond to a well-known genre. When clusters did not seem to have obvious names, McDonald would give them evocative but sometimes mysterious ones, like shiver pop ("a descriptive name for a subtly distinct cluster of indie pop, which needed a name") or destroy techno ("an invented name for a particularly hard-to-describe experimental techno cluster"). When these genre names surfaced in the Spotify interface, or in the year-end listening summaries the platform produced for its users, they were often a source of public contention and debate: listeners might be surprised to discover that their "favorite" genre had a name that neither they nor the artists involved had ever heard of.

Sometimes, competing labels would require McDonald to choose, emphasizing one aspect of a genre over another: such was the case with indie R&B, the name he eventually assigned to an emerging style of R&B notable for the whiteness of its audience relative to conventional R&B. Critics had made several attempts to name the genre, including PBR&B, a portmanteau of R&B and the initials of Pabst Blue Ribbon, a beer brand associated with the same audience (Harvey 2013). For a while, McDonald had chosen to go with R-neg-B, a name coined by another critic to emphasize the style's typical negativity (Wilson 2011), but eventually he changed the name to indie R&B, a tag with less implicit editorializing about the genre's audience and affect, though it maintained the racialized understanding of genre in which "indie" signified whiteness and "R&B" blackness (Sahim 2015).

These labels reflected a wide variety of "genres," not all of which were recognizable as such, referring sometimes to instruments (cello), high-level industry categories (pop), specific local traditions (forró), and even other clusters in the system (deep cello, which was a somehow intensified variant of cello). "I'm cheerfully unrigorous about what a genre can be," McDonald said in an interview, "Some of them are musicological, some are historical, and others are regional themes. A genre can be any listening mode I think people might want" (Kneschke 2017). Thus, his genres included activities like "sleep" (featuring white noise or quiet music) and "focus" (Eriksson and Johansson 2017; James 2017b).[12]

In interviews and press releases promoting his genre system, McDonald would describe this malleability as a virtue, reminiscent of the flexibility praised by the inventors of collaborative filtering: treating genre as an intrinsically emergent phenomenon rather than a set of strict boxes would free listeners (and potentially musicians) from its constraints. As he put it in a 2013 corporate blog post, "The resulting system's crucial, pragmatic quality is that it is dynamic and self-regulating on an ongoing basis," allowing artists and genres to evolve over time.

Although the labels were clearly the result of McDonald's active interpretation and open to debate, he insisted that the underlying clusters that he was labeling were objectively real: "The fact that there's a cluster of listening means that the genre is a real thing, even though I might have made up the name" (Johnston 2018). One might argue that the arbitrariness of labels applied to clusters only serves to bolster those clusters' claim to reality: While debates play out about whether shiver pop is a real genre, or whether something like cello or sleep should really count as a genre, the strong claim is not about the adequacy of the label (which, after all, is irrelevant to the internal working of the system) but about the reality of the pattern to which it is applied.

Like the sociologists described by Silber, McDonald used his spatial constructions in two registers: as a kind of objective production and as a setting for interpretive play. He would occasionally gloat on his Twitter account about the performance of his classifiers: "Next time somebody tells you 'algorithms' can't understand music, hand them this and confiscate their headphones," he tweeted, posting an image of part of his genre map, in which a set of regional hip-hop genres were all neatly stacked together. This stacking indicated an agreement between two forms of data analysis: the genres themselves had been constituted from listening patterns, and their placement reflected their typical sound. The fact that listener behavior and musical sound appeared to track with each other was taken as a sign that the system had grasped some underlying categorical reality. So although his map was not presented as an ultimate authority on the existence of genres, its connection to various forms of data analysis gave it a kind of ad hoc authority, which could be invoked at some moments and dismissed at others.

Crafting Genre

This generic use of "genre" was typical among people working on such classification systems. While genre theorists might find it odd or incorrect to call "sleep" or "deep cello" genres, for people like McDonald, the term was essentially synonymous with "cluster." Conventional genres simply served as a prototype for thinking about the many ways that similar music might be gathered together. From academic music informatics researchers, I heard the same thing: "genre recognition"—a long-standing analytic task in which researchers tried to guess a song's genre from its audio data—was being superseded by "tag prediction," in which software would predict which labels users had assigned to tracks on music streaming platforms like SoundCloud. Those labels sometimes included conventional genre names, but they also could include prominent instruments on a recording, its perceived mood, and an unbounded set of idiosyncratic and subjective other labels. Even Tomas's machine-listening system from the previous chapter was designed to be open about what a "genre" might be.

The inductive ethos of McDonald's clustering technique is widely shared in the world of data science, where the injunction to "listen to the data" often means using so-called unsupervised techniques to identify clusters and then interpreting what those clusters represent. Such techniques are typically opposed to a vision of top-down, hierarchical classification, in which categories are imposed from the outside—such practices are regarded as both unfair to the objects classified and prone to error. But these classificatory attitudes also correspond to ideas about the nature of the entities being classified.

When I showed McDonald's map to an executive at a competing info-mediary company—an older one, which was known for its hierarchical genre model—he mocked the idea: "Those hipsters," he said, "they want to pretend that anything can be related to anything else." And indeed, this was what it meant for music to be "infinitely connected," as McDonald had put it: there were countless dimensions along which music might be similar. This data-centric approach to musical classification produced a kind of "hyperactive kinship" (Helmreich 2003; Seaver 2015) among musical entities, facilitating new and surprising connections that did not necessarily depend on conventional ideas about musical relations. If genre was just another word for cluster, this meant that there were infinitely many possible genres, and many actually existing ones among those possibilities. The work of choosing which kinds of similarity would matter required the cultural judgment of people like McDonald.

But the suggestion that genre was just another word for "cluster" embodied a contestable theory about the ontology and pragmatics of genre—both what a genre was and what a genre was for. McDonald would not insist that his genres were the last word on musical classification: "The purpose of the map, as it is for the genres, isn't to end arguments but to invite exploration of music." While his algorithmic process participated in some of the typical realism of computational methods, he also argued, "This process isn't entirely accurate or precise, but music isn't either, and they both often seem to work." For the makers of music recommendation more generally, such tentativeness and pragmatism is a commonly held virtue, in contrast to dominant views of infallible artificial intelligence systems. This commitment also frequently means that apparently arbitrary choices do not need to be justified in relation to any absolute criterion of adequacy, and it allows for representations that continually change while never being strictly "wrong."

Although McDonald might insist on the tentative, arbitrary, and revisable nature of his genre classifications, the labels he produced nonetheless participated in broader discourses that interpreted them in the frame of a more rigid kind of genre realism. A corporate blog post from Spotify listed the "50 strangest genre names," as though a Spotify employee had not been responsible for coming up with terms like "abstracto" or "vintage swoon" in the first place (Van Buskirk 2015). It is not hard to imagine, as many critics have done (see, e.g., Pelly 2018), the performative effect such namings might have. Naming a cluster of artists "escape room" and telling listeners it is their favorite genre could teach them to interpret their own listening through this grid (Hu 2016). Publicly manifesting categories, through interfaces to listeners or through "artist dashboards" to musicians and music industry executives, could clearly encourage musicking practices to organize along those lines, although empirical research on the dynamics through which this might happen is still in its early stages. If we subscribe to Lena's (2012, 6) sociological theory of genre introduced in the previous chapter—"systems of orientations, expectations, and conventions that bind together industry, performers, critics, and fans"—it seems plausible that new understandings of genre might be shaped by new technologies of classification, provided that they are taken up by the relevant social actors. In theory, such genres might avoid pigeonholing artists into specific styles; in practice, such an outcome is by no means guaranteed.

The musicologist Eric Drott (2018a), writing about algorithmic genre detection, argues similarly that "the means by which specific, empirical genres are materialized and publicly circulated influences what genre is." Genres as clusters are quite different from the genres that preceded them. Historically, Drott notes, genre has been understood as the cause of musical similarity: artists participate in a genre knowingly and create music accordingly. The conquest of genre by similarity, strangely enough, results in a situation where artists may be part of a genre without realizing it; genre becomes an effect rather than a cause of musical similarity, Drott argues, becoming "ontologically subordinate" to mathematical measures.

The musicologist Tom Johnson (2019) has described this performative genre effect—by which similarity clustering comes to create the genres it nominally describes—as "genrecraft." He adapts the term from Barbara Fields and Karen Fields's (2012) "racecraft," which they use to describe the process by which racism produces race, scattering evidence for racial difference throughout the social world, which is then taken to show that race is natural and objective.

Here again we find spatial metaphorizing used to convey the reality of social phenomena, as the Fieldses define racecraft as a kind of "mental terrain": "Like physical terrain, racecraft exists objectively; it has topographical features that Americans regularly navigate, and we cannot readily stop traversing it. Unlike physical terrain, racecraft originates not in nature but in human action and imagination; it can exist in no other way" (Fields and Fields 2012, 18–19, quoted in Johnson 2019).[13] Here we find space used as a metaphor not for absolute objectivity but for an inter-subjective milieu, in which human action and classification takes place. Such arguments will be familiar to readers of theories of social construc-tion, articulation, performativity, reification, or materialization, with slightly different emphases depending on one's theoretical orientation. But of particular interest here is the role that spatial metaphorizing plays in making classification schemes seem "real." Johnson (2019, 6) picks up this spatial language in his discussion of genrecraft, writing of genre's "continuously reiterated landscapes," and describing the production of genres from data analysis practices predicated on the idea that there is an underlying genre topography to be found.

So, when Drott (2018a, 23) argues that "the collapse of genre into similarity entails a tacit reconceptualization of the musical field in which genres are embedded," which "transforms this field into a smooth, con-tinuous, and measurable space," the idea that social (or musical) space *is a space* is already a given.[14] His concern is with the way that space is constituted and measured because, as we have seen, there are choices to be made in the production of such spaces, and these choices can easily come to be seen as objective and natural, thanks to the intuitiveness of the spaces they create.

Imaginative Geographies

The purpose of McDonald's maps, as he had said, was to facilitate explo-ration of music beyond the familiar, broadening horizons in the music space—what people in the industry commonly call "music discovery." Not all music recommendation is oriented toward discovery: systems de-signed for lean-back listening are typically biased toward familiar music. But music discovery may be the closest thing to a universally shared value in the world of music recommendation. Academic research commonly takes the discovery of new music as the self-evident goal of recommender systems; record labels want listeners to find more of their catalog to lis-ten to; streaming services want listeners to find new value in their plat-forms; obscure artists want listeners to find their music (Celma 2010).[15] As Willow's head of engineering said during an industry panel on music discovery at a San Francisco conference: "We owe it to people to help them find music they love." When workers in music streaming feel bad about the ethical status of their work—that they may be furthering sur-veillance capitalism or commoditizing musical experiences—they often turn to discovery as an obvious good, a service to musicians struggling to be heard and to listeners who will benefit from broadened musical horizons, even if they don't know it.

As the language of "horizons" suggests, this valuing of discovery is closely tied to a spatial understanding of musical variety. As Spotify CEO Daniel Ek put it in a 2018 letter to investors: "In this new world, music has no borders. . . . We're working to democratize the industry and connect all of us, across the world, in a shared culture that expands our horizons."[16] We can hear in this line an echo of the internet ideology encountered in chapter 3—the idea that digital technologies remove old boundaries and encourage free exploration, replacing physical geography with a digital one. Yet looking through McDonald's map, we see the persistence of physical geography in the many genre names that index specific locations. These include widely recognized genres, like Miami bass or Chicago house, but also names that simply tie a country to a high-level genre, like Slovak hip-hop or Vietnamese pop.[17] Although popular discourses about the internet and large databases often consider them "postgeographic," allowing for novel or latent modes of connection that transcend physical proximity to emerge, they are often "reterritorialized" by the persistence of geographically based understandings of cultural variation.[18]

The central irony of the "postgenre" attitude, as music scholars have noted, is that it has occasioned an efflorescence of genre descriptors (Drott 2013; James 2017a; Johnson 2018). While claiming to transcend genre, postgenre artists accrue many genre labels, which serve to indicate how unbound by genre they are while nonetheless locating them ever more precisely in a space of genre fluidity. As the philosopher of music Robin James has argued, such freedom is not universally allowed but tends to accrue to white male artists: so, Diplo, a white DJ, is praised as exploratory for collaborating with musicians from around the world, while Pitbull, an internationally popular Latin American rapper who also blends many global styles of dance music, is pigeonholed by US audiences that understand Latin artists as embodying a "fixed particularity" (James 2017a, 28).

The makers of music recommendation take great pleasure in identifying new and obscure genres. During my summer at Whisper, many microgenres passed through the office stereo, like the post-ringtone recordings of PC Music described in the prologue. Such genres, like vaporwave or microsound, have proliferated in internet-mediated musical subcultures, often embracing an apparently "placeless" aesthetic—not being obviously from any geographical location in particular or having mysterious origins—while nonetheless reflecting prior geographical cultural dynamics; Georgina Born and Christopher Haworth (2017, 643) describe this as "a reconfiguration of both imaginary and physical music geographies." No longer is the variety of music around the world consigned to the grab bag of "world music" commonly critiqued by ethnomusicologists (e.g., Feld 2000). Instead, it is intensely typologized in categories that vary arbitrarily in their level of detail.

This is the other side of the anxiety of overload described in chapter 1: the pleasures of wide-ranging and fine-grained knowledge, of classification, avidity, and connoisseurship. As Johnson (2018, 150) writes, "Omnivorousness revels in heterogeneity and acts of overcoding, directing flows across filed-down but acknowledged porous borders." If omnivorousness is grounded in the recognition and overcoming of musical distinctions, then the ever-finer slicing up of genres provides more differences to be overcome and more pleasure to be had, for the classifiers, at least.

The cultural theorist Amanda Modell has argued that we should understand such musical mapping as a kind of "imaginative geography"—Edward Said's (1978) term for orientalist speculations about spaces figured as "far away." Elaborating on the work of Hortense Spillers (1987), Modell (2015, 6) writes: "Imaginative geographers imagine they are turning space into place, or populating a space with meaning. This ignores all the indigenous mappings that have taken place before the colonial encounter and continue to take place after it—it relies on the idea of space that does not signify anything. In a highly problematic process, imaginative geography reinforces what the cartographer already knows, that spaces do not mean or matter until the 'civilized' see and map them." The colonial quality of music discovery metaphors is plainly evident in McDonald's descriptions of his map and its purpose.[19] In fact, if we look to the literary critic Wayne Franklin's (1979) classic typology of colonial narrative styles in early US writing, we find them neatly replicated here.[20] First, there are "discovery narratives," which find their authors in awe of the vast resources they have encountered; Franklin notes that these narratives are often full of lists, like McDonald's sets of genres. As McDonald described Every Noise at Once: "There are probably things on this map you've never imagined. It probably contains things that you don't yet realize you love, and branching points where you will be amazed and thrilled to have veered." Then, in "exploratory narratives," explorers yearn to make use of the resources they've encountered. McDonald evokes this theme in describing the need to build recommender systems: "But for this new world to actually be appreciable, we have to find ways to map this space and then build machines to carry you through it along interesting paths."

Finally, in the "settlement narrative," we find the explorer negotiating the tensions between the apparent abundance of their environment and the challenges of actually living there. The anxiety of overload—the dark side of the musical promised land—fits well here.

As Modell suggests, these accounts of musical space are surprisingly devoid of inhabitants, like conventional colonial narratives. While McDonald described his job in a talk as "making the infinite musical unknown fractionally less unknowable," we might ask: unknown to whom? The colonial fantasy of *terra nullius* is more self-evidently false here, given that someone had to make and record all this music. We can understand McDonald not as literally claiming that this music is unknown to everyone but as occupying a particular musical location and relying on a set of readily available cultural tropes about mapmaking, geographical difference, and discovery. As he put it in his Seattle talk: "I sit at the center—as literally as there can be a literalness to this idea—of this universe of music as information." That center was, in one sense, his position relative to a large data-collecting apparatus, at one of the world's most popular music streaming companies, with access to an unprecedented amount of data about music and listening habits; but it was also a position in the postcolonial geography of music production and listening.

For some of my interlocutors, this position was a source of concern. Richard, an engineer at Whisper, once asked me: "We have to recommend Filipino music to people in the Philippines, but we have no Filipino staff—what should we do?" Neither he nor I were in positions to actually influence such decisions at the corporate level, and my suggestion, that perhaps his company didn't need to operate in the Philippines, was not tenable within an industry predicated on continuous expansion.[21]

The music space is multifarious. It is a kind of technical, abstract space, organized mathematically and derived from data. But it is also part of a cultural imaginary that links proximity to similarity, relying on a shared intuition of how the natural world is organized. As the makers of music recommendation navigate the tensions between these formal and informal senses of space, tacking from equations to intuitions and back again, they draw on other understandings of space. At times, they echo colonialist discourses of exploration and discovery; but like critical humanists, they also try to use spatial metaphors to recognize difference and imagine new relationships across it. In the following chapter, I turn my attention to another aspect of this spatial musical imaginary: the idea that the music space, for all its uncanny qualities, is something like a park or garden.

CHAPTER 6

Parks and Recommendation

We're Park Rangers

At the Billboard FutureSound Summit in 2012, a man named Tim Quirk was trying to explain his job. Quirk was the head of global content programming for Google's streaming music service, which at the time had the elaborate name Google Play Music All Access. The "programming" he was responsible for was not computer programming, but a kind of programming that predated it: deciding what music to play. Although the term "programming" was borrowed from broadcast radio (Hennion and Meadel 1986; Razlogova 2020), the rise of algorithmic recommendation meant that the job of a content programmer had become quite different. What did such a person do at a company where the music was nominally chosen by algorithms? It was, Quirk suggested, kind of complicated.

Earlier in his life, Quirk's job had been more straightforward. Through the 1980s and 1990s, he was the lead singer of the alt-rock band Too Much Joy, until he left performing to work in distribution, taking a string of jobs at digital music companies that would eventually lead him to Google. He recounted to his audience the standard history of the music industry told by people working in algorithmic recommendation: Once upon a time, the distribution of music was controlled by a set of influential "gatekeepers and tastemakers." Working at record labels, radio stations, and music shops, these people were tasked with being conspicuously "cool," relying on their cultural expertise to shape and respond to trends (see Negus 1995). Those cultural intermediaries, as sociologists would call them, had been radically disempowered by the rise of digital distribution, which democratized the production and the consumption of music: it was easier for people to release their own music and to listen to music of their choice, beyond the decisions made by DJs and their ilk.

While we might question some of this story's details, it remains commonplace among people in the industry, who rely on it as they try to make sense of their own jobs. If the gatekeepers and tastemakers had been displaced, then what was someone like Quirk, with his rock-band bona fides, doing? His job was both like and unlike those earlier intermediary archetypes: "That's one reason my job's name keeps changing," he said, "it didn't really exist before 1998. We're not exactly record store clerks, we're not exactly critics, and we're not exactly DJs, although our ranks include people who learned what they know doing each of those things" (quoted in Resnikoff 2014). Like most of the people we've heard from in this book, Quirk understood his task to be aiding listeners who were overwhelmed by their newfound freedom, to help them "through that maelstrom of musical choice" (quoted in Resnikoff 2014) whirling deep in the catalogs of on-demand streaming services. His responsibility, as he described it, was not exercising his own good taste but "imposing order on chaos" (quoted in Resnikoff 2014), organizing and managing a vast field of listening options: "Telling the entire world what it should and shouldn't listen to has become far less important than simply making this overgrown musical jungle navigable. Online music services need bushwhackers carving paths from one starting point to another. We're not gatekeepers. We're not tastemakers. We're park rangers" (quoted in Pham 2012). An essay in the online music magazine *Pitchfork* would describe Quirk's jungle metaphor as "unique" (Harvey 2014), but what was most striking about his self-description as a kind of trailblazing steward of the cultural wilderness was just how common it was.

Again and again, I heard people working on music recommender systems take up similarly pastoral metaphors to describe their work. Despite the supposed rationality of machine learning, the makers of music recommendation rarely described their work as orderly calculation. Instead, they were bushwhackers or park rangers, gardeners or farmers; they were explorers or guides, cartographers or surveyors. All these metaphorical professions set them apart from conventional visions of computer programming, but they also were meant to contrast with earlier modes of content programming—with the cultural intermediaries, like DJs, that they understood to be their precursors.

: :

In the previous chapter, I described how the abstract spaces of machine learning accrue persuasive power by joining the rationalistic guarantees of mathematization together with intuitions about the givenness of physical space. In this chapter, I expand on the cultural context of those intuitions, which are not merely universal, human experiences of embodiment but are tied to specific spatial archetypes, ranging from the national park to the garden to the frontier. These are ideologically loaded and symbolically dense cultural resources, which provide intuitions about the nature of space. As people working in music recommendation try to make sense of the purpose, substance, and ethical status of their work—to dwell in the abstract spaces of machine learning—they often rely on pastoral metaphors to do it.

These metaphors are "pastoral" in two senses. First, they represent the music space as a kind of bucolic landscape, a "green world" of organic growth and nonhuman agency, a resource to be carefully managed. Second, they figure the people who work on this space as caretakers, both for the land and for the people who might want to traverse it. Metaphors like these are commonly critiqued for being naturalizing—mystifying the material realities of computation and data collection. Here, I pursue a different line of interpretation: How does this sylvan language help the makers of music recommendation think about their work?

Pastoral metaphors provide a resource for workers to think about their moral responsibilities, the extent of their control, and the objectivity of their data. And although these metaphors may appear straightforwardly naturalizing, mystifying the social organization of algorithmic systems, I want to argue that they illuminate the experience of work within algorithmic systems today: the people who make music recommendation do not make it as they please but encounter the objects of their labor as lively, resistant materials that they do not absolutely control.

The Garden in the Machine

For most of my time as an intern at Whisper, I sat next to Ellie, who managed the company's quality assurance team. Quality assurance, or QA, is a conventional role in software development—it is often explained as trying to break the programs that programmers make by using them in aggressive or unexpected ways. At Whisper, the QA work that Ellie supervised, and which I participated in from time to time, had a different focus. Her team was responsible for tending to the company's data, examining the output of its radio algorithms, scanning its algorithmically generated charts of popular artists, and ensuring that everything was working as intended.

Because Whisper aggregated data from a wide array of sources, analyzing and synthesizing it through a complicated and ever-changing algorithmic apparatus, there was always the possibility of unanticipated errors. Ellie regularly checked on the company's popularity charts, which reflected listening data from music streaming and online chatter. If an artist suddenly changed position dramatically, that artist's name would be marked in red: such major shifts might reflect an actual, sudden increase in popularity, but it was very likely that the change was the result of an error somewhere in the system, which would need to be identified. A band like Queen, for instance, might accidentally receive a boost in popularity if Whisper's data scrapers mistook a news article about Queen Elizabeth II for one about the rock group. A quick human check was usually sufficient to determine whether such an error had occurred, and the relevant engineers could then try to implement a general fix to prevent it from happening again.

Although we sat next to each other, Ellie and I often communicated via instant messages on our laptops, keeping conversations going in the background while we browsed through algorithmic playlists, finding and resolving peculiar outputs. "I love music data gardening," she messaged me one day. As a manager, Ellie received the obscure or challenging edge cases that her interns were unsure about, and she reveled in the weirdness that one encountered upon leaving the world of popular artists. Today, she was cleaning up the data for a rapper named Boobie $oprano, and she said that she was feeling "Zen like." "Must maintain balance in the garden," she told me.

Ellie took great pleasure in her "data gardening," pruning the outputs of algorithms, tending to artist metadata, and weeding out errors. Like her colleagues, Ellie considered herself someone who really cared about music, and she manifested this care through her attunement with musical data.[1] If stereotypical QA work was destructive and adversarial, Ellie's data gardening appeared calm and careful. This work, which in other settings might be described as "janitorial" and frequently outsourced to underpaid remote workers (Irani 2015), was for Ellie an enjoyable opportunity to draw on and deepen her understanding of music across countless genres.[2]

While Ellie's data gardening happened in the "nontechnical" role of quality assurance, we can find related pastoral metaphors in use among technical machine-learning specialists as well.[3] In his book *The Master Algorithm*, the computer scientist Pedro Domingos suggests that we should understand machine learning by analogy with farming. If conventional programming is like factory manufacture, producing static, functional objects, the programmers of machine learning write software that "grows" its functionality. Domingos (2015, 7) writes: "In farming, we plant the seeds, make sure they have enough water and nutrients, and reap the grown crops. Why can't technology be more like this? It can, and that's the promise of machine learning. Learning algorithms are the seeds, data is the soil, and the learned programs are the grown plants. The machine learning expert is like a farmer, sowing the seeds, irrigating and fertilizing the soil, and keeping an eye on the health of the crop, but otherwise staying out of the way." In Domingos's account, programmers are like farmers who decide what to plant but do not control the details of how their plants grow. Instead, they work from a distance, "staying out of the way" while managing the resources necessary for growth and minding the system's outputs.

To be clear, this is a largely fantastical account of what farming is actually like, but for Domingos, the key quality of farming is this loose relationship with the crop. Like Quirk's park rangers, Domingos's farmers appear occupationally remote from the world of keyboards and computers where programming actually happens. And in both cases, this distance is the point: the pastoral metaphor is used to mark a break between the old way of doing things and the new. The old programmers were factory workers; the new ones are farmers. The old cultural intermediaries were gatekeepers; the new ones are park rangers.

Domingos participated in a longer history of computer scientists imagining computers as natural environments, in which programs might grow as though they were alive. In Stefan Helmreich's ethnography *Silicon Second Nature* (1998), he describes how "artificial life" researchers sought to populate computational "worlds" with programs that could evolve and breed. Among artificial life scientists, Helmreich (1998, 83) writes, "computers are cultivated to contain a world open with possibility." Programs "live" and "die" within parameters set by system designers, but not under their direct control. Helmreich's artificial life researchers compare themselves to gods, with the power to set and alter the laws of nature within the computer, to potentially intervene in the lives of their programs, and to create and destroy these "worlds" entirely (84).

By comparison with the gods of artificial life, Domingos's farmer is a relatively modest figure. He is not the ultimate power and authority in a computational universe, but rather someone whose control is bounded— who cannot create life from nothing but must cultivate it from a set of external resources. This attitude toward computing, Helmreich suggests, draws together two commonly opposed tropes: the "closed world" of computation, in which everything is deterministic and subject to rational mastery (Edwards 1996), and the "green world" beyond it, which is unbounded, lively, and a bit mystical. Here is a precursor to what I have been calling the "open plan" in this book: the idea that recommender systems might become a source of serendipity and growth, not pigeon-holing and constraint.

There is something culturally American about this wedding of closed and green worlds. In his classic book *The Machine in the Garden* (1964), the historian Leo Marx described how nineteenth-century Americans sought to reconcile two apparently contradictory values: on one side, the "pastoral ideal," an arcadian vision of living in harmony with nature; on the other, the "technological sublime," or an intense affective investment in the expansion of industry and machinery. A popular resolution to this tension emerged in the ideal of the "middle landscape"—a space that was neither the supposedly natural and harmonious countryside nor the relentless order and speed of the city, but "an industrial version of the pastoral design" (Marx 1964, 32; see Segal 1977), which brought the two together in uneasy union. The middle landscape was tied up with the ideology of the frontier, being a mediating space between the supposed order and rationality of civilization and the wilderness of a natural landscape figured (incorrectly) as devoid of human life and influence.[4]

Marx claimed that the balanced dream of the middle landscape vanished in the United States with the intensification and spread of industrialization. But in computational imaginaries of gardening and farming, we can see how a desire to marry the pastoral ideal and the technological sublime has been metaphorically taken up in the software industry. It is important to remember that the pastoral ideal is not "nature" and the technological sublime is not "technology"; both are cultural attitudes, toward harmonious living with a world beyond one's control and toward the ever-expanding scope of technical capacities.

Natural's Not in It

Natural metaphors remain ubiquitous in computing discourse, and they are an especially common object of critique for critical scholars of big data. Data is often described as a force of nature or as a natural resource (Puschmann and Burgess 2014). It arrives in a flood or a tsunami; it is as valuable as gold or oil (Lupton 2013; Seaver 2015; Watson 2015; Social Media Collective 2017). Like the gardeners, farmers, and park rangers I've already described, these metaphors seem to carry the work of data collection and analysis out of the office and into the outdoors.

Among critics of big data, the dominant concern about such "natural world" metaphors is the apparent absence of people: no one lives in the cloud (Hwang and Levy 2015). The internet researchers Cornelius Puschmann and Jean Burgess (2014, 1699) offer a clear version of this critique, arguing that natural metaphors reify and mystify data by obscuring its human origins: "The givenness of data is analogized through the givenness of natural resources, which can be mined or grown and which can act as a form of capital with no persistent ties to their creator." Although the etymology of the word "data" (from the Latin *dare*, "to give") suggests that it is given—simply an unproblematic resource to be used—this is not the case. The data of data science is made and it is taken, "created by humans and recorded by machines rather than being discovered and claimed by platform providers or third parties" (Puschmann and Burgess 2014, 1699). To talk about data like water, gold, or oil is to hide data's connections to all the people whose activities produce it: the users whose actions are logged, the cleaners who work to make data amenable to algorithmic analysis, and the engineers who organize the process.[5] Naturalizing metaphors in particular seem to obscure the variety of human agencies that go into making data exist, figuring it instead as the untainted, objective stuff of the outside world, innocent of human politics and concerns.

Critical analyses of metaphors are an old tradition in the relatively young field of internet research, and work on data metaphors continues that tradition's distinctively suspicious attitude toward metaphorical speech: "Danger! Metaphors at Work," begins the title of one now-classic piece by Sally Wyatt (2004). The typical problem, as Puschmann and Burgess (2014, 1701) diagnose it, is a mismatch between a metaphor's source and target domains: oil and water, for instance, have properties that data does not, which are then extended to data, "suggesting physicality, immutability, context independence, and intrinsic worth."

The language of "source" and "target" domains comes from George Lakoff and Mark Johnson's (1980) well-known cognitive theory of metaphor, which is widely cited in critical work on metaphors and technology. Metaphors, in this theory, structure not only communication but also thinking itself, providing a way for meaning to travel from one domain to another.[6] Such connections are conventionally designated in a recognizable all-caps style: "TIME IS A CONTAINER" or "ARGUMENT IS WAR" draw attention to sets of common phrases by which people—at least English-speakers—talk and think in metaphorical terms, bringing a host of preconceptions with them.[7]

In uses like Domingos's, the Lakoffian analysis is effectively done for us: MACHINE LEARNING IS FARMING. Algorithms are seeds, data is soil, trained models are plants, and so on. Thus presented, our critique is ready to hand: machine learning is *not* like farming, so stop pretending your machine is a garden.

One problem with Lakoffian metaphor theory, as its critics have noted, is that it tends to fix its metaphors in place, in stable, ahistorical configurations of meaning. These cross-domain mappings constitute a "coherent system of metaphoric concepts" (Lakoff and Johnson 1980, 9), which function something like the classical anthropological theory of "culture"—globally variable but internally consistent and holistic (Albro 2018). People working in this mode of analysis typically operate as though the meanings of a source domain are simply there to be shuttled over to the target domain.

So, if we wanted to critique Domingos, we might note that he does not seem particularly interested in or well informed about the empirical details of farming. Instead, he presents an idealized vision of life on the farm where everything works according to plan and farmers simply reap nature's bounty, which is both plentiful and objective. In actual farming (like in actual machine learning), projects can fail, resource flows can dry up, and growth and balance are the result of concerted, ongoing effort, frequently supported by outside subsidies. And while we might take Domingos to task for naturalizing data as soil, we could also note that the soil on farms is anything but natural—it is the product of substantial human and nonhuman labor. These issues do not derive from a mismatch between source and target domains, but from the way that the source domain is figured.

We can find similar issues in how critics make sense of these metaphors. To argue that data is not like gold, for instance, Puschmann and Burgess (2014, 1699) are put in the odd position of arguing that while the value of data is not intrinsic, the value of gold is. This is not a position we have to endorse, and it suggests a flaw in the way that critics typically engage with metaphors they object to. To follow another common example, if we want to argue that data is not like water, this requires us to make an argument about what water is like, and those arguments are often dubious and partial. Data is supposedly not like water because it is not a naturally occurring renewable resource but the constructed outcome of a great deal of human mediating labor. But making water appear plentiful, natural, and pristine is also the result of a great deal of human mediating labor (Ballestero 2019). While trying to denaturalize data, we naturalize water, committing the same error we seek to correct.

An alternative approach to metaphor understands these comparisons as essentially *creative*—not just carrying stable meanings from one domain to another, but generating or reasserting meanings in both domains at once (Albro 2018, 110). We may be more interested in data than in gold, water, or oil, but narrowly focusing on the implications of such comparisons for data will make us miss the way that these statements generate and reinforce meaning across domains. While Domingos is trying to make a point about machine learning, he is also participating in discourse about farming.

If we narrowly focus on the adequacy of metaphors, then we risk missing the work that metaphors do for the people who use them. To understand the significance of someone describing data as water or soil, we cannot presume that we already know what water or soil mean to them. Nor can we claim that any invocation of plants or landscape is "naturalization," as though nature has a fixed, singular meaning.[8]

Neither Raw nor Cooked

The critique of naturalizing data discourse is often framed as a rejection of "raw data." As the science studies scholar Geoffrey Bowker (2005, 184) once put it, in a frequently quoted quip, "Raw data is both an oxymoron and a bad idea; to the contrary, data should be cooked with care." There is no such thing as raw data, despite what metaphors like "data is soil" seem to imply, because by the time data appears it has always already been "cooked": it is shaped by the devices that capture it, by the interests of the people who set those devices and sift through their output, and by the broader social and technical context that determines what is captured and why. In other terms, data collection is theory-laden, and data never represents the "real world" in a natural, unmediated way.[9]

This distinction between the raw and the cooked—and the mapping of "raw" onto "nature"—is commonly traced to Claude Lévi-Strauss's structuralist opus *The Raw and the Cooked* (1969). There, Lévi-Strauss describes how the basic opposition between raw and cooked food is widely used as a model for thinking about all sorts of other distinctions and transformations—most significantly, between nature and culture. In the set of indigenous American myths Lévi-Strauss (1969, 164) analyzes, "cooking mark[s] the transition from nature to culture," setting the natural world apart from the cultural world by establishing how material from one can be transformed into the other. In this line of critique, naive data practitioners mistakenly take something cultural, or cooked, to be natural, or raw.

However, for Lévi-Strauss, what mattered about the raw-cooked dichotomy was not the content or correctness of those categories but the structure of their opposition: raw is to cooked as nature is to culture. His goal was not to criticize this mapping of domains onto each other, but to examine how such mapping could provide a model for thought: "how empirical categories . . . can nonetheless be used as conceptual tools" (Lévi-Strauss 1969, 1). The concrete distinction between raw and cooked food offered people around the world a model for difference and transformation between domains, which many of them used to shore up a distinction between the cultural human world and the natural world that surrounded them. Such a distinction may be critiqued for many reasons, but Lévi-Strauss was not trying to correct people—he was trying to understand the structure of their thinking.[10]

Although critics may refer to Lévi-Strauss when talking about raw and cooked data, they are rarely pursuing this kind of analysis. Instead, they are usually working in the Lakoffian mode, making and evaluating mappings between domains in terms of their adequacy. The anthropologist Tom Boellstorff (2013), for instance, digs deeper into structuralism than most writers on data metaphors, drawing on an elaboration of the raw-cooked dichotomy, where Lévi-Strauss (1966) adds a third term, "rotten," to create "the culinary triangle." In this set, rawness comes to signify unelaborated materials in general: raw materials can be elaborated culturally, by cooking, or naturally, by rotting. In a Lakoffian move, Boellstorff seeks out a data analogue for "rot" and finds it in the notion of "bit rot"—a technical term for the degradation of data as its material substrates age.

The media theorist Maria Eriksson (2016) picks up Boellstorff's term to describe the lively, error-prone musical data that people like Ellie manage. What Ellie described as "the garden," Eriksson calls "rotten data": this data is neither raw nor cooked but exists in a state of error and decay. Such errors are intrinsic to constantly shifting data, and they persist in the analytic engines of companies like Whisper, making computational outputs more unpredictable and less rational than they may seem. By bringing in the idea of "rot," Boellstorff (2013) aims to draw attention to the persistence of "the unplanned, unexpected, and accidental," identifying a third option beyond the assumed opposites of natural stability and cultural intentionality.

Following Lévi-Strauss's structuralist goals more closely, we could interpret metaphors like gardening and farming not as singular source domains from which arbitrary features are borrowed but as contrastive pairs. So, looking again, we note that Pedro Domingos says machine learning is like farming because it is not like factory manufacture. Tim Quirk says that content programming is like being a park ranger because it is not like being a gatekeeper.

In each of these cases, the apparently natural metaphor is doing something more than naturalizing: it is being used to mark a break between some new way of doing things and an old way. Claiming that machine learning is like farming while conventional programming is like factory manufacture is a way of introducing a rupture into a history of computing that we might otherwise describe as gradual and continuous. This is, structurally speaking, what Lévi-Strauss suggests that cooking metaphors do for the nature-culture distinction: they provide the people who use them with a model for drawing a line between themselves and the world around them. Similarly, thinking of content programmers as akin to park rangers severs them from common comparisons to DJs or record store clerks.

If the problem with natural metaphors for data is the absence of humans, then there is something peculiar about the figures I have described here: the scenes they invoke are not devoid of people. Instead, they are focused on people doing very specific kinds of work. Within the context of machine learning, these pastoral self-descriptions appear as efforts to account for work that requires managing tools, inputs, and outputs produced by outside agencies, over which workers have a limited sort of control.

In other words, these visions of parks, farms, and gardens are not simply naturalizing because parks, farms, and gardens are not simply natural: they are *pastoral*. Like Marx's middle landscape, they attempt to carve out a space somewhere between the presumed control and rationality of technology and the uncontrolled disarray of the wilderness. In practice, the pastoral metaphor locates data work not in an idealized nature but at the intersection of the natural (i.e., lively and exogenous), the cultural (i.e., arbitrary and expressive), and the technical (i.e., planned and instrumented). They express an ambivalent, partial control, which, as we can see in the words of Quirk and Domingos, is understood as something new—a break with earlier modes of programming content and computers, and an embrace of the open plan.

When Ellie analogized her work to gardening, she was not making a mistake or trying to mystify the data she tended to; she was thinking about relationships among workers, algorithms, and data flows. Where critics of metaphors tend to focus on objects, people like Ellie use them to think about relationships between people and objects; the core of the gardening metaphor, in practice, is the act of gardening itself, not data, algorithms, or workers in isolation. Pastoral metaphors account for a feeling of control at a remove. As the operation of algorithmic systems plays out over time, it is guided by the choices of the humans within it (themselves patterned in cultural form), but those choices interact with flows of data and bits of computational infrastructure not under their control: surprises still grow out of algorithmic systems as error or serendipity.[11]

These elements of the system are caught up in broader ecologies of meaning and resource flows: a text-scraping bot that gathers key terms from a website breaks when the website is redesigned; a fan club begins streaming songs on repeat, changing the significance of a "play"; a new technique for analyzing audio data is published at an academic conference; another team implements its bit of software in the wrong place and the outputs stop making sense. The data gardeners and park rangers work to provide order according to their particular understanding of order, responsive to these unexpected events that never stop.

The Garden Path

The people who are not explicitly present in these pastoral metaphors are, usually, the users whose interactions produce much of the data and who are the audience for recommendations. We might extend the data-is-soil metaphor to its breaking point and argue that users are equivalent to the microbes or worms without which the soil would be lifeless and unusable. But when users do appear in these metaphors, they usually show up as "visitors," to be guided through the music space. Quirk described his role as the production and maintenance of paths through the musical jungle: "Being a park ranger means our job isn't to tell visitors what's great and why. Our job is to get them from any given thing they like to a variety of other things they might. We may have our own favorite paths and being park rangers we probably even prefer the less crowded ones, but our job is to keep them all maintained so visitors to our park can choose their own adventure" (quoted in Resnikoff 2014). In chapter 2, I suggested that we might expand the analogy of recommender systems and traps to think specifically about pastoralists, who organize environments for their herds that simultaneously constrain and enable them. There, we saw pastoralism as a kind of loose enclosure that does not transfix its prey (like the gripping artworks that interested Alfred Gell) but surrounds it and sets conditions for its existence. In the figure of the path, we can see these two senses of pastoralism—tending to land and tending to animals—come together.

Quirk explained the influence that the people building his system had over their users: "They might not feel our hand on their backs as they wander, but it's there. It's just subtle." This is a kind of power that many critics of algorithmic personalization have explained by reference to Deleuze's (1992, 4) theory of control societies: "systems of variable geometry," which displace older and more clearly defined enclosures (like schools or prisons) with "self-deforming cast[s] that will continuously change from one moment to the other" (see Galloway 2004; Franklin 2015). The enclosures of the old music industry, manned by gatekeepers, give way to the apparent openness and freedom of the park, but park rangers subtly keep you on their paths.

The cultural theorist John Cheney-Lippold (2011, 177) has elaborated the Deleuzian argument as a form of "soft biopower": "Enclosure offers the idea of walls, of barriers to databases and surveillance technologies. Openness describes a freedom to action that at the same time is also vulnerable to surveillance and manipulation." If hard biopower works through the force of categorization, according to Cheney-Lippold, then soft biopower works at a remove, as "a guiding mechanism that opens and closes particular conditions of possibility that users can encounter" (175). It is power not through domination but through modulation.

Control societies are commonly posed as the successors to the sovereign and disciplinary societies famously analyzed by Michel Foucault (e.g., Galloway 2004, 27), reflecting the ascendance of computation as a tool of social ordering. Foucault scholars have suggested that we can also understand these techniques as a kind of "algorithmic governmentality": a mode of rationality "founded on the automated collection, aggregation and analysis of big data so as to model, anticipate and pre-emptively affect possible behaviors" (Rouvroy and Berns 2013).

Without straying too far from our concern with how these actors themselves understand what they're doing, we can find something useful to our present concerns in Foucault's writing about the genealogy of governmentality, where he traces this governmental ethos back to late antiquity, in the Christian pastorate—a form of power he calls, not coincidentally, "pastoral power." The critical theorist Rosalind Cooper (2019, 4) has argued that thinking of algorithms in terms of pastoral power helps us understand them not as distinctly new, but rather as part of "a long[ue] durée historical inclination" that spans most of "Western" civilization.[12]

Pastoral power is the "art of conducting, directing, leading, guiding, taking in hand, and manipulating men" (Foucault 2007, 165). Three defining qualities of Foucault's pastoral power are particularly relevant to the kind of power exercised through recommender systems. First, it is "defined by its beneficence": this power manifests as a kind of duty or obligation to care for the flock, "leading it to good pastures" and seeing to its overall well-being (Foucault 2007, 172). Second, unlike other powerful figures such as kings, the shepherd's pastoral power is not exercised on a bounded territory, but over a "multiplicity on the move" (171)— an intrinsically shifting and mobile flock, which means the shepherd's power is also shifting and mobile, with no recourse to something like sovereign power over a given domain. Third, this power over the flock (and obligation to care for it) means that the shepherd is concerned both for the flock as a whole and for each of its individual members, *omnes et singulatim*—each and every. This concern for the relationship between wholes and parts, for the way that power produces particular kinds of collectivities and individuals at once, came to animate much of Foucault's thinking on biopolitics.

We can find all three qualities abundant in the accounts that the makers of music recommendation give of their work: they understand themselves to be beneficent figures, even when using the language of trapping; they attend to clusters of users and music that are constantly shifting; and the "personalization" they seek to offer is aimed at both individual users and the overall collective. Recent critical theorists writing on technologies like recommender systems have tended to argue that "power is increasingly in the algorithm" (Lash 2007, 70), moving away from human control. But if, as I've been arguing throughout this book, algorithms are in fact populated by humans who make significant decisions and exercise some control over them, then such arguments make it hard to talk about these people. Foucault's writing on pastoral power helpfully points to a durable constellation of cultural values (the obligation to care, to manage a mobile and shifting collectivity by attending to its individual members, imagined with reference to the definitionally pastoral figure of the shepherd) for understanding the exercise of power by people like the makers of music recommendation. To be clear, this is not a defense of this form of power or how it is exercised: it is plainly possible for actors with beneficent intent to cause harm. But it is also useful for us to develop a deeper understanding of how these technical actors understand their ethical obligations and power to act. If we want to imagine alternatives to the recommender systems that currently populate our world, we need to think more deeply about who makes them, how they do it, and why.

The digital ethics scholars Luke Stark and Anna Lauren Hoffmann (2019) have also used the metaphors of data science as a way to imagine alternative ethical formations: in a study of professional ethics codes, they collected documents from various computing-related professional organizations as well as industries commonly used as metaphorical source domains for talking about computing, like forestry and petroleum engineering. They found that, in contrast to the codes of computer scientists, many of these other fields figured "stewardship" as a core ethical concern: foresters, for instance, describe an obligation to care for the world's forests.[13] Stark and Hoffmann (2019, 12) suggest that stewardship, or a "responsibility to broadly construed spaces, sites, or ideals," would be a welcome addition to the ethical imaginaries of computer scientists. Elaborating on the metaphor critiques discussed earlier, they write, "Analogizing digital data as 'natural' without stewardship discourses implicitly signals data—and the living people it involves—as open for rank exploitation" (Stark and Hoffmann 2019, 19).

In the pastoral discourses I've been describing here, we find an explicit emphasis on stewardship, as Stark and Hoffmann desire, and we also see some of stewardship's limits: a generic beneficence and understanding of one's own influence is, as they suggest, a starting point for ethics, not its culmination. In Quirk's analogy and the pastoral metaphor more broadly, we find an apparently ambivalent relationship to control on the part of people working within these algorithmic systems: they do not deny their power to shape user experience, to impose their own order on data, or to rearrange computational infrastructures. But their experience of control is not as a master planner from above but as an interactor within, where their attempts at ordering butt up against recalcitrant others.

When Ellie talks about data gardening, we learn about her position within an algorithmic system that is often chaotic. She exerts influence over unruly collections of data but in a limited way that "gardening" usefully captures. When Domingos talks about farming, he mystifies farmwork to introduce a break into the history of computing. When Quirk puts on the role of the park ranger, he tries to account for a kind of cultural intermediary power that has a new shape, which is influential but not absolute.

Pastoral figures metaphorize the programmer's place in the contemporary corporation: they are not in control of how the business works or how their users behave, but they often embrace a pastoral obligation, working where they are to facilitate exploration and growth. The early collaborative filters in systems like Ringo were fairly simple computational objects; the work of contemporary algorithmic systems unfolds complexly over time and in a variety of broader ecologies through which data, people, and techniques move. The pastoral metaphor usefully indexes the kinds of bounded control that are achieved within these systems. Algorithmic recommendations manifest connections that exceed and precede them, resisting and surprising their human minders: data comes already contoured by cultural worlds, and the spaces data gardeners tend are not entirely theirs to shape.

What Are We Really Doing Here?

Three years after I wound down my fieldwork among the makers of music recommendation, I finally managed to interview Greg. Greg was one of Whisper's founders, and for about seven years, he had studiously avoided my efforts to interview him. We crossed paths many times, at conferences, in the office, and on social media, but I had never gotten him alone with an audio recorder. Now, Greg had left Whisper to found a new company, and he was willing to talk.

We met in the coworking space that held his new company's temporary offices, on the fifteenth floor of an anonymous downtown skyscraper. He recalled the optimistic vision that had animated his earlier work: "The power of a really good recommendation, to me, was always the one defining mission of Whisper: The tiny artist gets more fans. The listener over here gets really excited about a brand-new discovery. That's really, at the end of the day, what the mission of Whisper was, and it never changed." Like the others we've heard from throughout this book, Greg was enthusiastic about music discovery, and he saw recommender systems as a way to broaden listeners' horizons and help less popular artists gather audiences. When Greg and his colleagues began to work on music recommendation, they were idealistic outsiders, building systems that not many people used: "To be honest, I was incredibly naive to think that this was even possible. Like, if we get this perfect, imagine how great it's going to be, to be a musician or a listener in the near future."

Over time, the makers of music recommendation succeeded: their work became central to the business of music streaming services, and more and more people used them more and more often. Measured by captivation metrics, at least, music recommendation finally seemed to work. Whisper was acquired for tens of millions of dollars, and the basic premises of algorithmic recommendation were woven deeper into the infrastructures of digital music circulation.

For many years, Greg's bio on social media read "Fruitlessly analyzing human preference since 1999." It was not uncommon to hear people whose livelihoods depended on building recommender systems express profound doubt that they could ever really work; that doubt alternated with an enthusiasm for making connections and finding new music, and it was belied by growing commercial success. I asked Greg about the joke, and he replied, "It's sort of like we're almost afraid of our own power, in a little way—I think."

Jokes like these reflected an ambivalence about overblown claims for machine learning—"I knew it was never going to be possible to have a perfect understanding of music"—as well as some discomfort with their makers' increasing ability to shape how music circulated. Greg reminisced about a hackathon project he had made early on, which he called Future of Music: "You'd run it on your laptop, on your own MP3 collection. It would actually do collaborative filtering on your collection and then delete all the songs that didn't fit your model, so it would delete 20 percent of your music. I actually ran it live on the demo stage and ended up deleting some of my music. It was pretty funny." Future of Music was another joke—a self-satire that imagined what would happen if faith in algorithmic recommendation were taken to an extreme. In it, we can see an anxiety about the power of recommendation and how, by anticipating listeners too narrowly, recommender systems might constrain people's listening instead of broadening it.

"Why did scientists do anything with music to begin with?," Greg asked me. "Any scientist that was working on music recs back in the midwhatever 2000s was doing it for the same reasons. It was because they wanted to connect people and music." This connective ethos was shared by many others in the software industry.[1] But now, reflecting on his success, Greg turned somber: "It's almost, like, what if that, but too much? And what's going to happen next?"

In his enthusiasm for connection and discovery, Greg had not anticipated what might happen when recommender systems came together with increasingly powerful platforms: "I spent a good total of, what now, thirteen years or so working on music recommendation, and two things came out of it that scared me a little bit. One was the amount of data we have on people. The other was what that can be used for—I was surprised by the anticonsumer uses of data analysis." As we've seen throughout this book, recommender systems have grown to encompass more data sources, profiling listeners in ever more flexible ways. These centralized collections of data pose privacy concerns, as critics have long argued; while a user's listening history may not seem especially sensitive, Greg pointed out that listening histories could in fact be quite revealing, hinting at a user's sexuality or political affiliation.

"Now," he said, "you can imagine, when those markets scale up, what kind of power do we have over people on the platform?" With the growing popularity of streaming music services, "It's a totally different ball game now. A company looks at this very powerful platform linking people to music, and they see that as a tool they can use to change things about that process." Algorithmic recommendation could be used not only to introduce listeners and artists to one another but also to shape a music industry that was increasingly dependent on algorithmic reach.

Whatever values engineers and scientists like Greg might have, they were constrained by their position within companies and industries. If the business unit decided to prioritize retaining listeners over introducing them to less popular music, there was little the engineering team could do. "I was conflicted," Greg told me, "What are we really doing here?"

: :

I was out of practice and had forgotten a key rule of ethnographic interviewing: the most interesting thing often happens just after you turn off the recorder.

As we walked out of the office, Greg told me that he had recently seen Richard, one of his former colleagues at Whisper I had known for many years. He mentioned our upcoming interview, and Richard seemed surprised: "You're meeting with Nick? I thought you didn't like him." Greg reassured me that this wasn't true—"I like you!"—and told me that he asked, "Why do you think that?" Richard answered, "Because you never let him interview you." "Oh no," Greg replied, "I do like him; I just don't believe in corporate anthropology."

Greg explained what this disbelief meant, pointing out the window of the coworking space, above the neighboring buildings and trees. "If you went to the Andes or something, you might get to some scientific truth about what's going on. But you'll never get the truth about a company like Wavelet or Wonder." The idea, I gathered, was that fieldwork in conventional anthropological field sites was straightforward: go to the village, and you can find out what you want to know. This was, of course, not true, but Greg was certainly not alone in thinking it.

Anthropologists of corporations, by contrast, were up against institutions that were definitionally secretive and hard to access—I knew this all too well. But more than that, they were dissimulating: "You'll never get the truth about companies like those—those truths are hidden under a layer of lies." Corporations are complex and ambivalent: they do not speak with one voice, and one employee's point of view may be straightforwardly contradicted by another's. I had dealt with this problem by adjusting my scope, getting to know the engineers and scientists who generally shared a worldview with one another and were willing to share it with me. But, I had learned, there was more to it than that: the makers of music recommendation, as they moved from the margins to the center of digital music distribution, had encountered conflict and limits to their ideals.

Many outside critics hope to find within recommender systems a singular logic that we might repudiate or repair. But that is not how they work. As one engineer put it, "Every industrial recommender system I've seen or worked on was a lumbering amalgam of recommendation techniques, cultural data, and product beliefs." These systems embody goals and theories that may seem incoherent or even at odds with each other.

As they pursued visions of open plans and musical connection, the makers of music recommendation found themselves caught up by their own success, put in positions of power that they did not really know how to manage. They responded with ambivalence: They joke and doubt. They embrace the promise of data and then disavow it. They profile users and try to help them change. They uneasily navigate the tension between care and control.

Greg and I got to the doorway, and I laughed nervously, as he cast doubt on the idea that it was even possible to write a book like this. He called out, "So . . . good luck!"

I walked away to the elevators.

Acknowledgments

I have been working on this book for a very long time. Since I first started thinking about music recommendation in 2009, my life has changed several times. Through all of it, including a few coast-to-coast moves, Christina Agapakis has been my closest and most patient interlocutor, partner, and friend. Thank you for literally everything.

I would never have gotten to this point without my teachers. My parents, Sonja Berggren and Patrick Seaver, always indulged my curiosity and gave me room to grow. Stephen Davis introduced me to interpretation. Dodie McDow recognized coherence in my intellectual aimlessness. Haun Saussy shepherded me into the world of scholarship when I truly had no idea what I was doing. William Uricchio and Henry Jenkins got me thinking about media, and Stefan Helmreich steered me into anthropological waters.

This book began at the University of California, Irvine, supervised by the extraordinary Bill Maurer. I am grateful to my mentors who pushed and pulled on my thinking as this project took shape: Tom Boellstorff, Geof Bowker, Kavita Philip, George Marcus, and Melissa Mazmanian. Through their courses and advice, Julia Elyachar, Keith Murphy, Kris Peterson, and Mei Zhan all helped me become a better anthropologist.

My fellow students at UC Irvine were an indispensable source of joy and commiseration. Thanks to my classmates Colin Cahill, Ben Cox, Padma Govindan, Georgia Hartman, and Beth Reddy. Chima Anyadike-Danes deserves special mention: his encyclopedic disciplinary knowledge helped me become a weirder thinker, and his influence permeates this book. Taylor Nelms, who remains one of the most brilliant anthropologists I know, shone a clarifying light on so many drafts. Lilly Irani,

Ellie Harmon, and Marisa Cohn pushed me to think more deeply about the work of making software.

This book could not have existed without my interlocutors in the field, who welcomed me into their offices and homes, were generous with their time, and put up with an endless stream of strange questions.

The research behind this book was funded by grants from the Wenner Gren Foundation (Dissertation Fieldwork Grant 8797) and the National Science Foundation (Doctoral Dissertation Research Improvement Grant 1323834). I was also lucky to be supported by the Intel Science and Technology Center for Social Computing, which provided some funding, but more importantly, a broad and brilliant network of peers and mentors: Morgan Ames, Mariam Asad, Solon Barocas, Ian Bogost, Jed Brubaker, Alex Campolo, Carl DiSalvo, Lynn Dombrowski, Paul Dourish, Mel Gregg, Judith Gregory, Tamara Kneese, Cory Knobel, Max Liboiron, Courtney Loder, Scott Mainwaring, Dawn Nafus, Lilly Nguyen, Helen Nissenbaum, Katie Pine, Winifred Poster, Erica Robles-Anderson, Phoebe Sengers, Luke Stark, Kaiton Williams, and Malte Ziewitz, among many others. Thanks to Jenny Fan, Norma Miranda, and Julio Rodriguez for their administrative support.

I wrapped up the project at Microsoft Research, where the Social Media Collective provided a nurturing home for writing and an enduring network of brilliant scholars. Thanks to Tarleton Gillespie, Nancy Baym, and Mary Gray for all of their support and mentorship through the years.

I am privileged now to work with many kind and supportive colleagues at Tufts University, where this book found its finish. Thanks to Rosalind Shaw and Nancy Bauer for welcoming me into the department and the school. Joe Auner, Amahl Bishara, Alex Blanchette, Liz Canter, Tatiana Chudakova, Ricky Crano, Moon Duchin, Sharon Kivenko, Sarah Luna, Zarin Machanda, Canay Özden-Schilling, Tom Özden-Schilling, Maria Sidorkina, Emilio Spadola, and Cathy Stanton, among many others, have been part of a wonderful scholarly community. Without the administrative expertise of Jamie Gorman and Lynn Wiles, I would have been lost. My students have been an inspiration and a constant spur to thought.

As I struggled to wrangle my attention and take care of myself, Cindy Blank-Edelman and Dusty Chipura provided much-needed guidance and support. Laura Portwood-Stacer helped me crack the shell of my dissertation and let a book out.

I am very grateful to the editorial staff of the University of Chicago Press for their help making this book real. Priya Nelson saw the promise in my project earlier than anyone else and brought me in. Joe Calamia picked me up and helped me bring a book out. My gratitude also goes to Jason Weidemann of the University of Minnesota Press for his editorial advice and enthusiasm. Thanks to Katherine Faydash for her careful copyediting, Derek Gottlieb for preparing the index, and Tasha Bigelow for proofreading assistance.

Over the years it has taken me to finish this book, I have been lucky enough to talk about its contents in so many venues and with so many people that I can scarcely remember them all. These people have shaped me and the book in ways large and small. Thanks to Mike Ananny, Ken Anderson, Andrea Ballestero, Dwai Banerjee, Ritwik Banerji, Michael Barany, Adia Benton, Georgina Born, danah boyd, Marisa Brandt, Sarah Brayne, Taina Bucher, Baki Cakici, Matei Candea, Jenny Carlson, Alberto Corsín Jiménez, Kate Crawford, Rebekah Cupitt, Anaar Desai-Stevens, Fernando Diaz, Stephanie Dick, Anne Dippel, Rachel Douglas-Jones, Kevin Driscoll, Joe Dumit, Blake Durham, Michael Ekstrand, Sam Weiss Evans, Laura Forlano, Maya Indira Ganesh, Stuart Geiger, James N. Gilmore, Danya Glabau, Wesley Goatley, Kaleb Goldschmitt, Joseph Guisti, Blake Hallinan, Orit Halpern, Alex Hanna, Eric Harvey, Christopher Haworth, Cori Hayden, C.-F. Helgesson, Anna Lauren Hoffmann, Rebecca Jablonsky, Caroline Jack, Robin James, Rae Jereza, Anna Jobin, Natalie Kane, Chris Kelty, Paul Kockelman, Jordan Kraemer, Jesse Kriss, Marcel LaFlamme, Martha Lampland, Débora Lanzeni, Lotta Larsen, Francis Lee, Jenn Lena, Celia Lury, Annette Markham, Wayne Marshall, Emily Martin, Shannon Mattern, Tressie McMillan Cottom, David Moats, Amanda Modell, Jeremy Morris, Dylan Mulvin, Chloe Nahum-Claudel, Mace Ojala, Grant Jun Otsuki, Anar Parikh, Heather Paxson, Chris Peterson, Justin Pickard, Trevor Pinch, Robert Prey, Elena Razlogova, David Ribes, John Rieffel, Evelyn Ruppert, Jathan Sadowski, Daniel Salas, Tomás Sánchez Criado, Christian Sandvig, Natasha Dow Schüll, Beth Semel, Gerald Sim, Alma Steingart, Marilyn Strathern, Lucy Suchman, Lana Swartz, Ezra Teboul, Angela VandenBroek, Janet Vertesi, Georgina Voss, Antonia Walford, Moira Weigel, and Ben Wurgaft. The online community of scholars and critics on Twitter has provided a constant source of entertainment, friendship, and anxiety.

An earlier version of chapter 2 appeared in my article "Captivating Algorithms: Recommender Systems as Traps," published in the *Journal of Material Culture* 24, no. 4 (2019): 421–36. Portions of chapter 3 are drawn from several previously published articles: "Seeing Like an Infrastructure: Avidity and Difference in Algorithmic Recommendation," *Cultural Studies* 35, nos. 4–5 (2021): 771–91; "The Nice Thing about Context Is That Everyone Has It," *Media, Culture & Society* 37, no. 7 (2015): 1101–9; and "Algorithmic Recommendations and Synaptic Functions," *Limn* 2

(2012): 46–49. Portions of chapter 4 were published in Russian translation as "Тардовская статистика, машинный слух и Big Data. Все, что воспринимаемо, лишь число," *Sociology of Power* 30, no. 3 (2018): 193–200. Portions of chapter 5 were published in "Everything Lies in a Space: Cultural Data and Spatial Reality," *Journal of the Royal Anthropological Institute* 27, supplement 1 (2021): 43–61. Part of chapter 6 appeared in "Care and Scale: Decorrelative Ethics in Algorithmic Recommendation," *Cultural Anthropology* 36, no. 3 (2021): 509–37. I thank the publishers for permission to use those materials here, and I thank the editors and reviewers for their help making my arguments cohere.

At a crucial moment in my revising, Stefan Helmreich, Deirdre Loughridge, and Lisa Messeri came together in a manuscript workshop to help me figure out what I was doing. As I brought this book to a finish, I was blessed with a set of generous and incisive readings: Tarleton Gillespie, Jonathan Sterne, Dan Greene, and two anonymous reviewers helped me to see what I had written in a clearer light and to draw out its strengths. Its remaining weaknesses are, of course, my own.

Before the pandemic sent us all home, much of this book was written and rewritten next to cups of coffee at Tamper Cafe in Medford. Thanks for the table space and the caffeine.

Finishing this book after the pandemic began would have been unfathomable without childcare support, and I am unfathomably grateful to Effie and John Agapakis for agreeing to spend much more time with their grandchildren than any grandparents should have to. Before the great turning-in, Nirmala and Ramesh Sharma and the staff of the Bright Horizons in Teele Square expertly nurtured and supported my children. Without them, this book could not exist.

Gus and Poppy have spent their entire lives under the shadow of this book, brightening my days and changing my life. Thanks for all of it.

Notes

Prologue

1. See Jennifer Kaufmann-Buhler's *Open Plan: A Design History of the American Office* (2020) for an account of the open plan's evolution since its midcentury origins.

2. Throughout this book, I have given pseudonyms to many of the organizations and people that participated in my research. Companies beginning with the letter *W* are pseudonymous, as are people introduced by first name alone. In some cases, details have been slightly altered or multiple entities joined into composites to maintain anonymity.

3. See Sherry Ortner's classic essay "On Key Symbols" (1973).

Introduction

1. The Verge, "Interview with Beats Music CEO Ian Rogers," YouTube video, 8:00, January 21, 2014, https://www.youtube.com/watch?v=EkwoGRZ3onk.

2. Throughout this book, quotations from the internet have been slightly altered to protect the identity of anonymized sources.

3. See my "What Should an Anthropology of Algorithms Do?" (Seaver 2018) for an extended treatment of this question.

4. See the reading list I assembled with Tarleton Gillespie (Gillespie and Seaver 2015) for evidence of the breadth and bulk of this work by the mid-2010s. More recent landmark books in the field include Safiya Umoja Noble's *Algorithms of Oppression* (2018), Taina Bucher's *If . . . Then: Algorithmic Power and Politics* (2018), and Virginia Eubanks's *Automating Inequality: How High-Tech Tools Profile, Police, and Punish the Poor* (2018).

5. For an extended treatment of this dichotomy and efforts to reimagine it, see my "Care and Scale: Decorrelative Ethics in Algorithmic Recommendation" (Seaver 2021a).

6. Readers may note that I have roughly followed this dramatic arc in the current chapter.

7. See my "Knowing Algorithms" (Seaver 2019) for more on the role of revelation in critical discourse about algorithms.

8. See Angèle Christin's "The Ethnographer and the Algorithm: Beyond the Black Box" (2020) for another approach to this question, emerging from sociological ethnography.

9. For a more extended treatment of ethnographic tactics, see my "Algorithms as Culture: Some Tactics for the Ethnography of Algorithmic Systems" (Seaver 2017).

10. Thomas Malaby's *Making Virtual Worlds: Linden Lab and Second Life* (2009) is a good example of what kinds of inquiry extended access at a specific software company can support, focused more on the social organization of the firm and its particular vision than a whole business sector.

Chapter 1

1. Nicholas Negroponte (1995, 149, 154), founder and director of the MIT Media Lab, described these systems as "digital butlers" or, uniquely, "digital sisters-in-law."

2. See Jonathan Cohn's "Female Labor and Digital Media" (2013) for an extended analysis of Maes's work in this period that connects it with "postfeminism." I elaborate more on the postdemographic framing of recommender systems in chapter 3.

3. Ironically, this claim is the reverse of what I more frequently heard from people working in the 2010s. By then, audio analysis was generally held to deliver more surprising results (often undesirably so), whereas ratings-based systems were taken to engender rather dull outcomes.

4. An earlier prototype of the system had been designed to recommend science fiction books (Maes 1994).

5. This figure also imagines a masculine, high-status user for recommendation—a concern I return to later.

6. The origins of the term are murky, but Patrick Burkart and Tom McCourt (2004, 359n1) report: "A long-time observer of the music industry [Seth Greenstein] told the authors that the RIAA [Recording Industry Association of America] used the term in 1989–1990 to obtain performance rights for digital transmissions."

7. For more on the orienting power of satellite visions, see Lisa Parks's *Cultures in Orbit* (2005).

8. The celestial jukebox was thus magical in an anthropological sense. Like the Trobriand gardening spells cataloged in Bronislaw Malinowski's *Coral Gardens and Their Magic* (1935), the celestial jukebox conjured an ideal situation in which mediation was "costless"—free of the "drudgery, hazards and investments which actual technical activity inevitably requires" (Gell 1988, 9). Gell continued: "Yam roots will strike down into the soil with the swiftness of a green parrot in flight, and the foliage above will dance and weave like dolphins playing in the surf," and anyone will be able to listen to their favorite song at any time in any place (9). Making a case for the similarity between magic and technology, Gell described magical statements like these as positing "an ideal standard, not to be approached in reality, towards which practical technical activity can nonetheless be organized" (8). Magic's efficacy, then, was not a matter of occult operations, but the orienting power of idealized visions, which downplayed their practical challenges. See Elish and boyd (2018) on magical discourses in machine learning and artificial intelligence and Singleton (2013) on this theme in relation to outer space and escape.

9. See the 2014 Nielsen Music U.S. report: https://www.nielsen.com/wp-content/uploads/sites/3/2019/04/nielsen-2014-year-end-music-report-us-1.pdf.

10. *A&R* is short for "artist and repertoire"—the people responsible for identifying and recruiting new artists for labels.

11. If I had chosen to focus on "choice," this analysis may have gone down the path

followed by the sociologist Dan Kotliar in his "Who Gets to Choose? On the Socio-Algorithmic Construction of Choice" (2021), which describes recommender systems as a form of "choice-inducing algorithm" operating in a broader "culture of choice" (Schwarz 2018). Although choice overload and information overload were generally treated as synonymous in the field, it is worth noting that they can be analytically distinguished: If choice overload emerges when a person is faced with a set of too many plausible options, then a recommender system can actually *produce* choice overload by presenting a user with a greater number of appealing items than they would have previously considered (Bollen et al. 2010).

12. Adorno (1976, 45) didn't much like jukeboxes either, seeing them, like satellites, as distracting attractions for the easily fooled: "Thus the jukebox in an empty pub will blare in order to lure 'suckers' with its false pretense of revelry in progress."

13. The webinar is archived here: Association for Computing Machinery, "'Recommender Systems: The Power of Personalization,' Joe Konstan," YouTube video, 58:37, July 16, 2013, https://www.youtube.com/watch?v=w8rLW6magqs.

14. While Konstan was working on GroupLens in the mid-1990s, Peter Pirolli and Stuart Card (1995), researchers at Xerox PARC, developed what they called "information foraging theory," which formalized this analogy, suggesting that humans seeking information could be understood using models borrowed from evolutionary ecologists and anthropologists studying human and animal foraging behavior. See also Marcia Bates's (1989) theory of "berrypicking" techniques in information retrieval.

15. On the semiotic potential of ant touch-glands, see Ursula Le Guin's 1983 short story "The Author of the Acacia Seeds," excerpted from the fictional *Journal of the Association of Therolinguistics*.

16. In the world of music recommendation, this story was repeated at the streaming radio company Pandora, which saw the return of its founder, Tim Westergren, who had famously guided the company through dire early days to temporary success (McGregor 2016).

17. Although Toffler is often credited with popularizing or even coining the term "information overload" today, Nick Levine (2017, 42–43) has shown that this reputation only emerged recently; in a steady stream of US journalistic accounts of information overload dating from the 1970s to the present, Toffler almost never appears until 1999.

18. Other cultural touchpoints here include J. G. Ballard's short story "The Overloaded Man" (1967), first published in 1961, which depicted a professor progressively abstracting his own mental processes away from the overwhelming detail of the world, and Gertrude Stein's (1998) last published work, "Reflection on the Atomic Bomb"—a fragment arguing that the only way to cope with the overwhelming force of nuclear weaponry was to ignore it altogether.

19. In a long historical continuity, Pope Francis cautioned about the perils of information overload in his 2015 papal encyclical *Laudato si'* (https://www.vatican.va/content/francesco/en/encyclicals/documents/papa-francesco_20150524_enciclica-laudato-si.html), warning that "the great sages of the past run the risk of going unheard amid the noise and distractions of an information overload."

20. Another interpretation, admittedly, would be that the fixed human capacity to cope with our collective media production was indeed overwhelmed at the advent of the printed word (or perhaps with the introduction of the codex) and things have only been getting worse since then.

21. We could describe overload in this context as the failure state of the flâneur—what happens when Walter Benjamin's (1999) prototypically idle male urban wanderer becomes overwhelmed by the setting he is meant to detachedly observe.

22. The shape of the modern research university itself, Wellmon (2015) claims, emerged in early nineteenth-century Germany as a collection of techniques for organizing and managing problems of academic scale.

23. Nonetheless, Peters's critical history of information traces out, at wide discursive scale, transformations in the term's meaning from its origins in medieval scholastic philosophy, through the emergence of statistics and telegraphy, to its contemporary ubiquity.

24. See Jonathan Sterne's *MP3: The Meaning of a Format* (2012, 78–88) for an account of Shannon's debts to earlier telephone system researchers, particularly in relation to the study of hearing.

25. This was not only a projection from cybernetics outward. In lectures in 1954 and 1955, psychoanalyst Jacques Lacan picked up the circuitous metaphors of cybernetics to describe how minds could be "jammed" like telephone lines (see Mills 2010).

26. Riedl and Resnick's presentation is archived online here: University of Michigan School of Information, "The Most Cited CSCW Paper Ever," YouTube video, 37:51, June 3, 2013, https://www.youtube.com/watch?v=iFL8rEoWic4.

27. Speaking as though he were back in 1994, Riedl joked that he hoped the Better Business Bureau wouldn't send them a cease and desist for trademark infringement. Breaking character at the end of the talk, he revealed that they in fact did receive a cease and desist from the Better Business Bureau, but that it was "one of the nicest cease and desists I've ever received."

28. Some version of this claim is usually found on Facebook's official, frequently updated explanation of how its newsfeed works: https://www.facebook.com/help/1155510281178725.

29. The talk is archived online here: ACM RecSys, "RecSys 2016: Paper Session 7—Algorithms Aside: Recommendation as the Lens of Life," YouTube video, 15:56, March 30, 2017, https://www.youtube.com/watch?v=Emgxg5Drr1k.

30. For a more extended critique of this naturalizing of filtering as a basic social activity, see Wendy Hui Kyong Chun's *Discriminating Data: Correlation, Neighborhoods, and the New Politics of Recognition* (2021).

31. Ironically enough, this argument for the omnipresence of filtering and the impossibility of any direct, uncontoured access to reality fits well with a substantial body of literature in media theory, anthropology, and science and technology studies (e.g., Bowker 2013). And more contemporary social theory is itself descended in one way or another from cybernetics (see, e.g., Paidipaty 2020).

Chapter 2

1. For more on the relationship between habits and new media, see Wendy Hui Kyong Chun's *Updating to Remain the Same* (2016).

2. Since I first drafted this chapter, these critiques have grown to the point that US senators have introduced bills to ban common behavioral design techniques; but even there, music recommendation has been exempted from regulation (Hawley 2019).

3. Quoted from captology.stanford.edu, as captured by the Internet Archive in April 2002.

4. In her book on machine gambling, Natasha Dow Schüll (2012, 293) describes similar appeals to user agency as a "ready-made ethical escape route" for the makers of slot machines confronted with the addictive consequences of their work.

5. For a similar theorization within the domain of advertising, see Franck Cochoy's (2007) "A Brief Theory of the 'Captation' of Publics."

6. See "Evaluating Collaborative Filtering Recommender Systems" (Herlocker et al. 2004) for a technical survey of evaluation techniques.

7. This metric exists and is called the "mean bias error."

8. Blake Hallinan and Ted Striphas give a more thorough account of the contest in their article "Recommended for You: The Netflix Prize and the Production of Algorithmic Culture" (2016).

9. The worst RMSE achieved during the Netflix Prize was 3.1679, achieved on purpose (to be so bad is challenging) by a team called Lanterne Rouge.

10. Sometimes, the pragmatism was quite literal. Mike's slide decks occasionally included a quote he attributed to the pragmatist philosopher William James: "What's true is what works."

11. While this factoid was commonly circulated at conferences, I was never able to find anyone who knew its source.

12. Such "front end" work is commonly feminized in the software industry more generally (see Posner 2017).

13. See Michael Ekstrand and Martijn Willemsen's "Behaviorism Is Not Enough" (2016) for an effort from within the recommender systems research community to push against this behaviorist framing in favor of letting users "speak."

14. In the case of search engines, Elizabeth Van Couvering (2007) argues that other goals than satisfaction are possible and desirable: a search engine that aimed to serve the public good, for instance, might act differently with regard to controversial material than one tuned solely to satisfaction.

15. Holes are hard for museums to accession, but so are other sorts of traps, which tend to unmake themselves in the act of trapping or to biodegrade and fade back into the environments where they are hidden. As a result, the traps registered in collections and photos are usually reproductions made specifically for collectors.

16. I would be remiss if I did not describe this particular trap in more detail. According to Hrdlička (1916, 547), these pits contained not only rabbit bait but also a man hidden underneath the bait, such that when the bird of prey swooped down, the man "would quickly seize the bird by the feet, pull it under the rafters into the dark, and wring its neck." This trap would be famously analyzed by Claude Lévi-Strauss in *The Savage Mind* (1966, 50).

17. Mason's counterpart at Oxford, Henry Balfour (1925), for instance, took an interest in the distribution of Melanesian fish traps—long narrow baskets, lined with the thorny ribs of calamus plants—as evidence for a particular pattern of migration across the islands, only to receive word from E. E. Evans-Pritchard that similar traps were being used to catch rats in South Sudan (Balfour 1932), suggesting that the basic mechanism had likely been invented multiple times in multiple places.

18. See Benedict Singleton's "On Craft and Being Crafty" (2014) for a discussion of the relationship between traps, design, and trickery.

19. In the posthumously published *Art and Agency* (1998, 68), Gell uses *captivation*

more narrowly than I do here, reserving it for one particular mechanism of enchantment, which finds the beholder of a work of art transfixed by imagining the expertise required to make it.

20. The structure of the Netflix Prize would also come to serve as a model for other machine-learning contests, encouraging enthusiasts and professionals around the world to try their hand at designing systems to identify birdcalls, rate chess players, or diagnose cancerous tumors. Kaggle, an Australian company founded shortly after the end of the Netflix Prize in 2010, is currently the most popular platform for hosting such contests.

21. Ironically, as the series' director noted in an interview, the show is now produced by Netflix: "It's all very exciting—a whole new bunch of *Black Mirror* episodes on the most fitting platform imaginable" (Birnbaum 2015).

22. I return to the question of pastoralism in chapter 6, where I discuss pastoral metaphors used by developers themselves.

23. Like any analogy, this one is not absolute: where start-ups aim for exponential growth, with the end goal of a successful "exit" or acquisition by a larger company, ecological understandings of pastoralism note that herds cannot grow out of control without threatening balance in the system (see also Rappaport 1967). In anthropological debates about whether pastoralism should be understood as a form of animal capitalism, this distinction has set them apart (Ingold 1980).

Chapter 3

1. See Jonathan Sterne's *The Audible Past* (2003, 172) for an account of the early twentieth-century erotics of headphone listening.

2. Ironically, the prize for the winner was a pair of Siege Stealth earbuds, in-ear headphones with hypermasculinist tactical branding, marketed to listeners who were "agro [*sic*] about music." Hype Machine, *Tumblr* post, April 6, 2020, http://hypem .tumblr.com/post/501086211.

3. Market researchers had, in fact, already been working along similar trajectories, toward fine-grained modeling of consumers based on purchasing habits rather than coarse demographic categories (Arvidsson 2002).

4. There is no easy answer here. Some critics have suggested solutions to racial bias in algorithmic systems that would require using explicit data about race. As Oscar Gandy (2011, 133) has argued, "not all efforts at segmentation and targeting are associated with commercial exploitation, marketplace discrimination and cumulative disadvantage": recognizing racialized patterns in music may not necessarily lead to negative outcomes, and ignoring them does not necessarily lead to positive ones.

5. Starbucks occupies a distinctive position in the history of what Anahid Kassabian (2013, 84–108) calls "ubiquitous listening." She dedicates a chapter of her book on background music to the close relationship between the coffee retailer and the world music label Putumayo. Rumors circulating in the music tech industry while I was in the field indicated that one streaming music service tested new versions of their smartphone application at an actual Starbucks in the southern United States, presumably to capture the opinion of indifferent listeners who were also socially and geographically distant from members of the trade press who might discover and report on such tests.

6. It goes without saying that this is not necessarily true: we could imagine avid fans of narrow styles of music or indifferent listeners who don't mind listening broadly.

7. Similarly, the media theorist Jonathan Cohn (2019) argues that the archetypal recommender system user is in fact a working mother, drawing on a retrospective interview with early RecSys originator Pattie Maes, who suggested that busy women were in particular need of the help that algorithmic recommendation might provide.

8. Peter, an enthusiastic listener of decidedly "uncool" genres of music, was described to me by a colleague as a "trans-savant"—someone who had essentially passed beyond the top of the pyramid, returning to the styles of music listened to by those at the bottom.

9. Thus occasioning media coverage with titles like "How Spotify's Music-Obsessed Culture Keeps Employees Hooked" (Titlow 2014). Critics often engage with music streaming services in these terms too: see *Spotify Teardown*, which draws the musical enthusiasm of that company's founders into question (Eriksson et al. 2019, 41).

10. Note the similarity between this argument for data mining and arguments for participant observation: what people say is not necessarily what they do. Tom would later advocate for a project comparing publicly stated "likes" on platforms like Facebook to actual listening behavior, which he took to be a listener's true likes.

11. Steve Woolgar's (1991) classic ethnographic study of user research in a computer firm in the late 1980s describes how user researchers maintained a privileged ability to speak on behalf of users; this boundary was not in effect during my fieldwork.

12. Critics of persona-based design practices (e.g., Massanari 2010) have described them as designing for "imaginary friends," noting that these figures are still typically defined by their use of particular product features.

13. Ironically, when Dourish's paper on context is cited by researchers in context-aware computing, it is often taken to be providing a pair of options, from which they reliably choose "representational" over Dourish's preferred "interactional" (e.g., Adomavicius and Tuzhilin 2011; but see Anand and Mobasher 2007 for an exception).

14. It is worth noting that this is a particularly Euro-American common sense. As Marilyn Strathern has argued: "Euro-Americans make sense of things by describing them as part of something else" (Schlecker and Hirsch 2001, 71).

Chapter 4

1. Thus, *signal processing* and *content analysis* were often taken as essentially synonymous in regard to music by my interlocutors, despite some definitions of signal processing that explicitly exclude questions of a signal's content (Sterne and Rodgers 2011, 33).

2. This is something that acoustic science—with its propensity for abstracting or cutting ears out of heads and attaching them to technical devices (Sterne 2003, 32)—has generally failed to appreciate.

3. Helmholtz was not the only source of this theory, but he was a very influential and popular proponent of it. For more on this history, see Alexandra Hui's *The Psychophysical Ear: Musical Experiments, Experimental Sounds, 1840–1910* (2013).

4. As should be clear by now, the original audio data is hardly "raw" in any absolute sense: "In audio, rawness is not a form of purity but a relative condition, a readiness to hand, an availability for subsequent processing" (Sterne and Rodgers 2011, 36).

5. For more on the role of sonification in scientific demonstration, see Alexanda Supper's "Data Karaoke: Sensory and Bodily Skills in Conference Presentations" (2015).

6. MFCCs are aurally equivalent to what the artist Harun Farocki calls "operational images," a concept Trevor Paglen (2014) has extended to techniques of machine learning.

7. He described this latter data set as "collaborative filtering" data, in recognition of its concern with interuser similarity, but it was quite abstracted away from the kinds of matrixes described in earlier chapters.

8. It is worth noting that the challenging complexity of software is not new with machine learning. In any moderately distributed software system—today, basically all of them—it is a challenge to figure out how they work, what they do, and whether they're working as intended. In one of the earliest ethnographies of software development, Georgina Born (1996, 109) described this issue as it manifested among the makers of experimental music software thirty years ago: "code is far from open and transparent to decode, even for the highly skilled authors themselves."

9. Note that Geertz adds physical and moral limits to the cognitive limits that tend to concern computer scientists.

Chapter 5

1. This is a persistent theme in the anthropology of science, developed by feminist scholars through the 1990s (e.g., Strathern 1992; Haraway 1997; Martin 1991).

2. For more on this history, see my essay "Bastard Algebra" (Seaver 2015).

3. For an extended treatment of the space and place distinction, see Lisa Messeri's *Placing Outer Space* (2016, esp. 13–16).

4. This is not unique to machine learning; as the mathematician Jordan Ellenberg (2014, 337) has noted: "Mathematicians ever since Descartes [and his analytic geometry] have enjoyed the wonderful freedom to flip back and forth between algebraic and geometric descriptions of the world."

5. The sociologist Dan Kotliar (2020b) describes this process as "the return of the social."

6. Looking to the top-left corner of figure 6, we might recognize an unremarked-on racialized corner, where an apparently Asian woman is located near the film adaptation of Alice Walker's *The Color Purple*. I have never seen this detail discussed by researchers. See Thao Phan and Scott Wark's "Racial Formations as Data Formations" (2021) for a discussion of similar dynamics to those I describe here in relation to race.

7. Another domain, which was out of the scope of my own research, is in the production of new market segments to sell to advertisers. For a discussion of how this plays out in one music analytics company, see the musicologist Eric Drott's "Music as a Technology of Surveillance" (2018b).

8. Even to see a three-dimensional space on a screen or printed page requires the

transformation of perspective, a representational technique that people learn to interpret as part of their enculturation in most contemporary societies.

9. It is worth noting that this is only a "curse" for those seeking to represent or analyze the space computationally, not for people living in it. Thanks to Jonathan Sterne for this observation.

10. See my "Everything Lies in a Space" (Seaver 2021b) for a longer treatment of such methods in the history of cognitive anthropology.

11. For more on the "embodied imagination" of scientific practitioners, see Natasha Myers and Joe Dumit's "Haptic Creativity and the Mid-Embodiments of Experimental Life" (2011).

12. While I have contrasted McDonald's genre categories with "conventional" musical genres, those conventions are themselves historically specific to the twentieth-century music industry, and as Eric Drott (2018a) notes, there is historical precedent for genre-like categorizations of music to be activity or location focused: the apparent novelty of "music for the gym" or "music for the office" is blunted by comparing it to eighteenth-century labels like *musica da chiesa* or *musica da teatro*.

13. The unpublished manuscript quoted in this paragraph was eventually published as "Chance the Rapper, Spotify, and Musical Categorization in the 2010s" (Johnson 2020).

14. Here is how the sociologist Gabriel Rossman (2015, 119) describes the same transformation: "Genre goes from being a set of fuzzy and overlapping categories to an irreducibly continuous set of multidimensional distances derived from a massive vector of content attributes [like a representation of musical sound] or a bipartite graph of consumers and objects [like the space produced by a collaborative filter]."

15. This was also the sentiment behind a third-party application called *Forgotify*, which would randomly play tracks from the Spotify catalog that had never been played before. Spotify declined to comment when the app went viral, noting that the company provided its own discovery tools. Likely this reticence to comment was due to the sobering statistic that drove *Forgotify*'s press coverage: 20 percent of the songs on Spotify, some four million of them at the time, had never been played (Palermino 2014).

16. Spotify Technology, Form F-1 registration, SEC filing, https://www.sec.gov/Archives/edgar/data/1639920/000119312518063434/d494294df1.htm.

17. For an ethnomusicological appraisal of such global genre formations, see Ward Keeler's "What's Burmese about Burmese Rap?" (2009).

18. See Robert Albro's "Writing Culture Doctrine" (2010) for an anthropological reflection of culture-as-terrain metaphors in the US military.

19. See Gavin Carfoot's "Musical Discovery, Colonialism, and the Possibilities of Intercultural Communication through Music" (2016) for a treatment of this theme in the music industry more broadly.

20. For a useful exposition of Franklin's typology, see Scott MacDonald's *The Garden in the Machine* (2001, 89–90).

21. See Dan Kotliar's "Data Orientalism: On the Algorithmic Construction of the Non-Western Other" (2020a) for a discussion of this dynamic in an Israeli data analytics firm, which also provides an excellent overview of work on "data colonialism" (Couldry and Mejias 2019).

Chapter 6

1. For more on the affective dimensions of contemporary tech work, see Sareeta Amrute's "Of Techno-Ethics and Techno-Affects" (2019); on care for data in particular, see Pinel, Prainsack, and McKevitt's "Caring for Data" (2020). Some of this discussion is excerpted from my "Care and Scale: Decorrelative Ethics in Algorithmic Recommendation" (Seaver 2021).

2. Ellie's "gardener" metaphor was notably feminized, in contrast to stereotypical tech worker titles like "plumber" or "rock star." On the feminization of maintenance work, see Shannon Mattern's "Maintenance and Care" (2018).

3. On the feminization of "nontechnical" roles in software development, see Miriam Posner's "JavaScript Is for Girls" (2017) and Mar Hicks' *Programmed Inequality* (2017).

4. In the US context, this idealization of the middle landscape was thus tied up with what would eventually be called "settler colonialism" (Wolfe 1999).

5. We can find similar metaphors used to describe the availability of streaming music as though it were a municipal service, like running water (e.g., Kusek and Leonard 2005), with similar critiques that this understanding obscure the human labor that goes into making music exist (Baade 2018, 20).

6. This sense is captured in a bit of academic etymological lore, commonly attributed to Paul Ricoeur (McLemee 2005) and reproduced semifictionally by Bruno Latour (1996, 59) in *Aramis, or, The Love of Technology*: "The word *metaphoros*, my friend, is written on all the moving vans in Greece."

7. This concern with the adequacy of domain matches has led some critics to suggest alternative metaphors, which might draw attention to qualities of data that dominant metaphors neglect. Sweat, smog, exhaust, nuclear waste, pets, and food (Gregg 2015; Shenk 1998; Noyes 2016; Doctorow 2008; Lupton 2016) are some alternatives that have been put forward to foreground the entanglement of data with human bodies and labor, its status as a by-product of other activities, or the risks it poses if not carefully managed.

8. As the historian Lorraine Daston (1992) has argued, both the practice and the critique of "naturalizing" appear to be modern inventions, and the qualities ascribed to nature (and its compared partners) have varied over the course of this modern history.

9. Antonia Walford (2017), drawing on fieldwork with environmental data collectors in the Amazon, argues that "rawness" in practice is not characterized by the absence of relations to the world, but rather by an excess of relations, which are trimmed back as data are "cooked." See also Cal Biruk's *Cooking Data* (2018).

10. Here, I depart from Boellstorff (2013), who takes Lévi-Strauss's "empirical" and "conceptual" to refer respectively to emic (i.e., ordinary and local) and etic (i.e., outsider analytic) forms of knowledge, rather than the concrete versus the abstract. This seems to me a misreading of Lévi-Strauss (1966), whose "science of the concrete" was concerned with the way that local empirical phenomena like cooking could provide equipment for local conceptual thinking. The etic position, in Lévi-Strauss's work, is concerned with the structure of relations among objects of thought, not with their "content," so to speak.

11. Managing such uncertainty is a signature feature of algorithmic data process-

ing, as the historian Theodora Dryer (2018) has argued, with roots in early twentieth-century statistical technologies.

12. While Foucault's historiography has been criticized, the historical details of his genealogy are less significant than the similarities between his description of pastoral power and the emic accounts of algorithmic power presented here.

13. Whether they achieve this goal is, of course, a separate question.

Epilogue

1. See "'Making the World More Open and Connected': Mark Zuckerberg and the Discursive Construction of Facebook and Its Users" (Hoffmann, Proferes, and Zimmer 2016) for an analysis of these rhetorics of openness and connection in the context of social media services.

Works Cited

Ackoff, Russell Lincoln. 1974. *Redesigning the Future: A Systems Approach to Societal Problems*. New York: Wiley.

Ad Age. 2007. "Ask.com: The Algorithm." June 14. https://adage.com/creativity/work/algorithm/4447.

Adomavicius, Gediminas, and Alexander Tuzhilin. 2015. "Context-Aware Recommender Systems." In *Recommender Systems Handbook*, 2nd ed., edited by Francesco Ricci, Lior Rokach, and Bracha Shapira, 191–226. Boston: Springer US.

Adorno, Theodor W. 1976. *Introduction to the Sociology of Music*. New York: Seabury Press.

Akrich, Madeleine. 1992. "The De-Scription of Technical Objects." In *Shaping Technology/Building Society: Studies in Sociotechnical Change*, edited by Wiebe E. Bijker and John Law, 205–24. Inside Technology. Cambridge, MA: MIT Press.

Albro, Robert. 2010. "Writing Culture Doctrine: Public Anthropology, Military Policy, and World Making." *Perspectives on Politics* 8 (4): 1087–93.

———. 2018. "Troping the Enemy: Metaphor, Culture, and the Big Data Black Boxes of National Security." *Secrecy and Society* 2 (1).

Amatriain, Xavier, and Justin Basilico. 2012. "Netflix Recommendations: Beyond the 5 Stars (Part 2)." *Netflix Tech Blog* (blog), June 20. https://netflixtechblog.com/netflix-recommendations-beyond-the-5-stars-part-2-d9b96aa399f5.

Amatriain, Xavier, Pablo Castells, Arjen de Vries, and Christian Posse. 2012. "Workshop on Recommendation Utility Evaluation: Beyond RMSE—RUE 2012." In *Proceedings of the Sixth ACM Conference on Recommender Systems*, 351–52. New York: Association for Computing Machinery.

Amatriain, Xavier, Josep M. Pujol, and Nuria Oliver. 2009. "I Like It . . . I Like It Not: Evaluating User Ratings Noise in Recommender Systems." In *User Modeling, Adaptation, and Personalization*, edited by Geert-Jan Houben, Gord McCalla, Fabio Pianesi, and Massimo Zancanaro, 247–58. Berlin: Springer.

Amoore, Louise, and Volha Piotukh. 2015. "Life beyond Big Data: Governing with Little Analytics." *Economy and Society* 44 (3): 341–66.

Amrute, Sareeta. 2019. "Of Techno-Ethics and Techno-Affects." *Feminist Review* 123 (1): 56–73.

Anand, Sarabjot Singh, and Bamshad Mobasher. 2007. "Contextual Recommendation." In *From Web to Social Web: Discovering and Deploying User and Content Profiles*, edited by Bettina Berendt, Andreas Hotho, Dunja Mladenic, and Giovanni Semeraro, 142–60. Lecture Notes in Computer Science. Berlin: Springer.

Ananny, Mike, and Kate Crawford. 2016. "Seeing without Knowing: Limitations of the Transparency Ideal and Its Application to Algorithmic Accountability." *New Media & Society*, December.

Anderson, Paul Allen. 2015. "Neo-Muzak and the Business of Mood." *Critical Inquiry* 41 (4): 811–40.

Andreessen, Marc. 2011. "Why Software Is Eating the World." *Wall Street Journal*, August 20, 2011, sec. Life and Style. https://www.wsj.com/articles/SB1000142405 3111903480904576512250915629460.

Arvidsson, Adam. 2002. "On the 'Pre-History of The Panoptic Sort': Mobility in Market Research." *Surveillance & Society* 1 (4): 456–74.

Asdal, Kristin, and Ingunn Moser. 2012. "Experiments in Context and Contexting." *Science, Technology & Human Values* 37 (4): 291–306.

Aspray, William. 1985. "The Scientific Conceptualization of Information: A Survey." *IEEE Annals of the History of Computing* 7 (2): 117–40.

Baade, Christina L. 2012. *Victory through Harmony: The BBC and Popular Music in World War II*. Oxford: Oxford University Press.

———. 2018. "Lean Back: Songza, Ubiquitous Listening and Internet Music Radio for the Masses." *Radio Journal: International Studies in Broadcast & Audio Media* 16 (1): 9–27.

Balfour, Henry. 1925. "Thorn-Lined Traps and Their Distribution." *Man* 25 (March): 33–37.

———. 1932. "Thorn-Lined Traps in the Pitt-Rivers Museum, Oxford." *Man* 32 (March): 57–59.

Ballard, J. G. 1967. *The Overloaded Man*. London: Panther Books.

Ballestero, Andrea. 2019. *A Future History of Water*. Durham, NC: Duke University Press.

Balsamo, Anne. 1996. "Myths of Information: The Cultural Impact of New Information Technologies." *Technology Analysis & Strategic Management* 8 (3): 341–48.

Barocas, Solon, and Andrew D. Selbst. 2016. "Big Data's Disparate Impact." *California Law Review* 104: 671–732.

Barthes, Roland. 1972. *Mythologies*. Translated by Annette Lavers. New York: Farrar, Straus and Giroux.

Bates, Marcia J. 1989. "The Design of Browsing and Berrypicking Techniques for the Online Search Interface." *Online Review* 13 (5): 407–24.

———. 2006. "Fundamental Forms of Information." *Journal of the American Society for Information Science and Technology* 57 (8): 1033–45.

Baym, Nancy K., Kelly B. Wagman, and Christopher J. Persaud. 2020. "Mindfully Scrolling: Rethinking Facebook after Time Deactivated." *Social Media + Society* 6 (2).

Beer, David. 2013. *Popular Culture and New Media: The Politics of Circulation*. London: Palgrave Macmillan.

Beer, Stafford. 1972. *Brain of the Firm: A Development in Management Cybernetics*. New York: Herder and Herder.

Bell, Robert M., Yehuda Koren, and Chris Volinsky. 2010. "All Together Now: A Perspective on the Netflix Prize." *CHANCE* 23 (1): 24–29.

Beniger, James. 1986. *The Control Revolution: Technological and Economic Origins of the Information Society.* Cambridge, MA: Harvard University Press.

Benjamin, Ruha. 2019. *Race After Technology: Abolitionist Tools for the New Jim Code.* Cambridge, UK: Polity.

Benjamin, Walter. 1999. *The Arcades Project.* Edited by Rolf Tiedemann. Translated by Howard Eiland and Kevin McLaughlin. Cambridge, MA: Harvard University Press.

Bennett, Toby. 2018. "'Essential—Passion for Music': Affirming, Critiquing, and Practising Passionate Work in Creative Industries." In *The Palgrave Handbook of Creativity at Work,* edited by Lee Martin and Nick Wilson, 431–59. Cham, Switzerland: Springer International Publishing.

Bien-Kahn, Joseph. 2016. "What Happens When 'Black Mirror' Moves beyond Inescapable Traps? It Gets Even Better." *Wired,* October 21. https://www.wired.com/2016/10/black-mirror-traps/.

Birnbaum, Debra. 2015. "Netflix Picks Up 'Black Mirror' for 12 New Episodes." *Variety* (blog), September 25. http://variety.com/2015/digital/news/netflix-black-mirror-new-episodes-1201602037/.

Biruk, Cal. 2018. *Cooking Data: Culture and Politics in an African Research World.* Durham, NC: Duke University Press.

Blair, Ann. 2003. "Reading Strategies for Coping With Information Overload ca. 1550–1700." *Journal of the History of Ideas* 64 (1): 11–28.

———. 2010. *Too Much to Know: Managing Scholarly Information before the Modern Age.* New Haven, CT: Yale University Press.

Blanke, Tobias. 2018. "The Geometric Rationality of Innocence in Algorithmic Decisions." In *Being Profiled,* edited by Emre Bayamlioğlu, Irina Baraliuc, Liisa Janssens, and Mireille Hildebrandt, 66–71. Amsterdam: Amsterdam University Press.

Bloch, Ernst. 1988. *The Utopian Function of Art and Literature: Selected Essays.* Translated by Jack Zipes and Frank Mecklenburg. Cambridge, MA: MIT Press.

Bloor, David. 1976. *Knowledge and Social Imagery.* Chicago: University of Chicago Press.

Boellstorff, Tom. 2013. "Making Big Data, in Theory." *First Monday* 18 (10).

Bollen, Dirk, Bart P. Knijnenburg, Martijn C. Willemsen, and Mark Graus. 2010. "Understanding Choice Overload in Recommender Systems." In *Proceedings of the Fourth ACM Conference on Recommender Systems,* 63–70. New York: Association for Computing Machinery.

Borchers, Al, Jon Herlocker, Joseph Konstan, and John Riedl. 1998. "Ganging Up on Information Overload." *Computer* 31 (4): 106–8.

Born, Georgina. 1996. "(Im)materiality and Sociality: The Dynamics of Intellectual Property in a Computer Software Research Culture." *Social Anthropology* 4 (2): 101–16.

Born, Georgina, and Christopher Haworth. 2017. "From Microsound to Vaporwave: Internet-Mediated Musics, Online Methods, and Genre." *Music and Letters* 98 (4): 601–47.

Bourdieu, Pierre. 1984. *Distinction.* Cambridge, MA: Harvard University Press.

———. 1985. "The Social Space and the Genesis of Groups." *Theory and Society* 14 (6): 723–44.

Bowker, Geof. 1993. "How to Be Universal: Some Cybernetic Strategies, 1943–70." *Social Studies of Science* 23 (1): 107–27.

———. 1994. "Information Mythology: The World of/as Information." In *Information Acumen: The Understanding and Use of Knowledge in Modern Business*, edited by L. Bud-Frierman, 231–47. London, Routledge.

———. 2005. *Memory Practices in the Sciences*. Cambridge, MA: MIT Press.

———. 2013. "The Ontological Priority of Mediation." In *Débordements: Mélanges offerts à Michel Callon*, edited by Madeleine Akrich, Yannick Barthe, Fabian Muniesa, and Philippe Mustar, 61–68. Sciences Sociales. Paris: Presses des Mines.

boyd, danah. 2012. "The Politics of 'Real Names.'" *Communications of the ACM* 55 (8): 29–31.

boyd, danah, and Kate Crawford. 2012. "Critical Questions for Big Data." *Information, Communication & Society* 15 (5): 662–79.

Boyer, Dominic. 2013. *The Life Informatic: Newsmaking in the Digital Era*. Ithaca, NY: Cornell University Press.

Boyer, Pascal. 1988. *Barricades mystérieuses & pièges à pensée: Introduction à l'analyse des épopées fang*. Paris: Société d'ethnologie.

Bruns, Axel. 2019. "Filter Bubble." *Internet Policy Review* 8 (4). https://policyreview .info/concepts/filter-bubble.

Bucher, Taina. 2018. *If . . . Then: Algorithmic Power and Politics*. Oxford: Oxford University Press.

Buolamwini, Joy, and Timnit Gebru. 2018. "Gender Shades: Intersectional Accuracy Disparities in Commercial Gender Classification." *Proceedings of Machine Learning Research* 81: 77–91.

Burkart, Patrick, and Tom McCourt. 2004. "Infrastructure for the Celestial Jukebox." *Popular Music* 23 (3): 349–62.

Burrell, Jenna. 2009. "The Field Site as a Network: A Strategy for Locating Ethnographic Research." *Field Methods* 21 (2): 181–99.

———. 2016. "How the Machine 'Thinks': Understanding Opacity in Machine Learning Algorithms." *Big Data & Society* 3 (1): 1–12.

Burton, Ian. 1963. "The Quantitative Revolution and Theoretical Geography." *The Canadian Geographer/Le Géographe Canadien* 7 (4): 151–62.

Bylin, Kyle. 2014. *Promised Land: Youth Culture, Disruptive Startups, and the Social Music Revolution*. N.p.: CreateSpace Independent Publishing Platform.

Candea, Matei. 2007. "Arbitrary Locations: In Defence of the Bounded Field-Site." *Journal of the Royal Anthropological Institute* 13 (1): 167–84.

Carfoot, Gavin. 2016. "Musical Discovery, Colonialism, and the Possibilities of Intercultural Communication through Music." *Popular Communication* 14 (3): 178–86.

Carr, E. Summerson, and Michael Lempert, eds. 2016. *Scale: Discourse and Dimensions of Social Life*. Oakland: University of California Press.

Celma, Òscar. 2010. *Music Recommendation and Discovery: The Long Tail, Long Fail, and Long Play in the Digital Music Space*. Berlin: Springer.

Chen, Judy. 2019. "Being Humans at Work: Through the Lens of 'Culture' among Tech and Culture Workers in the San Francisco Bay Area." BA honors thesis, Tufts University.

Cheney-Lippold, John. 2011. "A New Algorithmic Identity: Soft Biopolitics and the Modulation of Control." *Theory, Culture & Society* 28 (6): 164–81.

———. 2017. *We Are Data: Algorithms and the Making of Our Digital Selves*. New York: New York University Press.

Chesky, Brian. 2014. "Don't Fuck Up the Culture." *Medium*, April 21. https://medium .com/@bchesky/dont-fuck-up-the-culture-597cde9ee9d4.

Chow, Rey. 2012. *Entanglements, or, Transmedial Thinking about Capture*. Durham, NC: Duke University Press.

Christiansen, Jen. 2015. "Pop Culture Pulsar: The Science behind Joy Division's *Unknown Pleasures* Album Cover." *Scientific American*, October 13. https://blogs .scientificamerican.com/sa-visual/pop-culture-pulsar-the-science-behind-joy-division -s-unknown-pleasures-album-cover/.

Christin, Angèle. 2020. "The Ethnographer and the Algorithm: Beyond the Black Box." *Theory and Society* 49 (5–6): 897–918.

Chu, Julie Y. 2010. *Cosmologies of Credit: Transnational Mobility and the Politics of Destination in China*. Durham, NC: Duke University Press.

Chun, Wendy Hui Kyong. 2016. *Updating to Remain the Same: Habitual New Media*. Cambridge, MA: MIT Press.

———. 2018. "Queerying Homophily."

———. 2021. *Discriminating Data: Correlation, Neighborhoods, and the New Politics of Recognition*. Cambridge, MA: MIT Press.

Cochoy, Franck. 2007. "A Brief Theory of the 'Captation' of Publics: Understanding the Market with Little Red Riding Hood." *Theory, Culture & Society* 24 (7–8): 203–23.

Cohn, Jonathan. 2013. "Female Labor and Digital Media: Pattie Maes, Postfeminism, and the Birth of Social Networking Technologies." *Camera Obscura* 28 (2 [83]): 151–75.

———. 2019. *The Burden of Choice: Recommendations, Subversion, and Algorithmic Culture*. New Brunswick, NJ: Rutgers University Press.

Cooper, Rosalind. 2019. "Pastoral Power and Algorithmic Governmentality." *Theory, Culture & Society*, July, art. 026327641986057.

Coopmans, Catelijne. 2014. "Visual Analytics as Artful Revelation." In *Representation in Scientific Practice Revisited*, edited by Catelijne Coopmans, Janet Vertesi, Michael Lynch, and Steve Woolgar, 37–60. Cambridge, MA: MIT Press.

Cormen, Thomas H., Charles E. Leiserson, Ronald L. Rivest, and Clifford Stein. 2009. *Introduction to Algorithms*. 3rd ed. Cambridge, MA: MIT Press.

Corsín Jiménez, Alberto. 2018. "Spider Web Anthropologies: Ecologies, Infrastructures, Entanglements." In *A World of Many Worlds*, edited by Marisol de la Cadena and Mario Blaser, 53–82. Durham, NC: Duke University Press.

Corsín Jiménez, Alberto, and Chloe Nahum-Claudel. 2019. "The Anthropology of Traps: Concrete Technologies and Theoretical Interfaces." *Journal of Material Culture* 24 (4): 383–400.

Couldry, Nick, and Ulises A. Mejias. 2019. "Data Colonialism: Rethinking Big Data's Relation to the Contemporary Subject." *Television & New Media* 20 (4): 336–49.

Crane, Diana. 1972. *Invisible Colleges: Diffusion of Knowledge in Scientific Communities*. Chicago: University of Chicago Press.

Crary, Jonathan. 1999. *Suspensions of Perception: Attention, Spectacle, and Modern Culture*. Cambridge, MA: MIT Press.

Crombie, Alistair. 1990. *Science, Optics and Music in Medieval and Early Modern Thought*. London: Hambledon Press.

Cyert, Richard M., and James G. March. 1963. *A Behavioral Theory of the Firm*. Cambridge, MA: Wiley-Blackwell.

Daniels, Jessie. 2015. "'My Brain Database Doesn't See Skin Color': Color-Blind Racism in the Technology Industry and in Theorizing the Web." *American Behavioral Scientist* 59 (11): 1377–93.

Daston, Lorraine. 1992. "The Naturalized Female Intellect." *Science in Context* 5 (2): 209–35.

Davidow, Bill. 2013. "Skinner Marketing: We're the Rats, and Facebook Likes Are the Reward." *The Atlantic*, June 10. https://www.theatlantic.com/technology/archive/2013/06/skinner-marketing-were-the-rats-and-facebook-likes-are-the-reward/276613/.

Davis, Erik. 1998. *TechGnosis: Myth, Magic, and Mysticism in the Age of Information*. Berkeley, CA: Harmony Books.

Day, Ronald E. 2000. "The 'Conduit Metaphor' and the Nature and Politics of Information Studies." *Journal of the American Society for Information Science* 51 (9): 805–11.

Deleuze, Gilles. 1992. "Postscript on the Societies of Control." *October* 5: 3–7.

Derrida, Jacques. 2000. *Of Hospitality*. Translated by Rachel Bowlby. Stanford, CA: Stanford University Press.

Desrosières, Alain. 2012. "Mapping the Social World: From Aggregates to Individuals." *Limn* 2: 59–62.

Dilley, Roy. 1999. *The Problem of Context: Perspectives from Social Anthropology and Elsewhere*. Berghahn Books.

———. 2002. "The Problem of Context in Social and Cultural Anthropology." *Language & Communication* 22 (4): 437–56.

Doctorow, Cory. 2008. "Personal Data Is as Hot as Nuclear Waste." *The Guardian*, January 15, sec. Technology. http://www.theguardian.com/technology/2008/jan/15/data.security.

Dodge, Martin, and Rob Kitchin. 2001. *Mapping Cyberspace*. London: Routledge.

Domingos, Pedro. 2015. *The Master Algorithm: How the Quest for the Ultimate Learning Machine Will Remake Our World*. New York: Basic Books.

Doshi-Velez, Finale, and Been Kim. 2017. "Towards a Rigorous Science of Interpretable Machine Learning." February. https://arxiv.org/abs/1702.08608.

Dourish, Paul. 2004. "What We Talk about When We Talk about Context." *Personal and Ubiquitous Computing* 8 (1): 19–30.

Dredge, Stuart. 2015. "Spotify Debuts Discover Weekly Personalised 'Mixtape' Playlist." *MusicAlly* (blog), July 20. https://musically.com/2015/07/20/spotify-discover-weekly-personalised-mixtape-playlist/.

Dretske, Fred. 1981. *Knowledge and the Flow of Information*. Cambridge, MA: MIT Press.

Drott, Eric. 2013. "The End(s) of Genre." *Journal of Music Theory* 57 (1): 1–45.

———. 2018a. "Genre in the Age of Algorithms." Unpublished ms.

———. 2018b. "Music as a Technology of Surveillance." *Journal of the Society for American Music* 12 (3): 233–67.

———. 2018c. "Why the Next Song Matters: Streaming, Recommendation, Scarcity." *Twentieth-Century Music* 15 (3): 325–57.

Dryer, Theodora. 2018. "Algorithms under the Reign of Probability." *IEEE Annals of the History of Computing* 40 (1): 93–96.

Duranti, Alessandro, and Charles Goodwin. 1992. *Rethinking Context: Language as an Interactive Phenomenon.* Cambridge: Cambridge University Press.

Edmunds, Angela, and Anne Morris. 2000. "The Problem of Information Overload in Business Organisations: A Review of the Literature." *International Journal of Information Management* 20 (1): 17–28.

Edwards, Paul N. 1996. *The Closed World: Computers and the Politics of Discourse in Cold War America.* Cambridge, MA: MIT Press.

Eglash, Ron. 2002. "Race, Sex, and Nerds: From Black Geeks to Asian American Hipsters." *Social Text* 20 (2 [71]): 49–64.

Ekstrand, Michael D., and Martijn C. Willemsen. 2016. "Behaviorism Is Not Enough: Better Recommendations through Listening to Users." In *Proceedings of the 10th ACM Conference on Recommender Systems,* 221–24. New York: Association for Computing Machinery.

Elish, M. C., and danah boyd. 2018. "Situating Methods in the Magic of Big Data and AI." *Communication Monographs* 85 (1): 57–80.

Ellenberg, Jordan. 2014. *How Not to Be Wrong: The Power of Mathematical Thinking.* New York: Penguin.

Ellison, Katherine E. 2006. *The Fatal News: Reading and Information Overload in Early Eighteenth-Century Literature.* New York: Routledge.

English-Lueck, J. A., and Miriam Lueck Avery. 2017. "Intensifying Work and Chasing Innovation: Incorporating Care in Silicon Valley." *Anthropology of Work Review* 38 (1): 40–49.

Eppler, Martin J., and Jeanne Mengis. 2004. "The Concept of Information Overload: A Review of Literature from Organization Science, Accounting, Marketing, MIS, and Related Disciplines." *Information Society* 20 (5): 325–44.

Eriksson, Maria. 2016. "Close Reading Big Data: The Echo Nest and the Production of (Rotten) Music Metadata." *First Monday* 21 (7).

Eriksson, Maria, Rasmus Fleischer, Anna Johansson, Pelle Snickars, and Patrick Vonderau. 2019. *Spotify Teardown: Inside the Black Box of Streaming Music.* Cambridge, MA: MIT Press.

Eriksson, Maria, and Anna Johansson. 2017. "'Keep Smiling!': Time, Functionality and Intimacy in Spotify's Featured Playlists." *Cultural Analysis* 16 (1): 67–82.

Eubanks, Virginia. 2018. *Automating Inequality: How High-Tech Tools Profile, Police, and Punish the Poor.* New York: St. Martin's Press.

Eyal, Nir. 2014. *Hooked: How to Build Habit-Forming Products.* New York: Penguin.

Farman, Abou. 2017. "Informatic Cosmologies and the Anxieties of Immanence." *The Immanent Frame* (blog), October 25. https://tif.ssrc.org/2017/10/25/informatic-cosmologies-and-the-anxieties-of-immanence/.

Feld, Steven. 1996. "Waterfalls of Songs: An Acoustemology of Place Resounding in Bosavi, Papua New Guinea." In *Senses of Place,* edited by Steven Feld and Keith H. Basso, 91–136. Santa Fe, NM: School of American Research Press.

———. 2000. "A Sweet Lullaby for World Music." *Public Culture* 12 (1): 145–71.

Ferster, C. B, and B. F. Skinner. 1957. *Schedules of Reinforcement.* New York: Appleton-Century-Crofts.

Fields, Karen, and Barbara J. Fields. 2012. *Racecraft: The Soul of Inequality in American Life*. New York: Verso Books.

Fogg, B. J. 2003. *Persuasive Technology: Using Computers to Change What We Think and Do*. Boston: Morgan Kaufmann.

Fogg, B. J., Gregory Cuellar, and David Danielson. 2009. "Motivating, Influencing, and Persuading Users: An Introduction to Captology." In *Human Computer Interaction Fundamentals*, edited by Andrew Sears and Julie A. Jacko, 109–22. Boca Raton, FL: CRC Press.

Foucault, Michel. 1991. *The Foucault Effect: Studies in Governmentality*. Chicago: University of Chicago Press.

Franklin, Seb. 2015. *Control: Digitality as Cultural Logic*. Cambridge, MA: MIT Press.

Franklin, Wayne. 1979. *Discoverers, Explorers, Settlers: The Diligent Writers of Early America*. Chicago: University of Chicago Press.

Fricke, David, and David Fricke. 2012. "Jimmy Iovine: The Man with the Magic Ears." *Rolling Stone* (blog), April 12. https://www.rollingstone.com/music/music-news/jimmy-iovine-the-man-with-the-magic-ears-120618/.

Funk, Simon. 2006. "Netflix Update: Try This at Home." *The Evolution of Cybernetics* (blog), December 11. https://sifter.org/~simon/journal/20061211.html.

Gal, Susan, and Judith T. Irvine. 1995. "The Boundaries of Languages and Disciplines: How Ideologies Construct Difference." *Social Research* 62 (4): 967–1001.

Galison, Peter. 1994. "The Ontology of the Enemy: Norbert Wiener and the Cybernetic Vision." *Critical Inquiry* 21 (1): 228–66.

Galloway, Alexander R. 2006. *Protocol: How Control Exists after Decentralization*. Cambridge, MA: MIT Press.

Gandy, Oscar H. 2011. "Matrix Multiplication and the Digital Divide." In *Race After the Internet*, edited by Lisa Nakamura and Peter Chow-White, 128–45. New York: Routledge.

Garcia-Gathright, Jean, Christine Hosey, Brian St. Thomas, Ben Carterette, and Fernando Diaz. 2018. "Mixed Methods for Evaluating User Satisfaction." In *Proceedings of the 12th ACM Conference on Recommender Systems*, 541–42. New York: Association for Computing Machinery.

Geertz, Clifford. 1973. *The Interpretation of Cultures*. New York: Basic Books.

———. 1984. "Distinguished Lecture: Anti Anti-Relativism." *American Anthropologist* 86 (2): 263–78.

Gell, Alfred. 1988. "Technology and Magic." *Anthropology Today* 4 (2): 6–9.

———. 1996. "Vogel's Net: Traps as Artworks and Artworks as Traps." *Journal of Material Culture* 1 (1): 15–38.

———. 1998. *Art and Agency: An Anthropological Theory*. Oxford, UK: Clarendon Press.

Gillespie, Tarleton. 2010. "The Politics of 'Platforms.'" *New Media & Society* 12 (3): 347–64.

———. 2016. "Algorithm." In *Digital Keywords: A Vocabulary of Information Society and Culture*, by Benjamin Peters, 18–30. Princeton, NJ: Princeton University Press.

———. 2018. *Custodians of the Internet: Platforms, Content Moderation, and the Hidden Decisions That Shape Social Media*. New Haven, CT: Yale University Press.

Gillespie, Tarleton, and Nick Seaver. 2015. "Critical Algorithm Studies: A Reading List." *Social Media Collective* (blog), November 5. https://socialmediacollective.org/reading-lists/critical-algorithm-studies/.

Gladwell, Malcolm. 1999. "The Science of the Sleeper." *New Yorker*, September 26.

Goldberg, David, David Nichols, Brian M. Oki, and Douglas Terry. 1992. "Using Collaborative Filtering to Weave an Information Tapestry." *Communications of the ACM* 35 (12): 61–70.

Goldstein, Paul. 1994. *Copyright's Highway: From Gutenberg to the Celestial Jukebox.* Stanford, CA: Stanford University Press.

Golumbia, David. 2009. *The Cultural Logic of Computation.* Cambridge, MA: Harvard University Press.

Graham, Paul. 2012. "Startup = Growth." September. http://www.paulgraham.com/growth.html.

Gregg, Melissa. 2015. "Inside the Data Spectacle." *Television & New Media* 16 (1): 37–51.

Grossman, Lev. 2006. "You—Yes, You—Are TIME's Person of the Year." *Time*, December 25.

Gürses, Seda, and Joris van Hoboken. 2018. "Privacy after the Agile Turn." In *The Cambridge Handbook of Consumer Privacy*, edited by Evan Selinger, Jules Polonetsky, and Omer Tene, 579–601. Cambridge, UK: Cambridge University Press.

Gusterson, Hugh. 1997. "Studying Up Revisited." *PoLAR: Political and Legal Anthropology Review* 20 (1): 114–19.

Guyer, Jane, Naveeda Khan, and Juan Obarrio. 2010. "Introduction: Number as Inventive Frontier." *Anthropological Theory* 10 (12): 36–61.

Haber, Alejandro F. 2009. "Animism, Relatedness, Life: Post-Western Perspectives." *Cambridge Archaeological Journal* 19 (3): 418–30.

Haimson, Oliver L., Jed R. Brubaker, Lynn Dombrowski, and Gillian R. Hayes. 2015. "Disclosure, Stress, and Support During Gender Transition on Facebook." In *Proceedings of the 18th ACM Conference on Computer Supported Cooperative Work & Social Computing*, 1176–90. New York: Association for Computing Machinery.

Hallinan, Blake, and Ted Striphas. 2016. "Recommended for You: The Netflix Prize and the Production of Algorithmic Culture." *New Media & Society* 18 (1): 117–37.

Hannerz, Ulf. 2003. "Being There . . . and There . . . and There! Reflections on Multi-Site Ethnography." *Ethnography* 4 (2): 201–16.

Harari, Yuval Noah. 2014. *Sapiens: A Brief History of Humankind.* New York: HarperCollins.

———. 2017. *Homo Deus: A Brief History of Tomorrow.* New York: HarperCollins.

Haraway, Donna 1979. "The Biological Enterprise: Sex, Mind, and Profit from Human Engineering to Sociobiology." *Radical History Review* 1979 (20): 206–37.

———. 1988. "Situated Knowledges: The Science Question in Feminism and the Privilege of Partial Perspective." *Feminist Studies* 14 (3): 575.

———. 1991. "A Cyborg Manifesto: Science, Technology, and Socialist-Feminism in the Late Twentieth Century." In *Simians, Cyborgs, and Women: The Reinvention of Nature*, 149–81. New York: Routledge.

———. 1997. *Modest_Witness@Second_Millennium.FemaleMan_Meets_OncoMouse.* New York: Routledge.

Harvey, Eric. 2014. "Station to Station: The Past, Present, and Future of Streaming Music." *Pitchfork*, April 16. https://pitchfork.com/features/cover-story/reader/streaming/.

Hawley, Josh. 2019. "Sen. Hawley Introduces Legislation to Curb Social Media Addiction." Senator Josh Hawley, July 30. https://www.hawley.senate.gov/sen-hawley-introduces-legislation-curb-social-media-addiction.

Hayles, N. Katherine. 1999. *How We Became Posthuman: Virtual Bodies in Cybernetics, Literature, and Informatics.* Chicago: University of Chicago Press.

Helmholtz, Hermann von. 1995. "On the Physiological Causes of Harmony in Music." In *Science and Culture: Popular and Philosophical Essays,* edited by David Cahan, 46–75. Chicago: University of Chicago Press.

Helmreich, Stefan. 1998. *Silicon Second Nature: Culturing Artificial Life in a Digital World, Updated With a New Preface.* Berkeley: University of California Press.

———. 2003. "Trees and Seas of Information: Alien Kinship and the Biopolitics of Gene Transfer in Marine Biology and Biotechnology." *American Ethnologist* 30 (3): 340–58.

———. 2007. "An Anthropologist Underwater: Immersive Soundscapes, Submarine Cyborgs, and Transductive Ethnography." *American Ethnologist* 34 (4): 621–41.

———. 2016. "Gravity's Reverb: Listening to Space-Time, or Articulating the Sounds of Gravitational-Wave Detection." *Cultural Anthropology* 31 (4): 464–92.

Hennion, Antoine, and Cecile Meadel. 1986. "Programming Music: Radio as Mediator." *Media, Culture & Society* 8 (3): 281–303.

Herlocker, Jonathan, Joseph Konstan, Loren Terveen, and John Riedl. 2004. "Evaluating Collaborative Filtering Recommender Systems." *ACM Transactions on Information Systems (TOIS)* 22 (1): 5–53.

Heyck, Hunter. 2015. *Age of System: Understanding the Development of Modern Social Science.* Baltimore: Johns Hopkins University Press.

Hicks, Mar. 2017. Programmed Inequality: How Britain Discarded Women Technologists and Lost Its Edge in Computing. Cambridge, MA: MIT Press.

Hoffman, Alex. 2012. "Context Culture: The Next Music Revolution." *Hypebot* (blog), November 13. https://www.hypebot.com/hypebot/2012/11/context-culture-the-next-music-revolution.html.

Hoffmann, Anna Lauren, Nicholas Proferes, and Michael Zimmer. 2016. "'Making the World More Open and Connected': Mark Zuckerberg and the Discursive Construction of Facebook and Its Users." *New Media & Society,* 20 (1): 199–218.

Houghton, Bruce. 2013. "Beats Music: Daisy Gets a Name, Hiring More Staff." *Hypebot* (blog), August 12. https://www.hypebot.com/hypebot/2013/08/beats-music-daisy-gets-a-name-hiring-more-staff.html.

Hrdlička, Aleš. 1916. "Indian Trap Pits along the Missouri." *American Anthropologist* 18 (4): 546–47.

Hu, Cherie. 2016. "What Is 'Escape Room' and Why Is It One of My Top Genres on Spotify?" *Festival Peak* (blog), December 16. https://festivalpeak.com/what-is-escape-room-and-why-is-it-one-of-my-top-genres-on-spotify-a886372f003f.

Hughes, Thomas P. 1987. "The Evolution of Large Technological Systems." In *The Social Construction of Technological Systems: New Directions in the Sociology and History of Technology,* edited by Wiebe E. Bijker, Thomas P. Hughes, and Trevor J. Pinch, 51–82. Cambridge, MA: MIT Press.

Hui, Alexandra. 2013. *The Psychophysical Ear: Musical Experiments, Experimental Sounds, 1840–1910.* Cambridge, MA: MIT Press.

Humphrey, Caroline. 1985. "Barter and Economic Disintegration." *Man* 20 (1): 48–72.

Hwang, Tim, and Karen Levy. 2015. "'The Cloud' and Other Dangerous Metaphors." *The Atlantic*, January 20. https://www.theatlantic.com/technology/archive/2015/01/the-cloud-and-other-dangerous-metaphors/384518/.

Ingold, Tim. 1974. "On Reindeer and Men." *Man* 9 (4): 523.

———. 1980. *Hunters, Pastoralists and Ranchers: Reindeer Economies and Their Transformations*. Cambridge Studies in Social and Cultural Anthropology. Cambridge: Cambridge University Press.

Irani, Lilly. 2015. "Justice for 'Data Janitors.'" *Public Books* (blog), January 15. https://www.publicbooks.org/justice-for-data-janitors/.

Irani, Lilly, and Rumman Chowdhury. 2019. "To Really 'Disrupt,' Tech Needs to Listen to Actual Researchers." *Wired*, June 26. https://www.wired.com/story/tech-needs-to-listen-to-actual-researchers/.

Irvine, Judith T. 2016. "Going Upscale: Scales and Scale-Climbing as Ideological Projects." In *Scale: Discourse and Dimensions of Social Life*, edited by E. Summerson Carr and Michael Lempert, 213–32. Oakland: University of California Press.

Iyengar, Sheena S., and Mark R. Lepper. 2000. "When Choice Is Demotivating: Can One Desire Too Much of a Good Thing?" *Journal of Personality and Social Psychology* 79 (6): 995–1006.

Jackson, Myles. 2006. *Harmonious Triads*. Cambridge, MA: MIT Press.

Jacoby, Jacob. 1975. "Perspectives on a Consumer Information Processing Research Program." *Communication Research* 2 (3): 203–15.

James, Robin. 2013. "Race and the Feminized Popular in Nietzsche and Beyond." *Hypatia* 28 (4): 749–66.

———. 2017a. "Is the Post- in Post-Identity the Post- in Post-Genre?" *Popular Music* 36 (1): 21–32.

———. 2017b. "Songs of Myself." *Real Life*, May 31. https://reallifemag.com/songs-of-myself/.

Jennings, David. 2007. *Net, Blogs and Rock "n" Roll: How Digital Discovery Works and What It Means for Consumers*. London: Nicholas Brealey.

Jensen, Casper Bruun. 2010. "Asymmetries of Knowledge: Mediated Ethnography and ICT for Development." *Methodological Innovations Online* 5 (1): 72–85.

Johnson, Thomas. 2018. "Analyzing Genre in Post-Millennial Popular Music." PhD diss., City University of New York.

———. 2019. "Genrecraft: Chance the Rapper, Spotify, and Musical Categorization in the 2010s." Unpublished manuscript.

———. 2020. "Chance the Rapper, Spotify, and Musical Categorization in the 2010s." *American Music* 38 (2): 176–96.

Johnston, Maura. 2018. "How Spotify Discovers the Genres of Tomorrow." *Spotify for Artists* (blog), June 7. https://artists.spotify.com/en/blog/how-spotify-discovers-the-genres-of-tomorrow.

Jones, Graham M. 2014. "Secrecy." *Annual Review of Anthropology* 43 (1): 53–69.

Kafka, Peter. 2017. "Amazon? HBO? Netflix Thinks Its Real Competitor Is . . . Sleep." *Vox*, April 17. https://www.vox.com/2017/4/17/15334122/netflix-sleep-competitor-amazon-hbo.

Kassabian, Anahid. 2013. *Ubiquitous Listening: Affect, Attention, and Distributed Subjectivity*. Berkeley: University of California Press.

Kaufmann-Buhler, Jennifer. 2020. *Open Plan: A Design History of the American Office*. London: Bloomsbury Publishing.

Kay, Lily. 1997. "Cybernetics, Information, Life: The Emergence of Scriptural Representations of Heredity." *Configurations* 5 (1): 23–91.

Keeler, Ward. 2009. "What's Burmese about Burmese Rap? Why Some Expressive Forms Go Global." *American Ethnologist* 36 (1): 2–19.

Kelkar, Shreeharsh. 2020. "Are Surveillance Capitalists Behaviorists? No. Does It Matter? Maybe." *Culture Digitally* (blog), December 7. https://culturedigitally.org/2020/12/are-surveillance-capitalists-behaviorists-no-does-it-matter-maybe/.

Killen, Andreas. 2006. *Berlin Electropolis: Shock, Nerves, and German Modernity*. Berkeley: University of California Press.

Kimmel, Eric A., and Trina Schart Hyman. 2014. *Hershel and the Hanukkah Goblins*. 25th anniversary ed. New York: Holiday House.

Kitchin, Rob, and Tracey Lauriault. 2014. "Towards Critical Data Studies: Charting and Unpacking Data Assemblages and Their Work." SSRN Scholarly Paper ID 2474112. Rochester, NY: Social Science Research Network. https://papers.ssrn.com/abstract=2474112.

Kline, Ronald R. 2015. *The Cybernetics Moment: Or, Why We Call Our Age the Information Age*. Baltimore: Johns Hopkins University Press.

Kneschke, Tristan. 2017. "On Wandering the Paths of a Spotify Analyst's Mad Music Map." *PopMatters* (blog), February 10. https://www.popmatters.com/on-wandering-the-paths-of-a-spotify-analysts-mad-music-map-2495400875.html.

Knijnenburg, Bart P., and Martijn C. Willemsen. 2015. "Evaluating Recommender Systems with User Experiments." In *Recommender Systems Handbook*, edited by Francesco Ricci, Lior Rokach, and Bracha Shapira, 309–52. Boston: Springer US.

Knijnenburg, Bart P., Martijn C. Willemsen, Zeno Gantner, Hakan Soncu, and Chris Newell. 2012. "Explaining the User Experience of Recommender Systems." *User Modeling and User-Adapted Interaction* 22 (4): 441–504.

Koppman, Sharon. 2016. "Different Like Me: Why Cultural Omnivores Get Creative Jobs." *Administrative Science Quarterly* 61 (2): 291–331.

Koren, Yehuda, Robert Bell, and Chris Volinsky. 2009. "Matrix Factorization Techniques for Recommender Systems." *Computer*, no. 8: 30–37.

Kotliar, Dan M. 2020a. "Data Orientalism: On the Algorithmic Construction of the Non-Western Other." *Theory and Society* 49 (5): 919–39.

———. 2020b. "The Return of the Social: Algorithmic Identity in an Age of Symbolic Demise." *New Media & Society* 22 (7): 1152–67.

———. 2021. "Who Gets to Choose? On the Socio-Algorithmic Construction of Choice." *Science, Technology, & Human Values* 46 (2): 346–75.

Kracauer, Siegfried. 1987. "Cult of Distraction: On Berlin's Picture Palaces." Translated by Thomas Y. Levin. *New German Critique*, no. 40: 91–96.

Kusek, David, and Gerd Leonhard. 2005. *The Future of Music*. Boston: Berklee Press.

Lakoff, George, and Mark Johnson. 1980. *Metaphors We Live By*. Chicago: University of Chicago Press.

Latour, Bruno. 1992. "Where Are the Missing Masses? The Sociology of a Few Mundane Artifacts." In *Shaping Technology/Building Society: Studies in Sociotechnical Change*, edited by Wiebe E. Bijker and John Law, 225–58. Cambridge, MA: MIT Press.

———. 1993. *We Have Never Been Modern*. Translated by Catherine Porter. Cambridge, MA: Harvard University Press.

———. 1996. *Aramis, or, The Love of Technology*. Cambridge, MA: Harvard University Press.

Lee, Richard Borshay. 1979. *The !Kung San: Men, Women and Work in a Foraging Society*. Cambridge: Cambridge University Press.

Lefebvre, Henri. 1992. *The Production of Space*. Translated by Donald Nicholson-Smith. Malden, MA: Wiley-Blackwell.

Le Guin, Ursula K. 1983. "The Author of the Acacia Seeds." In *The Compass Rose*, 3–14. New York: Bantam.

Lena, Jennifer C. 2012. *Banding Together: How Communities Create Genres in Popular Music*. Princeton, NJ: Princeton University Press.

Leslie, Ian. 2016. "The Scientists Who Make Apps Addictive." *The Economist*, October 20. https://www.economist.com/1843/2016/10/20/the-scientists-who-make-apps-addictive.

Levine, Nick. 2017. "The Nature of the Glut: Information Overload in Postwar America." *History of the Human Sciences* 30 (1): 32–49.

Lévi-Strauss, Claude. 1966. *The Savage Mind*. Translated by Doreen Weightman and John Weightman. Chicago: University of Chicago Press.

———. 1969. *The Raw and the Cooked*. Translated by John Weightman and Doreen Weightman. Chicago: University of Chicago Press.

Lindenmayer, David B., Richard J. Hobbs, Gene E. Likens, Charles J. Krebs, and Samuel C. Banks. 2011. "Newly Discovered Landscape Traps Produce Regime Shifts in Wet Forests." *Proceedings of the National Academy of Sciences* 108 (38): 15887–91.

Lippman, Alexandra. 2020. "Listening." In *Transmissions: Critical Tactics for Making & Communicating Research*, edited by Kat Jungnickel, 211–27. Cambridge, MA: MIT Press.

Liu, Alan. 2004. *The Laws of Cool: Knowledge Work and the Culture of Information*. Chicago: University of Chicago Press.

Loeb, Shoshana. 1992. "Architecting Personalized Delivery of Multimedia Information." *Communications of the ACM* 35 (12): 39–47.

Logan, Beth. 2000. "Mel Frequency Cepstral Coefficients for Music Modeling." *International Symposium on Music Information Retrieval* 28 (5).

Lupton, Deborah. 2013. "Swimming or Drowning in the Data Ocean? Thoughts on the Metaphors of Big Data." *This Sociological Life* (blog), October 29. https://simplysociology.wordpress.com/2013/10/29/swimming-or-drowning-in-the-data-ocean-thoughts-on-the-metaphors-of-big-data/.

———. 2016. "Digital Companion Species and Eating Data: Implications for Theorising Digital Data–Human Assemblages." *Big Data & Society* 3 (1).

Lury, Celia, and Sophie Day. 2019. "Algorithmic Personalization as a Mode of Individuation." *Theory, Culture & Society* 36 (2): 17–37.

Lynch, Jason. 2018. "Netflix Thrives by Programming to 'Taste Communities,' Not Demographics." *Adweek*, July 29. https://www.adweek.com/tv-video/netflix-thrives-by-programming-to-taste-communities-not-demographics/.

Lynch, Michael. 1988. "The Externalized Retina: Selection and Mathematization in the Visual Documentation of Objects in the Life Sciences." *Human Studies* 11 (2–3).

MacDonald, Scott. 2001. *The Garden in the Machine: A Field Guide to Independent Films about Place*. Berkeley: University of California Press.

Mackenzie, Adrian. 2017. *Machine Learners: Archaeology of a Data Practice*. Cambridge, MA: MIT Press.

Maes, Pattie. 1994. "Agents That Reduce Work and Information Overload." *Communications of the ACM* 37 (7): 30–40.

Mahmud, Lilith. 2012. "'The World Is a Forest of Symbols': Italian Freemasonry and the Practice of Discretion: Freemasonry and the Practice of Discretion." *American Ethnologist* 39 (2): 425–38.

Malaby, Thomas. 2009. *Making Virtual Worlds: Linden Lab and Second Life*. Ithaca: Cornell University Press.

Malazita, James W., and Korryn Resetar. 2019. "Infrastructures of Abstraction: How Computer Science Education Produces Anti-Political Subjects." *Digital Creativity* 30 (4): 300–312.

Malinowski, Bronislaw. 1935. *Coral Gardens and Their Magic*. Vol. 2. New York: George Allen and Unwin.

March, James G., and Herbert A. Simon. 1958. *Organizations*. New York: Wiley.

Marcus, George E. 1995. "Ethnography in/of the World System: The Emergence of Multi-Sited Ethnography." *Annual Review of Anthropology* 24 (1): 95–117.

Margolis, Jane, and Allan Fisher. 2002. *Unlocking the Clubhouse: Women in Computing*. Cambridge, MA: MIT Press.

Markham, Annette N. 2003. "Metaphors Reflecting and Shaping the Reality of the Internet: Tool, Place, Way of Being." Unpublished ms. http://markham.internetinquiry.org/writing/MarkhamTPW.pdf.

Martin, Andrew J. 2011. "Headphones with Swagger (and Lots of Bass)." *New York Times*, November 19, sec. Business. https://www.nytimes.com/2011/11/20/business/beats-headphones-expand-dr-dres-business-world.html.

Martin, Emily. 1991. "The Egg and the Sperm: How Science Has Constructed a Romance Based on Stereotypical Male-Female Roles." *Signs* 16 (3): 485–501.

Marx, Leo. 1964. *The Machine in the Garden: Technology and the Pastoral Ideal in America*. Oxford University Press.

Masco, Joseph. 2006. *The Nuclear Borderlands: The Manhattan Project in Post–Cold War New Mexico*. Princeton, NJ: Princeton University Press.

Mason, Otis T. 1900. "Traps of the Amerinds—A Study in Psychology and Invention." *American Anthropologist* 2 (4): 657–75.

Massanari, Adrienne L. 2010. "Designing for Imaginary Friends: Information Architecture, Personas and the Politics of User-Centered Design." *New Media & Society* 12 (3): 401–16.

Mattern, Shannon. 2018. "Maintenance and Care." *Places Journal*, November.

McDonald, Glenn. 2013. "How We Understand Music Genres." *The Echo Nest Blog* (blog), June 7. https://blog.echonest.com/post/52385283599/how-we-understand-music-genres.

McGregor, Jena. 2016. "Why Yet Another Internet Company Is Bringing Back Its Founder." *Washington Post*, March 30. https://www.washingtonpost.com/news/on-leadership/wp/2016/03/30/why-yet-another-internet-company-is-bringing-back-its-founder/.

McKinnon, Susan. 2006. *Neo-Liberal Genetics: The Myths and Moral Tales of Evolutionary Psychology*. Chicago: Prickly Paradigm Press.

McLemee, Scott. 2005. "Of Metaphors and Moving Vans." *Inside Higher Ed*, June 2. https://www.insidehighered.com/views/2005/06/02/metaphors-and-moving-vans.

McNee, Sean M., John Riedl, and Joseph A. Konstan. 2006. "Being Accurate Is Not Enough: How Accuracy Metrics Have Hurt Recommender Systems." *CHI'06 Extended Abstracts on Human Factors in Computing Systems* (April): 1097–1101.

McQuillan, Dan. 2015. "Algorithmic States of Exception." *European Journal of Cultural Studies* 18 (4–5): 564–76.

McRobbie, Angela. 2004. "Post-Feminism and Popular Culture." *Feminist Media Studies* 4 (3): 255–64.

Mermelstein, Paul. 1976. "Distance Measures for Speech Recognition, Psychological and Instrumental." In *Pattern Recognition and Artificial Intelligence,* edited by C. H. Chen, 374–88. New York: Academic Press.

Merry, Sally Engle. 2016. *The Seductions of Quantification: Measuring Human Rights, Gender Violence, and Sex Trafficking.* Chicago Series in Law and Society. Chicago: University of Chicago Press.

Messeri, Lisa. 2016. *Placing Outer Space: An Earthly Ethnography of Other Worlds.* Durham, NC: Duke University Press.

Milgram, Stanley. 1970. "The Experience of Living in Cities." *Science* 167 (12): 1461–68.

Miller, George A. 1956. "The Magical Number Seven, Plus or Minus Two." *Psychological Review* 63 (2): 81–97.

———. 2003. "The Cognitive Revolution: A Historical Perspective." *Trends in Cognitive Sciences* 7 (3): 141–44.

Miller, James G. 1960. "Information Input Overload and Psychopathology." *American Journal of Psychiatry* 116: 695–704.

———. 1978. *Living Systems.* New York: McGraw-Hill.

Mills, Mara. 2010. "Deaf Jam: From Inscription to Reproduction to Information." *Social Text* 28 (1 [102]): 35–58.

Modell, Amanda. 2015. "Mapping the Music Genome: Imaginative Geography in Pandora Internet Radio and the Genographic Project." *Media Fields* 10.

Mohr, John W. 1998. "Measuring Meaning Structures." *Annual Review of Sociology* 24 (1): 345–70.

Mookerji, R. R. 1939. "A Nicobarese Rat-Trap." *Man* 39: 8–9.

Moore, Henrietta. 2010. "Forms of Knowing and Un-Knowing: Secrets about Society, Sexuality and God in Northern Kenya." In *Secrecy and Silence in the Research Process,* edited by Róisín Ryan-Flood and Rosalind Gill, 49–60. New York: Routledge.

Morgan, Mary S. 2020. "Inducing Visibility and Visual Deduction." *East Asian Science, Technology and Society* 14 (2): 225–52.

Morris, Jeremy Wade, and Devon Powers. 2015. "Control, Curation and Musical Experience in Streaming Music Services." *Creative Industries Journal* 8 (2): 106–22.

Motajcsek, Tamas, Jean-Yves Le Moine, Martha Larson, Daniel Kohlsdorf, Andreas Lommatzsch, Domonkos Tikk, Omar Alonso, Paolo Cremonesi, Andrew Demetriou, Kristaps Dobrajs, Franca Garzotto, Ayşe Göker, Frank Hopfgartner, Davide Malagoli, Thuy Ngoc Nguyen, Jasminko Novak, Francesco Ricci, Mario Scriminaci, Marko Tkalcic, and Anna Zacchi. 2016. "Algorithms Aside: Recommendation as the Lens of Life." In *Proceedings of the 10th ACM Conference on Recommender Systems,* 215–19. New York: Association for Computing Machinery.

Moussallam, Manuel, Antoine Liutkus, and Laurent Daudet. 2015. "Listening to Features." January. http://arxiv.org/abs/1501.04981.

Mullaney, Tim. 2015. "'Everything Is a Recommendation.'" *MIT Technology Review,* March 23. https://www.technologyreview.com/2015/03/23/168831/everything-is-a -recommendation/.

Myers, Natasha, and Joe Dumit. 2011. "Haptic Creativity and the Mid-Embodiments of Experimental Life." In *A Companion to the Anthropology of the Body and Embodiment,* edited by Frances E. Mascia-Lees, 239–61. Oxford, UK: Blackwell.

Nahum-Claudel, Chloe. 2017. *Vital Diplomacy: The Ritual Everyday on a Dammed River in Amazonia.* New York: Berghahn Books.

Nakamura, Lisa. 2000. "'Where Do You Want to Go Today?': Cybernetic Tourism, the Internet, and Transnationality." In *Race in Cyberspace,* edited by Beth E. Kolko, Lisa Nakamura, and Gilbert B. Rodman, 15–26. New York: Routledge.

Nakamura, Lisa, and Donna Haraway. 2003. "Prospects for a Materialist Informatics: An Interview with Donna Haraway." *Electronic Book Review* (blog), August 30. https://electronicbookreview.com/essay/prospects-for-a-materialist-informatics -an-interview-with-donna-haraway/.

Negroponte, Nicholas. 1995. *Being Digital.* New York: Vintage.

Negus, Keith. 1995. "Where the Mystical Meets the Market: Creativity and Commerce in the Production of Popular Music." *Sociological Review* 43 (2): 316–41.

Nelson, Alondra. 2002. "Introduction: Future Texts." *Social Text* 20 (2): 1–15.

Noble, Safiya Umoja. 2018. *Algorithms of Oppression: How Search Engines Reinforce Racism.* New York: NYU Press.

Noble, Safiya Umoja, and Sarah T. Roberts. 2019. "Technological Elites, the Meritocracy, and Post-Racial Myths in Silicon Valley." In *Racism Postrace,* edited by Roopali Mukherjee, Sarah Banet-Weiser, and Herman Gray, 113–34. Durham, NC: Duke University Press.

Noyes, Katherine. 2016. "5 Things You Need to Know about Data Exhaust." *Computerworld,* May 13. https://www.computerworld.com/article/3070475/5 -things-you-need-to-know-about-data-exhaust.html.

Olson, Valerie. 2018. *Into the Extreme: U.S. Environmental Systems and Politics beyond Earth.* Minneapolis: University of Minnesota Press.

Ortner, Sherry. 1973. "On Key Symbols." *American Anthropologist* 75 (5): 1338–46.

Oudshoorn, Nelly, Els Rommes, and Marcelle Stienstra. 2004. "Configuring the User as Everybody: Gender and Design Cultures in Information and Communication Technologies." *Science, Technology, & Human Values* 29 (1): 30–63.

Packer, George. 2013. "Change the World." *New Yorker,* May 20.

Pagano, Roberto, Paolo Cremonesi, Martha Larson, Balázs Hidasi, Domonkos Tikk, Alexandros Karatzoglou, and Massimo Quadrana. 2016. "The Contextual Turn: From Context-Aware to Context-Driven Recommender Systems." In *Proceedings of the 10th ACM Conference on Recommender Systems,* 249–52. New York: Association for Computing Machinery.

Paglen, Trevor. 2014. "Operational Images." *E-Flux* 59. https://www.e-flux.com/ journal/59/61130/operational-images/.

Paidipaty, Poornima. 2020. "'Tortoises All the Way Down': Geertz, Cybernetics and 'Culture' at the End of the Cold War." *Anthropological Theory* 20 (1): 97–129.

Palermino, Chris Leo. 2014. "Forgotify Plays Spotify's 4 Million Unheard Songs."

Billboard, February 12. https://www.billboard.com/articles/business/5901260/
forgotify-plays-spotifys-4-million-unheard-songs.

Parks, Lisa. 2005. *Cultures in Orbit: Satellites and the Televisual.* Durham, NC: Duke
University Press.

Pasquale, Frank. 2015. *The Black Box Society.* Cambridge, MA: Harvard University
Press.

Pateman, Carole. 1988. *The Sexual Contract.* Stanford, CA: Stanford University
Press.

Peate, Iorwerth C. 1934. "Severn Eel-Traps." *Man* 34 (October): 153–54.

Pelly, Liz. 2018. "Streambait Pop." *The Baffler* (blog). December 11. https://thebaffler
.com/downstream/streambait-pop-pelly.

Peters, John Durham. 1988. "Information: Notes toward a Critical History." *Journal
of Communication Inquiry* 12 (2): 9–23.

———. 2004. "Helmholtz, Edison, and Sound History." In *Memory Bytes: History,
Technology, and Digital Culture,* edited by Lauren Rabinovitz and Abraham Geil,
177–98. Durham, NC: Duke University Press.

Peterson, Richard A., and Roger M. Kern. 1996. "Changing Highbrow Taste: From
Snob to Omnivore." *American Sociological Review* 61 (5): 900–907.

Pfaffenberger, Bryan. 1992. "Social Anthropology of Technology." *Annual Review of
Anthropology* 21 (1): 491–516.

Pham, Alex. 2012. "Discovery: The Key to Digital Fortune." *FutureSound White Paper: Why Discovery, Data and Licensing Are Key to the New Music Business.* Billboard.
https://www.billboard.com/music/music-news/billboards-futuresound-white-paper
-why-discovery-data-and-licensing-are-1082961/.

Phan, Thao, and Scott Wark. 2021. "Racial Formations as Data Formations." *Big Data
& Society* 8 (2).

Phillips, P. Jonathon, Fang Jiang, Abhijit Narvekar, Julianne Ayyad, and Alice J.
O'Toole. 2011. "An Other-Race Effect for Face Recognition Algorithms." *ACM
Transactions on Applied Perception* 8 (2): 14:1–14:11.

Pinch, Trevor J., and Wiebe E. Bijker. 1984. "The Social Construction of Facts and
Artefacts: Or How the Sociology of Science and the Sociology of Technology
Might Benefit Each Other." *Social Studies of Science* 14 (3): 399–441.

Pinel, Clémence, Barbara Prainsack, and Christopher McKevitt. 2020. "Caring for
Data: Value Creation in a Data-Intensive Research Laboratory." *Social Studies of
Science* 50 (2): 175–97.

Pirolli, Peter, and Stuart Card. 1995. "Information Foraging in Information Access
Environments." In *CHI '95 Mosaic of Creativity,* 51–58. New York: Association for
Computing Machinery.

Posner, Miriam. 2017. "JavaScript Is for Girls." *Logic Magazine,* no. 1. https://logicmag
.io/intelligence/javascript-is-for-girls/.

Powers, Devon. 2012. "Long-Haired, Freaky People Need to Apply: Rock Music,
Cultural Intermediation, and the Rise of the 'Company Freak.'" *Journal of Consumer Culture* 12 (1): 3–18.

Prey, Robert. 2015. "Henri Lefebvre and the Production of Music Streaming Spaces."
Sociologica 9 (3): 1–22.

———. 2017. "Nothing Personal: Algorithmic Individuation on Music Streaming
Platforms." *Media, Culture & Society* 40 (7): 1086–1100.

Pu, Pearl, Li Chen, and Rong Hu. 2011. "A User-Centric Evaluation Framework for

Recommender Systems." In *Proceedings of the Fifth ACM Conference on Recommender Systems*, 157–64. New York: Association for Computing Machinery.

Puschmann, Cornelius, and Jean Burgess. 2014. "Metaphors of Big Data." *International Journal of Communication* 8: 1690–1709.

Rappaport, Roy A. 1967. "Ritual Regulation of Environmental Relations among a New Guinea People." *Ethnology* 6 (1): 17–30.

Razlogova, Elena. 2020. "Provincializing Spotify: Radio, Algorithms and Conviviality." *Radio Journal: International Studies in Broadcast & Audio Media* 18 (1): 29–42.

Reinert, Hugo, and Tor A. Benjaminsen. 2015. "Conceptualising Resilience in Norwegian Sámi Reindeer Pastoralism." *Resilience* 3 (2): 95–112.

Resnick, Paul, Neophytos Iacovou, Mitesh Suchak, Peter Bergstrom, and John Riedl. 1994. "GroupLens: An Open Architecture for Collaborative Filtering of Netnews." In *Proceedings of the 1994 ACM Conference on Computer Supported Cooperative Work*, 175–86. New York: Association for Computing Machinery.

Resnikoff, Paul. 2014. "Google Executive: 'You Cannot Devalue Music. It's Impossible.'" *Digital Music News* (blog), June 25. https://www.digitalmusicnews.com/2014/06/25/devaluationmyth/.

Reuters. 2017. "A Quick Guide to Apple Music, Spotify, and More Top Music Streaming Services." *Fortune*, September 11. https://fortune.com/2017/09/11/spotify-apple-music-tidal-streaming/.

Riedl, John, and Joseph Konstan. 2002. *Word of Mouse: The Marketing Power of Collaborative Filtering*. New York: Business Plus.

Riles, Annelise. 2001. "Encountering Amateurism: John Henry Wigmore and the Uses of American Formalism." *Northwestern University School of Law Public Law and Legal Theory Papers Working Paper* 39. https://law.bepress.com/nwwps-plltp/art39.

Roberts, Jessica, and Michael Koliska. 2014. "The Effects of Ambient Media: What Unplugging Reveals about Being Plugged In." *First Monday* 19 (8).

Robinson, Sandra. 2018. "Databases and Doppelgängers: New Articulations of Power." *Configurations* 26 (4): 411–40.

Rosaldo, Michelle Zimbalist. 1980. "The Use and Abuse of Anthropology: Reflections on Feminism and Cross-Cultural Understanding." *Signs* 5 (3): 389–417.

Rosenberg, Daniel. 2003. "Early Modern Information Overload." *Journal of the History of Ideas* 64 (1): 1–9.

Rossman, Gabriel. 2012. *Climbing the Charts: What Radio Airplay Tells Us about the Diffusion of Innovation*. Princeton, NJ: Princeton University Press.

Rouvroy, Antoinette, and Thomas Berns. 2013. "Algorithmic governmentality and prospects of emancipation: Disparateness as a precondition for individuation through relationships?" Translated by Liz Carey Libbrecht. *Réseaux* 177 (1): 163–96.

Rowe, Peter G. 1991. *Making a Middle Landscape*. Cambridge, MA: MIT Press.

Said, Edward W. 1978. *Orientalism*. New York: Pantheon Books.

Samuels, David W., Louise Meintjes, Ana Maria Ochoa, and Thomas Porcello. 2010. "Soundscapes: Toward a Sounded Anthropology." *Annual Review of Anthropology* 39 (1): 329–45.

Schilit, Bill, Norman Adams, and Roy Want. 1994. "Context-Aware Computing Applications." In *1994 First Workshop on Mobile Computing Systems and Applica-*

tions, edited by Luis-Felipe Cabrera and Mahadev Satyanarayanan, 85–90. Los Alamitos, CA: IEEE Computer Society Press.

Schlecker, Markus, and Eric Hirsch. 2001. "Incomplete Knowledge: Ethnography and the Crisis of Context in Studies of Media, Science and Technology." *History of the Human Sciences* 14 (1): 69–87.

Schrempp, Gregory. 2012. *The Ancient Mythology of Modern Science: A Mythologist Looks (Seriously) at Popular Science Writing*. Montréal: McGill-Queen's University Press.

Schüll, Natasha Dow. 2012. *Addiction by Design: Machine Gambling in Las Vegas*. Princeton, NJ: Princeton University Press.

Schwartz, Barry. 2004. *The Paradox of Choice: Why More Is Less*. New York: HarperCollins.

Schwarz, Ori. 2018. "Cultures of Choice: Towards a Sociology of Choice as a Cultural Phenomenon." *British Journal of Sociology* 69 (3): 845–64.

Seabrook, John. 2014. "Spotify: Friend or Foe?" *New Yorker*, November 17. https://www.newyorker.com/magazine/2014/11/24/revenue-streams.

Seaver, Nick. 2014. "Computers and Sociocultural Anthropology." *Savage Minds* (blog), May 19. https://savageminds.org/2014/05/19/computers-and-sociocultural-anthropology/.

———. 2015. "Bastard Algebra." In *Data, Now Bigger & Better!*, edited by Bill Maurer and Tom Boellstorff, 27–45. Chicago: Prickly Paradigm Press.

———. 2017. "Algorithms as Culture: Some Tactics for the Ethnography of Algorithmic Systems." *Big Data & Society* 4 (2).

———. 2018. "What Should an Anthropology of Algorithms Do?" *Cultural Anthropology* 33 (3): 375–85.

———. 2019. "Knowing Algorithms." In *Digital STS: A Field Guide for Science & Technology Studies*, edited by Janet Vertesi and David Ribes, 412–22. Princeton, NJ: Princeton University Press.

———. 2021a. "Care and Scale: Decorrelative Ethics in Algorithmic Recommendation." *Cultural Anthropology* 36 (3): 509–37.

———. 2021b. "Everything Lies in a Space: Cultural Data and Spatial Reality." *Journal of the Royal Anthropological Institute* 27 (S1): 43–61.

Segal, Howard P. 1977. "Leo Marx's 'Middle Landscape': A Critique, a Revision, and an Appreciation." *Reviews in American History* 5 (1): 137–50.

Shannon, Claude E. 1948. "A Mathematical Theory of Communication." *Bell System Technical Journal* 27 (3): 379–423.

Shardanand, Upendra. 1994. "Social Information Filtering for Music Recommendation." Master's thesis, Massachusetts Institute of Technology.

Shardanand, Upendra, and Pattie Maes. 1995. "Social Information Filtering: Algorithms for Automating 'Word of Mouth.'" In *Proceedings of the SIGCHI Conference on Human Factors in Computing Systems*, 210–17. New York: Association for Computing Machinery.

Shenk, David. 1998. *Data Smog: Surviving the Information Glut*. New York: HarperOne.

Silber, Ilana Friedrich. 1995. "Space, Fields, Boundaries: The Rise of Spatial Metaphors in Contemporary Sociological Theory." *Social Research* 62 (2): 323–55.

Silberbauer, George B. 1980. *Hunter and Habitat in the Central Kalahari Desert*. Cambridge, MA: Cambridge University Press.

Simmel, Georg. 1906. "The Sociology of Secrecy and of Secret Societies." *American Journal of Sociology* 11 (4): 441–98.

———. 1969. "The Metropolis and Mental Life." 1903. In *Classic Essays on the Culture of Cities*, edited by Richard Sennett. Englewood Cliffs, NJ: Prentice-Hall.

Singleton, Benedict. 2013. "Maximum Jailbreak." *e-flux* 46. https://www.e-flux.com/journal/46/60088/maximum-jailbreak/.

———. 2014. "On Craft and Being Crafty." PhD diss., Northumbria University.

Skinner, B. F. 1971. *Beyond Freedom and Dignity*. Indianapolis, IN: Hackett Publishing.

Social Media Collective. 2017. "Metaphors of Data: A Reading List." *Social Media Collective* (blog). https://socialmediacollective.org/reading-lists/metaphors-of-data-a-reading-list/.

Spillers, Hortense J. 1987. "Mama's Baby, Papa's Maybe: An American Grammar Book." *Diacritics* 17 (2): 65–81.

Stahl, William A. 1999. *God and the Chip: Religion and the Culture of Technology*. Waterloo, ON: Wilfrid Laurier University Press.

Steege, Benjamin. 2012. *Helmholtz and the Modern Listener*. Cambridge: Cambridge University Press.

Stefik, Mark J., ed. 1997. *Internet Dreams: Archetypes, Myths, and Metaphors*. Cambridge, MA: MIT Press.

Stein, Gertrude. 1998. "Reflection on the Atomic Bomb." In *Gertrude Stein: Writings 1932–1946*, edited by Catharine R. Stimpson and Harriet Chessman, 823. New York: Library of America.

Sterne, Jonathan. 2003. *The Audible Past: Cultural Origins of Sound Reproduction*. Durham, NC: Duke University Press.

———. 2006. "The MP3 as Cultural Artifact." *New Media & Society* 8 (5): 825–42.

———. 2012. *MP3: The Meaning of a Format*. Durham, NC: Duke University Press.

Sterne, Jonathan, and Tara Rodgers. 2011. "The Poetics of Signal Processing." *differences* 22 (2–3): 31–53.

Strathern, Marilyn. 1992. *After Nature: English Kinship in the Late Twentieth Century*. Cambridge: Cambridge University Press.

———. 1996. "Cutting the Network." *Journal of the Royal Anthropological Institute* 2 (3): 517–35.

———. 2014. "Reading Relations Backwards." *Journal of the Royal Anthropological Institute* 20 (1): 3–19.

Suchman, Lucy A. 2007. *Human-Machine Reconfigurations*. 2nd ed. Cambridge: Cambridge University Press.

Supper, Alexandra. 2015. "Data Karaoke: Sensory and Bodily Skills in Conference Presentations." *Science as Culture* 24 (4): 436–57.

Susser, Daniel, Beate Roessler, and Helen Nissenbaum. 2018. "Online Manipulation: Hidden Influences in a Digital World." *Georgetown Law Technology Review* 4.1: 1–45.

Swancutt, Katherine. 2012. "The Captive Guest: Spider Webs of Hospitality among the Nuosu of Southwest China." *Journal of the Royal Anthropological Institute* 18 (S1): S103–16.

Tidline, Tonyia. 1999. "The Mythology of Information Overload." *Library Trends* 47 (3): 485–506.

Tiku, Nitasha. 2013. "'Culture Fit' Is a Shitty Excuse for Marginalizing Women in

Tech." *Valleywag*, August 23. http://valleywag.gawker.com/culture-fit-is-a-shitty
-excuse-for-marginalizing-wome-1186914306.

Titlow, John Paul. 2013. "Screw Algorithms! The New Music Service from Beats
Uses Celebrity Curators to Show You New Music." *Fast Company*. October 10.
https://www.fastcompany.com/3019830/screw-algorithms-the-new-music-service
-from-beats-uses-celebrity-curators-to-show-you-new-mu.

———. 2014. "How Spotify's Music-Obsessed Culture Keeps Employees Hooked."
Fast Company, August 20. https://www.fastcompany.com/3034617/how-spotifys
-music-obsessed-culture-makes-the-company-rock.

Toffler, Alvin. 1970. *Future Shock*. New York: Random House.

Traweek, Sharon. 1992. "Border Crossings: Narrative Strategies in Science Studies and
among Physicists in Tsukuba Science City, Japan." In *Science as Practice and Culture*, edited by Andrew Pickering, 429–66. Chicago: University of Chicago Press.

Turner, Fred. 2009. "Burning Man at Google: A Cultural Infrastructure for New
Media Production." *New Media & Society* 11 (1–2): 73–94.

———. 2010. *From Counterculture to Cyberculture: Stewart Brand, the Whole Earth Network, and the Rise of Digital Utopianism*. Chicago: University of Chicago Press.

TV Tropes. n.d. "Clutching Hand Trap." https://tvtropes.org/pmwiki/pmwiki.php/
Main/ClutchingHandTrap.

Tyler, Stephen A. 1969. *Cognitive Anthropology*. New York: Holt, Rinehart and
Winston.

Umesh, S., L. Cohen, and D. Nelson. 1999. "Fitting the Mel Scale." In *Proceedings of
the 1999 IEEE International Conference on Acoustics, Speech, and Signal Processing*,
217–20. Piscataway, NJ: Institute of Electrical and Electronics Engineers.

Ungerleider, Neal. 2017. "Forecasting the Future and Explaining Silicon Valley's
New Religions." *Fast Company*, February 13. https://www.fastcompany.com/
3066813/yuval-harari-inside-homo-deus-and-silicon-valleys-new-religions.

Van Buskirk, Eliot. 2012. "Voice Is Not Content: WTFPod, Jams, and the New
Music Revolution." *Evolver.Fm* (blog), August 13. http://evolver.fm/2012/08/13/
voice-is-not-content-wtfpod-jamscontext-and-the-new-music-revolution/.

———. 2015. "50 Genres with the Strangest Names on Spotify." *Spotify Insights*
(blog), September 30. https://insights.spotify.com/us/2015/09/30/50-strangest
-genre-names/.

Van Couvering, Elizabeth. 2007. "Is Relevance Relevant? Market, Science, and War:
Discourses of Search Engine Quality." *Journal of Computer-Mediated Communication* 12 (3): 866–87.

van Dijck, José. 2014. "Datafication, Dataism and Dataveillance: Big Data between
Scientific Paradigm and Ideology." *Surveillance & Society* 12 (2): 197–208.

Walford, Antonia. 2017. "Raw Data: Making Relations Matter." *Social Analysis* 61 (2):
65–80.

Watson, Sara. 2015. "Metaphors of Big Data." *DIS Magazine* (blog). http://
dismagazine.com/discussion/73298/sara-m-watson-metaphors-of-big-data/.

Weaver, Warren. 1949. "The Mathematics of Communication." *Scientific American* 181
(1): 11–15.

Weiner, James F. 1994. "Myth and Metaphor." In *Companion Encyclopedia of Anthropology*, edited by Tim Ingold, 591–612. New York: Routledge.

Welker, Marina. 2014. *Enacting the Corporation: An American Mining Firm in Post-
Authoritarian Indonesia*. Berkeley: University of California Press.

Wellmon, Chad. 2015. *Organizing Enlightenment: Information Overload and the Invention of the Modern Research University*. Baltimore: Johns Hopkins University Press.

Whitman, Brian. 2012. "How Music Recommendation Works—and Doesn't Work." *Variogram* (blog), December 11. https://notes.variogr.am/2012/12/11/how-music-recommendation-works-and-doesnt-work/.

Wiener, Norbert. 1948. "Cybernetics." *Scientific American* 179 (5): 14–19.

Wilson, Japhy. 2013. "'The Devastating Conquest of the Lived by the Conceived': The Concept of Abstract Space in the Work of Henri Lefebvre." *Space and Culture* 16 (3): 364–80.

Wolfe, Patrick. 2006. "Settler Colonialism and the Elimination of the Native." *Journal of Genocide Research* 8 (4): 387–409.

Woolgar, Steve. 1990. "Configuring the User: The Case of Usability Trials." *Sociological Review* 38 (S1): 58–99.

Wyatt, Sally. 2004. "Danger! Metaphors at Work in Economics, Geophysiology, and the Internet." *Science, Technology, & Human Values* 29 (2): 242–61.

Ziewitz, Malte. 2016. "Governing Algorithms: Myth, Mess, and Methods." *Science, Technology & Human Values* 41 (1): 3–16.

Zuboff, Shoshana. 2019. *The Age of Surveillance Capitalism: The Fight for a Human Future at the New Frontier of Power*. New York: PublicAffairs.

———. 2020. "You Are Now Remotely Controlled." *New York Times*, January 24, sec. Opinion. https://www.nytimes.com/2020/01/24/opinion/sunday/surveillance-capitalism.html.

Index

Page numbers in italics refer to figures and tables.

Lightning Source UK Ltd.
Milton Keynes UK
UKHW010757081122
411812UK00003B/102

9 780226 702261